SWEET BITTER BLUES

SWEET BITTER
BLUES

WASHINGTON, DC'S HOMEMADE BLUES

PHIL WIGGINS AND FRANK MATHEIS
FOREWORD BY ELIJAH WALD

UNIVERSITY PRESS OF MISSISSIPPI / JACKSON

The University Press of Mississippi is the scholarly publishing agency of the Mississippi Institutions of Higher Learning: Alcorn State University, Delta State University, Jackson State University, Mississippi State University, Mississippi University for Women, Mississippi Valley State University, University of Mississippi, and University of Southern Mississippi.

www.upress.state.ms.us

The University Press of Mississippi is a member of the Association of University Presses.

First printing 2020
∞

Library of Congress Cataloging-in-Publication Data

Names: Wiggins, Phil, author. | Matheis, Frank, author. | Wald, Elijah, author of foreword.
Title: Sweet bitter blues : Washington, DCs homemade blues / Phil Wiggins and Frank Matheis ; foreword by Elijah Wald.
Other titles: American made music series.
Description: Jackson : University Press of Mississippi, 2020. | Series: American made music series | Includes bibliographical references and index. | Summary: "Sweet Bitter Blues: Washington, DCs Homemade Blues depicts the life and times of harmonica player Phil Wiggins and the unique, vibrant music scene around him, as described by music journalist Frank Matheis. Featuring Wigginss story, but including information on many musicians, the volume presents an incomparable documentary of the African American blues scene in Washington, DC, from 1975 to the present. At its core, the DC-area acoustic "down home" blues scene was and is rooted in the African American community. A dedicated group of musicians saw it as their mission to carry on their respective Piedmont musical traditions: Mother Scott, Flora Molton, Chief Ellis, Archie Edwards, John Jackson, John Cephas, and foremost Phil Wiggins. Because of their love for the music and willingness to teach, these creators fostered a harmonious environment, mostly centered on Archie Edwardss famous barbershop where Edwards opened his doors every Saturday afternoon for jam sessions. Sweet Bitter Blues features biographies and supporting essays based on Wigginss recollections and supplemented by Matheiss research, along with a foreword by noted blues scholar Elijah Wald, historic interviews by Dr. Barry Lee Pearson with John Cephas and Archie Edwards, and previously unpublished and rare photographs. This is the story of an acoustic blues scene that was and is a living tradition"Provided by publisher.
Identifiers: LCCN 2019046222 (print) | LCCN 2019046223 (ebook) | ISBN 9781496826916 (hardback) | ISBN 9781496826923 (trade paperback) | ISBN 9781496826930 | ISBN 9781496826947 | ISBN 9781496826954 | ISBN 9781496826961
Subjects: LCSH: Wiggins, Phil. | Blues musiciansWashington (D.C.)Biography. | Harmonica playersWashington (D.C.)Biography. |Blues (Music)Washington (D.C.)History and criticism. | BISAC: MUSIC / Genres & Styles / Blues | LCGFT: Autobiographies.
Classification: LCC ML419.W415 A3 2020 (print) | LCC ML419.W415 (ebook) | DDC 781.64309753dc23
LC record available at https://lccn.loc.gov/2019046222
LC ebook record available at https://lccn.loc.gov/2019046223

British Library Cataloging-in-Publication Data available

Two authors, two grandmas

In gratefulness to my grandmother Effie Mae Carter who
kept me hanging outside the Green Liberty Baptist Church.
—Phil Wiggins

In loving memory of my Oma, Berta Lehmann,
who adopted and raised me.
—Frank Matheis

CONTENTS

FOREWORD

—Elijah Wald, March 2019

The Washington, DC, blues scene has never received much attention. Memphis, Chicago, New Orleans, and Houston produced blues stars when the music was a major black pop style—the B in R&B—but the Washington scene had nothing to do with that. Developing as part of the folk-blues revival of the 1960s, it has remained firmly rooted in older, acoustic traditions.

This book gives a good sense of that scene and of the close-knit, familial feeling that has made it special. It reminds us that Washington nurtured new careers for Mississippi John Hurt and Skip James, and introduced the world to the marvelous John Jackson. It pays tribute to local heroes like John Cephas, Archie Edwards, Flora Molton, Mother Scott, and Eleanor Ellis.

The only thing I might change would be to give more props to the artist who, in my view, is the most innovative and interesting musician to emerge from the Washington scene and for many years has been its central figure: a fellow named Phil Wiggins.

I've been listening to Phil since the 1980s, and was always astonished by the originality of his playing. Growing up around acoustic blues, I've heard a lot of fine musicians, but pretty much all the ones who arrived after the 1960s have recycled older styles. There is nothing wrong with that, at all, and I appreciate the way this book recognizes the talents of dedicated craftspeople who learned classic styles and kept them alive. But Phil did something different. He writes about it like it was nothing special, saying he enjoyed Sonny Terry's and Walter Horton's playing, but just never happened to learn their licks. I believe it really feels that way to him: like he played with some good older musicians, tried to shape his sound to complement theirs, and happened to end up with his own sound. But in a field as large and full of brilliant artists as acoustic blues, coming up with a genuinely original sound is a very unusual accomplishment.

I got to know Phil a little when I was a fellow teacher at a couple of blues camps, and one of the great pleasures of this book was getting a better sense of where he comes from: his personal history and his experiences around the older players on the DC scene. There were some surprises, but mostly it was back-story to things that are pretty obvious if you spend time around him—like how much his life and art are about listening and caring about other people. I cannot think of a more generous person on the blues scene, whether toward his students, his peers, his friends, or—most strikingly in a world of fragile and overbearing egos—toward whoever he is playing with at any moment.

In a way, reading this book is kind of like seeing Phil onstage or at a jam session: there are lots of other people and he kind of stands off to one side a lot of the time, nodding his appreciation for each of them, taking his solo when it comes around, then stepping back, smiling his quiet smile. Like it's kind of his book, but he's just part of this bigger story. That's one of the things I most admire about him, and I'm not complaining. I'm just saying: there are a bunch of good players between these covers, but I'm here to listen to Phil.

PREFACE

—Frank Matheis

One Saturday afternoon in 1981, my then girlfriend, now my wife and photographic contributor to this project, Bibiana Huang Matheis, and I walked into Kramerbooks on Dupont Circle in Washington, DC. As we entered, intending to just browse a bit, there was amazing music playing—acoustic blues guitar and harmonica, not what you would expect in a bookstore. First, I thought it was a record by the famed blues duo Sonny Terry and Brownie McGhee, whose music I loved. When the song ended and there was a short pause, I realized that it was actually live music. Two musicians were playing upstairs in the second-floor balcony area. Bewildered, we went upstairs. There indeed was a duo of handsome guys in classy Fedora hats playing East Coast fingerpicking style guitar and harmonica. They weren't Sonny and Brownie but were every bit as good.

There was nobody else upstairs. They played for about an hour to an audience of just us two, as nobody from below was even curious enough to see who was playing music in the store—thrilling roots music, truehearted, emotive down-home blues. We had lots of time to chat and they were friendly and open, asking us where we were from, because we are both immigrants with accents. When I said I was from Germany, the affable pair got excited to tell us that they had just made their first album, *Living Country Blues USA, Vol.1*, by "Bowling Green" John Cephas and "Harmonica" Phil Wiggins, on a German record label. They had the LP right there and we bought one for $8. They said that we were among the first to get one. I still have it, signatures and all.

We moved away from the Washington, DC, area a year later, but over the decades I kept up with Cephas & Wiggins's ascending career. Whenever they came to New York festivals or clubs we tried to make the shows. Later, I often spun their music on my roots and blues radio show on WKZE-FM and WVKR-FM, and reviewed their albums and CDs in music magazines and websites. After John Cephas passed away, I met up with Phil again in New York. In 2012, Alvin Youngblood Hart invited Phil Wiggins, Corey Harris, and Guy Davis to perform with him at Jazz at Lincoln Center in Manhattan. We went to the show and backstage Phil indicated that he needed to get to Pennsylvania for a gig the following day. I offered to give him a ride, eager to spend some undisturbed time together since I was planning to write a feature article about him for *Living Blues* magazine. During that long drive, we had the opportunity to reconnect. We then worked on the interviews for the article through most of 2013. The *Living Blues* cover story finally appeared in 2014, titled "Phil Wiggins—On His Own but Not Alone." During this period, we formed a true friendship. Most importantly, we decided to team up to write a book to tell Phil's story, his life and times in the "real homemade blues" in and around Washington, DC, and the world, as well as to document the acoustic blues scene of which Phil has been an integral part for more than forty years. He tells the story of the DC acoustic blues from the perspective of a musician, always with poignant insight and plainspoken narrative.

Before we started, we sought the counsel of University of Maryland professor Barry Lee Pearson, an influential blues folklorist and regional blues expert who is a longtime trusted friend of Phil's and an important voice for the regional folk and blues music. He gave us simple and clear advice: Just let the musician tell his story. That's what we did. This is Phil's book—his story, his narrative, a summary of multiple interviews—and I wrote it all out. Sometimes in the process of writing this book, people have implied that I am somehow "telling Phil Wiggins's story" as his biographer. Not so. Phil does not need anybody to speak for him. He tells his own story very well. I am proudly just his scribe.

Sweet Bitter Blues has two primary components. Phil's story is told in first-person narrative, in his own voice, as he told it to me in numerous interviews over four years; essentially all other sections are by me, including biographies and supporting essays, with additional essays with Eleanor Ellis about Flora Molton and two by Dr. Barry Lee Pearson, who conducted extensive interviews with Archie Edwards and John Cephas, which he graciously contributed to this book.

In large part we relied on Phil's recollections and memories, supplemented by research to validate dates, times, and places. In some cases the dates are approximate, simply because, after forty years of performing, it was difficult for Phil to remember all details. We tell his story sequentially, but during the many hours of interviews he told it to me in multiple recollections, moving back and forth through time. I did my utmost to piece the sections together faithful to his own words and meaning, and to fact-check as well as possible.

My primary objective was to capture Phil's words, meanings, and essence just as he told his own story, no less, no more. That was my main job, as well as to fill in facts and details behind Phil's narrative about the people and organizations with whom he interacted. This is not a typical biography or autobiography filled with personal details. Nothing salacious or sensational. It is a musical biography.

The inevitable question will arise, "Why is so-and-so not in this book?" We are not attempting to present the entire history of everybody who was involved with blues in Washington, DC. You will not find much about Michael Stewart, Max Ochs, Cathy Ponton King, John Fahey, Danny Gatton, Roy Buchanan, the Nighthawks, Catfish Hodge, Tom Principato, and all the other fine musicians who ever played the blues in DC. Not even much about other African American blues compatriots like Charlie Sayles, Memphis Gold, Chuck Brown, or Napoleon Turner, or great jazz players who lived in DC like Duke Ellington and Jelly Roll Morton, or soul stars like Marvin Gaye. Instead, we are focusing on the life and times of Phil Wiggins and his own community, the people and organizations he and the others interfaced with, people who were in some way part of the local traditional blues in the African American community.

We interviewed many musicians who were part of the Washington, DC, blues scene and the organizations that supported it, to tell their recollections of the place and times. The memories of those who were involved forge the history of this music scene from the mid-1970s to now.

In the course of writing this book I have been greatly enriched by knowing Phil as a friend, writing partner, and musician. He is a humble, kind, and decent man of considerable talent. I am honored to have Phil's trust and confidence, foremost as a friend, fellow music aficionado, and now writing partner for this book.

In 2017 it was a great honor for me to be by Phil's side when he was awarded the National Heritage Fellowship by the National Endowment of the Arts, the highest honor the United States bestows on its traditional artists. As Phil wowed the audience at the Library of Congress ceremony with his eloquent, always plainspoken but poignant speech, I could not help but remember a phrase that the former DC mayor Walter Washington once said about the local bluesman Bill Harris: "He brought honor on himself." I got to know Phil very well in the course of writing this book and I know that Phil brings honor on himself, not just through his music, but by who he is deep down to the core as a human being.

There is much more to say on almost every aspect of Phil's story over the last four decades, beyond what we could cover here. I hope readers will forgive any omissions of people and events.[1] We also wrote much more than could fit into this book. For more essays and photographs, visit www.sweetbitterblues.com. To hear some of the music by the people written about, a CD titled *Carrying On the Legacy* featuring music by contemporary Piedmont blues musicians has been issued on the Patuxent Music record label (Patuxent CD-321).

SWEET BITTER BLUES

Phil Wiggins, 2016. Photo by Frank Matheis.

INTRODUCTION

Washington, DC, an Epicenter of the Acoustic Blues

Washington, DC, is also known as "Chocolate City" because it is perhaps the blackest city in America, with the largest population percentage of African Americans. Phil calls it "a Southern town." Bluesman Bill Harris, known for his pig-hollers and nylon string guitar, the proprietor of the old Pigfoot blues club in Northeast DC, used to affectionately refer to it as "Chocolate City with vanilla suburbs." During the Great Migration of black Americans from the rural South to the cities of the North, from the early twentieth century to 1970, the population of Washington, DC, exploded as many blacks headed north to seek economic opportunities and escape harsh Jim Crow segregation laws. Like other large northern cities, the influx of southern rural folks brought along the blues musicians; but, unlike Chicago, Memphis, and St. Louis, the District of Columbia never developed a comparable electric blues scene and maintained its rural, country blues in the songster and so-called Piedmont blues traditions of the mid-Atlantic region. The acoustic blues scene is still going strong in and around Washington, DC, today.

At its core, the DC area acoustic "down-home" blues scene was and is rooted in the African American community, with a small group of musicians, proud and beloved men and women, who saw it as their mission to carry on their respective musical traditions: Mother Scott, Flora Molton, Chief Ellis, Archie Edwards, John Jackson, John Cephas & Phil Wiggins. Because of their love for the music and willingness to teach, these fine musicians created a harmonious environment, mostly centered on Archie's famous barbershop, where Archie Edwards opened his doors every Saturday afternoon for jam sessions. In the barbershop, and in the whole DC area scene, issues that were pervasive in other places never came up. Nobody was judged by their skill level, their skin color, their age, or gender...everybody was welcomed, everybody was met with open arms and a spirit of friendship pervaded. White musicians like Eleanor Ellis, sometimes Neil Harpe and Ben Andrews, were integral to the scene. Others were active nearby in the city but never interacted with the locals centered around the barbershop scene.

The 1960s folk and blues revival helped trigger white folks' interest in acoustic traditional music and many music fans found their way to the true blues, often first through white musicians or seminal folk record collections like the influential *Anthology of American Folk Music*, a six-album compilation released in 1952 by Moses Asch's Folkways Records. The eager new listeners then traced their way to the Appalachian and African American originators, wanting to hear the people who actually passed along, wrote, and performed the music. The interest in folk and country blues was peaking in the United States and Europe among an entirely new audience, but the DC musicians were as yet untapped. By the early 1970s, Mother Scott, Flora Molton, Elizabeth Cotten, Archie Edwards, John Jackson, John Cephas, and others were all actively playing as true folk musicians—mostly within their own localities for house parties, fish fries, or as street performers and for occasional festivals and concerts. Yet, at this point in time, many of these musicians had not received the same recognition and respect that had already been bestowed on many of their roots and blues peers around the country. None enjoyed the international fame that would follow in later years.

The DC musicians who are no longer with us have left an important legacy: "Carry on this music. Keep it going." This book aims to do just that. It documents the music community in and around DC as Phil lived and experienced it. It is about the generation that continued this musical legacy and the facilitating forces that helped shape the local scene. Who better to tell that story than a musician who lived the history, was part of it, and continues the legacy of this musical tradition to this day, as performer and educator? We happily tell the story that the Washington, DC, acoustic blues scene was and is a living tradition, and we tip our hats to those who made it happen.

Sweet Bitter Blues is also the title of a blues melody written by John Cephas with lyrics by Otis Williams, who served the University of Maryland for twenty-six years as director of the Nyumburu Cultural Center. Otis Williams was an influential songwriter, singer, promoter, teacher, and blues poet. He touched the lives of many, and he often invited Cephas & Wiggins to perform at the University of Maryland. Phil recalled, "Otis Williams had a beautiful voice and I don't mean just the sound of it. His voice was beautiful, deep, melodic, lyrical, steeped in African American culture. But his voice was also beautiful in the sense that it gave life to beautiful ideas. To hear that Griot's voice encouraged me to find and to use my own voice both in singing and making songs, has always given me inspiration and confidence to carry my music on and especially since John's passing."

John Cephas and Phil Wiggins recorded "Sweet Bitter Blues" as the title cut of a 1994 album, for which University of Maryland professor Barry Lee Pearson wrote the liner notes. It's a symbolic example of real, homegrown local blues, a DC-area blues in every way, what they used to call "old down-home blues."

The two simple words "sweet" and "bitter" could also be used to generally define the acoustic blues style played along the East Coast, a gentle and melodic blues style native in the Carolinas and Virginia over to Tennessee, but practiced along the entire mid-Atlantic region. Julia Olin, director of the National Council for the Traditional Arts (NCTA), perhaps gave the cleanest definition as "the melodic, delicate, lyrical blues of this region. It's not as percussive as other forms of blues. It's not out of the cotton fields. It even sounds fun." The rich musical tradition in the East Coast country blues owes much to ragtime, traditional Appalachian Mountain music, African American string music, spirituals and gospel, rural African American dance music, and the early white country music of the 1930s. This blues style features intricate fingerpicking with alternating bass and a simultaneous syncopated melody picked on the treble strings. Other characteristics of the East Coast or Piedmont style of solo acoustic guitar blues are light, bouncy rhythms, emphasis on virtuosity and professionalism, use of passing notes and chords, frequent instrumental breaks, adherence to twelve-bar and other standardized forms, and generally consistent thematic lyrics—songs with an underlying "story." There are many exceptions, of course. One characteristic of the style is the prominence and influence of blind performers, who took to performing as a means of income: Blind Blake, Blind Boy Fuller, Blind Willie McTell, the Reverend Gary Davis, Sonny Terry, Blind Joe Taggart, and Blind Willie Walker, and many others along the East Coast. This was also true for musicians with other disabilities, like Peg Leg Howell, Peg Leg Sam, and Brownie McGhee. Piedmont blues has a certain sweetness in the guitar style, but the themes of these blues can be about the sacred or the profane, about hardship, struggle, murder, pain, suffering, drinking, trouble with the opposite sex, and more. It's the blues where if you don't understand or listen to the words, the singing and melody sound so lovely and sweet, but if you do hear and understand them you can feel the bite. To paraphrase Tom Waits, it's ". . . beautiful melodies telling me terrible things."

> Well, it's sweet bitter blues
> Walk all around my bed
> Sometimes I wonder, am I alive or dead.

THE SO-CALLED PIEDMONT BLUES

Piedmont blues, East Coast blues, mid-Atlantic blues: it has many names, but, in its essence it is the pure, ethereal, original music of rural African Americans from the Eastern United States during the 1920s and 1930s and takes its roots in the earliest American string music traditions. This music was brought to Washington, DC, when rural African Americans moved to the city and brought their traditional musical styles with them.

Piedmont is a French word meaning foothill, derived from the Latin *pes montium*. It includes the geographic plateau that runs along the Eastern Seaboard between the foothills of the Appalachians (mostly along the Blue Ridge Mountains) and the coastal lowlands. The Piedmont encompasses a large geographic area that includes parts of Alabama, Georgia, North and South Carolina, Virginia, Maryland, Pennsylvania, and New Jersey.

The East Coast has a rich tradition of acoustic blues, mostly guitar-centric. Great instrumentalists refined the regional guitar style, with intricate syncopated fingerpicking patterns. This book cannot cover a suitable history of these famous players and singers of the 1920s and '30s, and the interested reader is best advised to read up and listen to these wonderful musicians, including the widely emulated Arthur "Blind" Blake, a ragtime and blues guitarist; Blind Willie McTell, a twelve-string player in the Piedmont style with amazing fingerpicking and slide skills from Georgia; the influential Reverend Gary Davis from South Carolina, who taught many white musicians during his time in New York in the 1960s; North Carolina's Blind Boy Fuller, one of the most popular players; and the guitar and harmonica duo of Sonny Terry and Brownie McGhee, who were highly influential. There were many more, such as Frank Hovington in Delaware, Buddy Moss, Curley Weaver, Barbecue Bob. There are many books written and many albums recorded. The history of the acoustic East Coast blues is an adventurous and exciting musical journey filled with some of the finest music in the blues.

Piedmont blues is a convenient way to define a regional musical style by giving it a stylistic and geographic identity, comparable to Delta blues or Chicago blues. It sounds good, although it is perhaps imperfect. East Coast or mid-Atlantic blues might be better descriptions. Yet, Piedmont blues is now widely accepted, and for this book we also embrace it.

Some have expressed the belief that the acoustic Piedmont blues tradition died with the first wave of original players of the 1930s and '40s. When confronted with these declarations, Phil Wiggins, utterly unconvinced of the demise of this particular musical tradition, simply responded, "I say they need to get out more."

John Cephas stated:

> Phil and I, we're committed to traditional music in the hope that we can keep it alive and interest some younger people in it. The type of music we play is the grass roots of most American music and we have a heartfelt interest to do everything we can to try to preserve it. White people have their country music, but the blues we play is the black man's country music. It was born in the black community, out in the

country at house parties and country breakdowns where people would get together and dance all night long. But today, anybody can learn the blues. If you are a musician, color doesn't make any difference. You can learn the blues if you are black, white, gray, grizzly, or green. For me, it's part of my heritage. It's in my blood. This is the black folks' folk music, but it is also all our music. It's an American tradition.[1]

Yet, race is today an undeniable external factor. Blues is an African American cultural contribution to the world, a black musical form and an inherent part of the African American experience. Today, black musicians can feel a form of estrangement, as this music, which had its origins in the black experience, is now in a white-dominated world. The blues press, blues forums, record labels, academia, and radio DJs are predominantly white—as is the audience.

The term *Piedmont* declares a collective identity, but it does not mean that Piedmont blues is played or perceived in any one single way. Some, like John Cephas, proudly proclaimed that he played the "Piedmont blues of Virginia" and he made it his mission to propagate this blues to future generations. He taught that term to his students and actively used it in his vocabulary. One of his students, Valerie Turner, now calls her duo Piedmont Blūz. Virginia bluesman John Jackson conversely said, "We just liked songs. We didn't call them Piedmont. We just played songs at home and if we heard a song from someone else, we learned how to play it. My favorite singer on the radio was Jimmie Rodgers, so I learned some of his songs."[2] Phil Wiggins said:

> People like John Jackson had a particular picking style and incorporated elements
> of country music and Appalachian folk music and songs that had also been popular
> among the entire population of the region, and sometimes they've taken pop songs
> of the period and included them, like Jimmie Rodgers and such. . . . John didn't call
> himself a Piedmont blues musician, even if he was one by today's popular defini-
> tion. While his fingerpicking and gentle singing style was definitely befitting the
> Piedmont style, he played a wide-ranging repertoire of various songs from country,
> folk, gospel, and even pop music genres. In that sense, he was as much a songster as
> a Piedmont blues singer and instrumentalist.

The term *songster* usually refers to a musician of the pre-blues days, a Vaude-ville performer, traveling medicine show minstrel, or itinerant musician who played a wide-ranging repertoire of music. A "songster" in black usage is simply someone who is known as a good singer. The repertoire could be anything—all blues, or a variety of genres. The term has been given a new meaning by writers, a meaning contrasted to "bluesman" or "blues singer." Today, it is often associated with someone who can please an audience with whatever type of music they like. Black songsters often had a special song list for white audiences, catering to their tastes and preferences. Howard Armstrong, for example, played German and Polish songs that his particular audience liked. It has been often cited that just because the early musicians recorded certain songs on record, that does not mean that this was all they played in life. Johnny Shines, who traveled with and recorded Robert Johnson's songs, frequently spoke of the fact that they played all kinds of music, some not blues at all, in order to earn tips. This was confirmed many times over by Robert Junior Lockwood, Honeyboy Edwards, and many others. Their commercial recordings were merely a snap-shot of the wider repertoire of these musicians.

The integration of new songs, whether blues or not—as in the case of John Jackson, who heard country songs on the radio and incorporated them into his repertoire—did not mean the end of traditional blues. It was just a normal evolution. He adapted the country pop songs of the period and played them in his own regional style. Over time, some late twentieth-century regional musi-cians incorporated songs typically found in other parts of the country, such as Delta blues. DC bluesman John Cephas played a mixed repertoire of both Pied-mont and Delta blues, for example. The point is that regional blues offers wide diversity, not just in styles but artist preferences, tastes, and personal influences, whatever they may be.

Phil Wiggins also stated his musical partner John Cephas didn't call it Pied-mont blues "until Dr. Barry Lee Pearson told him that's what he was playing. Then he started to refer to it as Piedmont." Archie Edwards is frequently quoted as having said, "I play what they call the old Piedmont style, but I call it East Vir-ginia blues, 'cause that's where I learned it when I was growing up in the country. It's fingerpicking, where you use your thumb and your fingers but I don't use any picks. I just play with my fingers. John Hurt, he played about the same way, but he called it cotton-picking style."[3] Phil Wiggins noted:

> John Cephas, he loved to play an occasional Delta style. He became a sort of an ambassador of the Piedmont style—he had a hard time comparing the two different styles without making the Piedmont style seem better in a way and more difficult and much more of an accomplishment to play. But I guess that's human nature. He took pride in that. But I laugh, because he said a lot of people played Delta style because they couldn't play the so-called Piedmont style. But I don't know, at the same time, John loved Delta style and he played some of it. He played all sorts of different styles of music. There are different styles, but people flow between one and the other.

The Piedmont blues is a style of playing, a traditional blues that originated from the general geography of the region; but it's the musical tradition of the player, rather than the geographic origin of the musician. Today, you can be called a Piedmont blues player no matter where you live or where you are from, provided you play that distinctive fingerpicking guitar style. Mary Flower lives in Portland, Oregon, and is defined as a Piedmont player. Lots of musicians play the Piedmont blues nationwide—Paul Geremia, Jorma Kaukonen, Andy Cohen, Woody Mann, Stefan Grossman, Ry Cooder, Roy Book Binder, and many more.

There are also musicians all over the world who emulate East Coast blues greats such as Blind Blake, Blind Boy Fuller, and others, having learned from records, and who faithfully reproduce the complicated guitar playing from the original old 78-rpm recordings, note for note. Gifted players like Ari Eisinger, Frank Fotusky, and Tom Feldman, to mention but a few, are wonderfully capable of replicating the old masters. This is an important part of keeping the blues alive, but it encapsulates the music in a historical vacuum. In the Washington, DC, area the music was passed down from generation to generation in the African American community of Virginia, West Virginia, the Carolinas, and beyond. The black musicians of DC continued this musical tradition, playing the songs of their own rural heritage in a new music community that they created in DC, and then taught these songs to their students and friends. The students of these folk musicians are carrying on this music today in an organic traditional folk music scene. Many are featured in this book.

IT TAKES A TRIBE

What made Washington, DC, so special that it could sustain a thriving country blues scene for more than forty years? It was a convergence of cultural forces. Archie Edwards's barbershop, famous for Saturday afternoon jam sessions, was and is a central meeting point for blues musicians young and old, black and white. Dr. Barry Lee Pearson, the "Professor of the Blues" at the University of Maryland, is an ever-present supporter and chronicler, as was Otis Williams. Smithsonian Folkways Records is centered in Washington and the annual Smithsonian Folklife Festival has been one of the biggest gatherings of traditional acoustic blues in the world. There were supportive organizations like the National Council for the Traditional Arts (NCTA) and the Travellin' Blues Workshop, newspapers like the *Unicorn Times*, musical venues such as Ontario Place, the Childe Harold, and Food-for-Thought. On FM radio, you had the voice of the blues in DC, the dapper Nap Turner on WPFW, who frequently spun the records of the local musicians. FM stations like WAMU and WHFS also played blues and helped popularize the genre.

One main reason for the unprecedented continuation of the acoustic blues in this region has been the willingness of the older generation to carry on the traditions. Many musicians in the center of the local blues were later teachers at the popular annual blues camp at the nearby Augusta Heritage Center of Davis & Elkins College in Elkins, West Virginia, a cultural institution of immense importance to the development of folk blues in the region. John Jackson, John Cephas, Phil Wiggins, Eleanor Ellis, and others were all active teachers who taught blues workshops at the Augusta Heritage Center and other programs nationwide; and they all had local students. John Cephas was a founding member of the DC Blues Society, an organization dedicated to preserving traditional blues. This nurturing environment is still one of the most unique in the U.S. acoustic blues today, and has contributed significantly to the progress of this genre in the region. Even small record labels like Patuxent Music, operated by Tom Mindte, which are willing to issue roots music by local and regional musicians, are important contributors. As bluesman Robert Johnson said, "There is a great long story to tell . . ."

Before we start with Phil telling his own story, let's reflect on the decade prior to Phil's career: the 1960s, the era when blues elders were being rediscovered and were playing in DC.

THE PRECEDING YEARS: JOHN HURT, SKIP JAMES, AND ELIZABETH COTTEN

Phil Wiggins started his musical career in DC in the early 1970s, when the acoustic blues scene in the African American community was burgeoning. In the decade earlier, three important blues artists who achieved international fame resided in the city: Elizabeth Cotten, John Hurt, and Skip James.

Of course, there were countless others who remained unrecognized. Considering that the blues, as a genre, dates back to the 1920s, and even earlier, it stands to reason that many great musicians must have graced the city, some resident and some itinerant. The 78-rpm recordings made by blues musicians down South, during the heyday of "race records," sold in small quantities to the black audience in the 1930s Depression era. After the old-time blues faded from interest among its original African American audience by the 1950s, most blues musicians in this style slipped into obscurity, many never having achieved fame and fortune. Those plantation musicians who were "rediscovered" during the 1960s "blues revival" were found because they left a legacy in the form of 78-rpm records, made in earlier decades, which gave them a historical marker. Son House, Skip James, John Hurt, Booker "Bukka" White, and many others were found only because they had become subjects of interest to a group of fervent young white blues fans and devoted record collectors, who knew of them only from their scratchy old records, as mysterious ghostlike figures from the past. The blues record collectors descended on Mississippi and other points south to find and bring back these players, launching a second career for these old musicians, most of whom lived in poverty and had given up playing music decades earlier.

Musicians who never cut a record often remained unknown, no matter how good they were, with no record to lead to them, no material on which to base a cult following. But these musicians existed, carrying on the regional styles and continuing the music generation to generation. While the blues fans and collectors were looking far away all over the South for objects of their romanticized imagination, surely there were wonderful blues players right here all along in their backyard in DC or rural Virginia and Maryland.

The early 1960s record-collector and blues revivalist clique predated Phil's involvement with the local African American blues scene by a full decade. The white college fans and the record collector and blues aficionado world was contemporary, but far separated from the local, community-rooted black down-home blues scene. There was and is a gap between black and white DC, and sometimes it might as well be a million miles wide. This was reflected in the blues community as well. The same folks who had no qualms about roaming through Mississippi in the great hunt for their blues idols never crossed the Anacostia River. This schism remains to this day. In the course of interviewing for this book, Frank Matheis received an outraged message from the president of a local record company declaring, "What African-American blues scene? There was no African-American blues scene in Washington, DC!"[4]

While this book focuses on people who in some way interacted with the down-home African American blues scene in Washington, the city has a rich history and many contemporaries that were important musically and culturally. Duke Ellington had blues singers in his bands or accompanied them in the studio in the 1920s: Gussie Alexander, Florence Bristol, Alberta Jones, Ozie McPherson (Ozie Ware), Alberta Prime, and Walter Richardson. Sis Quander also sang with his band. There were other early Washington-area blues singers, especially on the vaudeville stage, such as the Howard Theatre. Jelly Roll Morton was resident in Washington in the late 1930s and performed solo, doing a lot of blues material, as he showed in his 1938 sessions for Alan Lomax.[5] Significantly, the city was a center of blues research, especially through the blues recording activity coordinated by the Library of Congress and undertaken by the Lomaxes and others. Lead Belly, Josh White, and others performed in Washington frequently in the 1940s, and Eleanor Roosevelt became a serious patron of Josh White in the late 1940s. Professor, poet, and literary critic Sterling Brown taught for years at Howard University and wrote about blues lyrics as well as composing wonderful blues-themed poetry.

There was also a core of influential local record collectors, archivists and record producers and their friends: Joe Bussard, Dick Spottswood, Tom Hoskins, Bill Givens, Pete Whelan, and John Fahey. Dick Spottswood is still a celebrated local radio personality and roots music proponent, who has catalogued and been responsible for the reissue of many thousands of recordings. He recorded Frank Hovington and many others, and was well known to John Cephas.

There were also numerous small local blues record labels: Fonotone Records in Frederick, Maryland, 1956–69, operated by Joe Bussard; Origin Jazz Library by Pete Whelan and Bill Givens; Piedmont by Dick Spottswood; Adelphi by Gene Rosenthal. The only label that actually took interest in the local scene, of which Phil Wiggins was part, was Trix Records by Peter B. Lowry, who recorded numerous Piedmont artists. Cephas & Wiggins recorded with Trix in 1980, but the record never paid off financially for them. Most other local labels largely ignored the scene that is the subject of this book. Other than the "rediscovery" of Morton in the late 1930s, this research and collecting activity largely ignored any indigenous blues scene. Joe Bussard mainly concentrated on John Fahey, but he also recorded some local black artists. By the 1960s, blues artists were being "imported" to create a "local scene" of sorts to make up for the supposed nonexistence of an indigenous scene.

Had local record producers and collectors looked regionally, they would surely have uncovered local musicians of great skill and stature. In Virginia, for example, there were John Jackson, John Tinsley, James Lowry, Marvin and Turner Foddrell, Luke Jordan, Rabbit Muse, and many more. Serious folklorists did take an interest. Chuck Perdue, for example, met John Jackson in 1965 giving a guitar lesson at a Fairfax, Virginia, gas station and took him under his wing to help get his career launched. Dr. Kip Lornell has taught courses in American music and ethnomusicology at George Washington University, and is a primary chronicler of the Piedmont blues along with Dr. Barry Lee Pearson at the University of Maryland.[6]

During the 1940s and 1950s, Alec Seward of Newport News made some records in New York City; Silas Pendleton from Rappahannock, Virginia, was field-recorded by folklorist Horace Beck; and John Tinsley of Franklin County made a single recording. Spurred by the folk revival of the 1960s, other artists with Virginia ties were located, including Richmond-born songster Bill Williams, a brilliant guitarist who claimed he had toured with Blind Blake. Peter Lowry recorded Pernell Charity of Sussex County, and Kip Lornell recorded a number of musicians for the Blue Ridge Institute, most notably the Foddrell family.[7]

History has brought out a range of perspectives about the good and the bad, heroes and villains, when it comes to the "rediscovery" of the old blues musicians. The fact is that local record collectors and labels contributed significantly to change the course of history of folk music and country blues in America and the world. The folk and blues revival sparked global interest in the genre. It's hard to imagine that there could have been a market for this roots music today if it hadn't been for these early proponents, if the great musicians such as John Hurt, Skip James, Booker "Bukka" White, Son House, Sleepy John Estes, Johnny Shines, and many more had not been brought back from a long musical hiatus to grace the world's stages. Now, more than five decades later, there is still worldwide interest in the traditional blues. The blues revival, and all that came after, paved the way for the blues artists in Washington, DC, who would emerge a decade later, the people who are the subjects of this book.

John Hurt

The popular blues press of the time referred to him by his marketing stage name as "Mississippi" John Hurt, but in Archie's barbershop at 2007 Bunker Hill Road NE he was simply called "John." For the years 1963–66 that Hurt lived in DC with his wife Jessie and two grandchildren, he was in two worlds—in his new career in the white music establishment, with his handlers and managers; and, his private life in the black community where he could feel at "home"[8] and where he had a special friend, Archie Edwards, and many more, including Philadelphia Jerry Ricks who often visited Washington, DC. Hurt used to get his hair cut at Archie Edwards's barbershop, and he and Archie often played together at the barbershop's famed jam sessions. Archie was his friend and musical kin whom he referred to as "Brother Arch." John Hurt had a regular gig at the Ontario Place Coffee House, and the relationship between Edwards and Hurt would be one of the building blocks of the blues scene in Archie's barbershop, the center of the DC acoustic blues scene, and would impact the region's music for decades to come.

Hurt, from Avalon, Mississippi, was one of the great "rediscovered" artists of the golden era of country blues and one of the most beloved figures in folk music. His music is so accessible that even people who claim not to like the blues have an affinity for this bluesman and songster. Perhaps it was because of his melodically elegant and subtle style, his lilting, wistful music that touches people's hearts with his syncopated, refined, and intricate alternating bass fingerpicking style, with fluid left-hand arpeggios—a style similar to the East Coast fingerpicking often called Piedmont blues. He played with a light beat and a gentle sweetness—accompanied by his soothing voice. You could feel the love in his music and he was often described as an affable, kind, sweet, unassuming old man, always in a worn old felt hat. He played with a smile and put a smile on those fortunate enough to have heard him play in his lifetime. He may have been diminutive in size, but he remains an adored giant of folk music to this day. According to photographer and folk music manager Dick Waterman, John Hurt once told him his biggest wish in the whole wide world: "If I was to have just one wish and I knew that wish was to come true, I would wish . . . I would wish that everyone in this world would love me just like I love everyone in the world."[9]

Surely that wish has come true. Now, five decades after his death, he remains one of the most beloved figures in folk music.

John Smith Hurt was born in 1892 in Teoc, Mississippi, in the hill country above the Delta region, and was raised in nearby Avalon, a small rural community. He only had four years of formal education, worked as a sharecropper, and was a self-taught guitarist. As published in the liner notes of the 1997 Rounder album *Mississippi John Hurt: Legend*, John Hurt in 1963 said:

> I learned to play guitar at age of nine. A week after that my mother bought me a second-hand guitar at the price of $1.50. No guitar has no more beautifuler sound. At age of 14, I went to playing for country dances. Also, private homes. At this time, I was working very hard on a farm near Avalon, Mississippi. In the years of '28 and '29, I recorded for the Okeh Recording Company at Memphis, Tennessee, in '28, in New York in '29.[10] After that I came back to my home in Mississippi. Worked hard on a farm for my living. Worked on the river with the U.S. Engineers, also work some on the railroad and on W.P.A. project. Now I'm on the road again with the Piedmont Record Company.

In an often-told story, he was long forgotten, perhaps assumed deceased, faded into musical obscurity, the way of many of the musicians who recorded sides for the "race records" of the 1920s and '30s, sold to the African American blues audience. There was no mass appeal for these rural blues records in the jazz era and most were released regionally in small quantity pressings.

In 1963 Tom Hoskins, aka "Fang," brought Hurt to DC to launch his new career. Hurt, by then just over seventy years old but still musically skilled, played the Newport Folk Festival and the Philadelphia Folk Festival. He actively toured the college and coffeehouse concert circuit. He was a guest on the biggest TV talk show of the time, Johnny Carson's *Tonight Show*; featured in *Newsweek*, *Down Beat*, *Time*, and the *New York Times*; and celebrated as the "Dramatic rediscovery of a near legendary musician." Young white kids flocked to his shows and concerts. Many articles were written. Vanguard Records issued a series of albums. His songs were also recorded for the Library of Congress and included in countless compilations. The 1928 OKeh recordings were reissued. Yet, he returned to Mississippi in 1966, only a few short years after being rediscovered, where he soon died of a heart attack.[11] He did not have much to show for the three years of fame.

Photographer and music manager Dick Waterman acknowledged, "John never felt at home in white society and every time that we drove into a new city, he would anxiously scan the streets to find 'someone that looks like me.'"[12] In Hurt's DC years, there were places where he could go and simply feel at home, with people who did not have ulterior motives, where he was not a novelty and where he did not have to be anyone other than himself. One of those places was Archie's barbershop and one of those people was Archie Edwards.

In 1978 German record producer and photographer Axel Küstner interviewed Archie, who spoke of John Hurt:[13]

> I used to do a lot of his stuff. Mississippi John Hurt—I worked with him in person, here in Washington. He lived here for about three years, and I met him when he was performing down at the Ontario Place (a coffeehouse) in Washington, D.C. Since I had learned some of his music when I was a kid, we just started playing together. His "Stack O'Lee" and "Candy Man Blues" I learned when I was a kid. But what made me so interested in him was that 35 years after learning some of his music, I met him. Then we worked together for three years and he went back to Mississippi and passed away. The last three years of his lifetime I was his buddy. I learned quite a few of his songs during the time that he and I worked together. He asked me to learn them and teach them to other people. He asked me not to let his music die, you know. Said if I could learn it and could pass it on to someone else he would still be alive. It was quite a coincidence about me being a country blues musician who had admired him all this long time and getting a chance to meet him. It was quite a story, but I guess it was something that was supposed to happen. I started to do my own writing back in '63 and '64 after I met John Hurt. When I was playing his music and other people's music, he said, "Brother, I see you are a good guitar player but write you some stuff. Write some stuff for yourself." He said, "My stuff and Blind Lemon all that's been played. Write something that nobody has ever written." So, I started writing my own stuff.

As part of his extensive interviews with Dr. Barry Lee Pearson, Archie Edwards explained:[14]

> It was a beautiful thing between me and John Hurt, because for the last three years of his life he'd come to my house when he wasn't on the road, or I'd go to his house. Or we'd go to the barbershop, and we'd sit and play all night long until the sun came up. We just had ourselves a hell of a good time. When I met him, it was like I'd known him all my life. We sounded so much alike. Now John and I had several things that we were doing just alike, even though he was from Mississippi and I was from Virginia. Most people thought I was his understudy, but I was playing that way before I met him. That knocked him for a loop. He didn't know anybody was still picking the guitar like him. I worked with John Hurt for about three years then he went back to Mississippi and passed away. I used to go down there on Rhode Island Ave. and pick him up because he lived at #30 Rhode Island Avenue, Northwest. So, if he wasn't on the road I would call him and tell him, "John, I'll come down and pick you up. We can go to the barbershop." So, we would go over there and he would sit

and play the guitar for my customers. Sometimes he'd have the whole barbershop full of people. We've had them all the way out the street, in the back and the front. I would be cutting a head of hair and if he played a song I felt he needed some backing on, I just put the tools down and pick up the guitar and follow him. So, we had a lot of fun there. Big audiences would come to hear me and John play and the people tell me about that now sometimes. "Man, I remember a time back in the sixties when you was doing big business here and John Hurt would come in here and play" . . . When we got together, we had some fun. We drank up many half pints. I didn't say nothing about that. But, it's a shame so many dead men go to the trashcan. I never heard him say a curse word and I never knew him to do anything to anybody. But he would take a drink and smoke cigarettes. That's as far as he would go. I never knew him to speak an evil word against anybody. He was a very cool guy. So, it was an honor to meet a guy like that.

Archie told Dr. Barry Lee Pearson, ". . . Mississippi John Hurt asked me, he said, 'Brother Arch, whatever you do, teach my music to other people.' He said, 'Don't make no difference what color they are, teach it to them. Because I don't want to die and you don't want to die. Teach them my music and teach them your music.'"[15]

That's what Archie Edwards did. The jams at Archie's barbershop became regular events over decades to come, and the central meeting point for the acoustic blues scene in Washington. Archie's legacy is carried on through the local musicians who carry on traditional music.

Skip James

The bluesman Nehemiah "Skip" James, from Bentonia, Mississippi, was another of the "rediscovered" artists who had been transplanted late in life to Washington. The bluesman, known for his wistful and stirring falsetto singing, and a prime "rediscovery" target for these early blues aficionados of the folk and blues revival in the early 1960s. His famed 1931 Paramount recording session included eighteen songs, shrouded in mystery and intrigue, such as "Devil Got My Woman," "22–20 Blues" and "Hard Time Killing Floor Blues." Part of his haunting sound came from the "Bentonia guitar tuning"—Open-D minor, that he had learned from local musician Henry Stuckey (1897–1966). Like Robert Johnson (who emulated James), Skip James evoked devil imagery in his songs, which was as intriguing to the new white college-aged audience as his guitar styling and eerie falsetto. His somber and ethereal delivery was spine-chilling and strange, almost scary. James cut right through the aesthetic milieu of white middle-class sensibilities with dissonant, even primal music and slashing lines like, "I'd rather be the devil than be that woman's man. / 'Cause nothing but the devil changed my baby's mind." James' songs were stark, filled with elemental imagery, often violent, tormented by the eternal conflict of the sacred and profane.

Skip James lived in Washington, DC, from 1966 to 1968 and he immortalized this period in his song "Washington, D.C. Hospital Blues":

> In the hospital, now
> In Washington D.C.
> Ain't got nobody
> To see about me

Skip James had been seriously ill before coming to DC and was actually hospitalized when he was found in Tunica, Mississippi. His ailment continued during his time in DC, where it landed him in the hospital that was to become famous in song. He later moved to Philadelphia, where he died in 1969.

Skip James was known to be strong-willed, and on occasion ornery. Washington record collector, musicologist, and radio host Dick Spottswood said, "He didn't suffer fools or take *no* kind of shit."[16] A complex person who had been a sharecropper and preacher, along with more disreputable pursuits, James was a rough-hewn survivor whose path through life gave him a razor-sharp edge. His biographer Stephen Calt reported that James had even admitted to murder. He was definitely not a poster child for the blues revival 78-rpm record crowd, who had wanted these old musicians to fulfill some imaginary ideal of what the blues was and where it came from.

John Hurt and Skip James were often headliners at the Ontario Place, a DC coffeehouse where Archie Edwards also performed. One of the co-owners, Leland Talbot, related that Skip James had told him, while out in Olney, Maryland, that he got into playing blues to ". . . cloud women's minds."[17]

James shared many other stages with Hurt, including at the 1964 Newport Folk Festival. Like Hurt, he entered into unfavorable business contracts and, despite many bookings and concert appearances, lived month to month without great financial success, until he received $10,000 in royalties when the rock group Cream covered his song "I'm So Glad" in 1966.

Unlike Hurt, Skip James did not integrate in the local African American blues scene; and by all accounts, James did not hold other musicians, including John Hurt, in high esteem. Perhaps due to his illness or other factors, he worked the same clubs and sometimes jammed with Archie at the barbershop, but never established strong friendships locally. He gave some lessons to the local musician Ed Morris, who wrote, "Skip James is the greatest artist ever to come from the Mississippi Delta"[18] in the liner notes of the debut album by Skip James after his reemergence in 1964, even though Bentonia is actually not in the Delta region. Not unusually, James did not embrace Morris with equal enthusiasm.

Archie Edwards reminisced in an interview with Dr. Barry Lee Pearson:

> Skip James, he was a character. We had another time when Mississippi John Hurt, Skip James, and me were doing shows at the Ontario Place. John did a show, next week Skip did a show, then it was my turn to do a show. Skip called me up to come with him on his show, but I told him if I played on his show then the people wouldn't come out to see me on my own show. Anyway, I went down with him and you know, he got so drunk I wound up doing his whole show. And, the next week, when I did my show, nobody showed up. They said, "We already saw you last week." I think about ten people showed up.[19]

Yet, Skip James was an important contributor to the local scene, and even years after he left the city, his impact on the blues scene remained, as John Cephas would carry on his songs in the Cephas & Wiggins repertoire. Whereas Archie Edwards emulated John Hurt, John Cephas was influenced by Skip James. John Cephas even taught Skip James's guitar style to his students and he became a proponent of the James style.

Phil Wiggins reminisced:

> John actually did not know about Skip James. He had never met him, even though they were in D.C. at the same time. We were on the way to a faraway gig, I can't remember to where, it was in the early '90s. It was a long drive and I brought along a cassette tape of the original Paramount recordings. John was impressed. He listened to it over and over until we actually got tired of hearing it. Then, he took the cassette back home and listened to it again and again until he figured out the D-minor tuning, that sad style that Skip James used. Eventually John became an expert on Skip James. And we covered quite a few of his songs. We played "Sickbed Blues," "Hard Time Killing Floor Blues," "Illinois Blues," "I'd Rather Be the Devil," and some others. John loved that music style and he really mastered it.

John Cephas told Dr. Barry Lee Pearson:

> I was fascinated by Skip James. I loved his sound and tried to learn how to do it. I guess the first song I learned was "Sickbed Blues." . . . But on tour, I could really identify with the words, and I kept trying to get the sound. And then he does a lot of numbers in E-minor so it was hard for musicians that wanted to copy him. They couldn't figure out how he was getting such an eerie sound out of his guitar, but it was his tuning. It was a real sad sound. I think right now, after Blind Boy Fuller and Reverend Gary Davis, he's about my favorite. We do quite a few numbers from his repertoire, "Cherry Ball," "Special Rider" and several others.[20]

Skip James, the tragic figure, the exalted and the vanquished, made his imprint in Washington, DC, and in many ways, the fact that he lived there during the time of the blues revival helped solidify the city as a center of the acoustic blues.

Elizabeth "Libba" Cotten

Elizabeth "Libba" Cotten was born in Chapel Hill, North Carolina, in about 1894. She taught herself to play guitar on a dirt street in what is now Carrboro, along the railroad tracks where she could hear the whistle from the trains. She bought the guitar with the money she made cooking and cleaning around Lloyd Street, where she also chopped wood and carried water, earning seventy-five cents, and later a dollar, a day. She was only a girl when she lived on Lloyd Street at the turn of the twentieth century, the time of Jim Crow. But the songs she wrote there would carry her far away, all the way to the stage at Carnegie Hall, where the world heard her sing about the lonely sound of a passing train.[21]

Beginning in 1940, Cotten, one of America's favorite folk singers, lived with her daughter and grandchildren in Washington, DC. Hers is an amazing story as she may never have been "discovered" had she not coincidentally ended up working in the household of one of America's foremost folk music families, the Seegers, under the most fortuitous circumstances: In 1946 or 1947, Ruth Crawford Seeger, the family matriarch and the first woman to be awarded a Guggenheim Fellowship Award for Music,[22] was shopping at a Lansburgh's department store, a major chain in the DC area. In the store, her young child Peggy, who would later become a prominent folk singer and political activist, was separated from her mother and lost. Elizabeth Cotten found the child, comforted her, and brought her back to her mother. This incident led to a friendly relationship between Ruth Crawford Seeger and a job offer for Elizabeth Cotten to work in the Seeger household as a nanny. Over the next years, she was exposed to much music in the Seeger household and she eventually revealed that she had also played guitar as a child. The Seegers bestowed her one of Peggy's guitars and Elizabeth Cotten started to relearn the instrument, which she played left-handed by turning the guitar over with the strings reversed.[23] She played the treble strings with her thumb and the bass strings with her other fingers, developing a truly distinctive guitar style and sound. Her song "Freight Train" is a fingerpicker's classic, and her arrangements of tunes like "Oh, Babe, It Ain't No Lie" are standards now in the folk repertoire.

From late 1957 to early 1958, Peggy's brother Mike Seeger, one of America's foremost musician-folklorists and musicologists, and half-brother to Pete Seeger, made her first recording in a bedroom in Elizabeth's home in Washington, DC. Mike Seeger, who would be her friend, supporter, and advocate for life, visited about a half a dozen times for the recording. In 1958, *Folksongs and Instrumentals with Guitar* (also issued as *Negro Folk Songs and Tunes*) was released (later reissued on Folkways as *Freight Train and Other North Carolina Folk Songs and Tunes*). In January 1960, Elizabeth Cotten had her first concert with Mike Seeger at a joint performance at Swarthmore College. Thereafter, she joined the so-called "rediscovered" folk and blues artists and joined the stage with people like John Jackson, Sleepy John Estes, John Lee Hooker, Jesse Fuller, Muddy Waters, and many more.[24]

Her two most popular songs were "Freight Train" and "Shake Sugaree," both of which were widely covered by other musicians, and which ended up becoming her way to financial success. Unlike some of the other artists who did not have the same fate, Elizabeth Cotten was under the protection of the Seeger family, who looked out for her interests, and she received all of the income due to her. She was able to buy a nice home and live in comfort. Peter, Paul and Mary; Bob Dylan; the Grateful Dead and many others covered her songs . . . and she was paid the full royalties. Her music was included in movie soundtracks and on PBS' *Shining Time Station*—all that for a musician whose public career started at the age of sixty-eight. She became a key figure in the folk revival of the 1960s, a National Heritage Fellow and a Grammy winner for *Elizabeth Cotten Live!*, which won the 1985 Grammy for Best Ethnic or Traditional Recording. She played the Philadelphia Folk Festival and the 1964 Newport Folk Festival, along with Joan Baez and Mavis Staples.

One of her most financially rewarding events was when Peter, Paul and Mary recorded "Freight Train," and Peter Yarrow called and asked to give full credit for the song to Elizabeth Cotten, even though they had added something.[25]

Elizabeth Cotten died on June 29, 1987. She started her career at an age when some people start their retirement, and she remains as one of the most beloved folk and blues singers of the twentieth century, an American cultural treasure. Her albums on Arhoolie and Smithsonian Folkways record labels continue to sell to this day, as her music lives on.

PART ONE

Phil's Story

The music that I like to play feels like home—it's what I know. It is where I came from. It's time for me to tell my own story and to talk about the music and the people who played it, as I lived and experienced it. There is always somebody externally telling me about our music—my music—judging, pontificating and directing—but I learned the real blues from real bluesmen and women in my own community. It is important that we, in the black community, tell our own story, to talk about from where this music derives–to tell the story of the Washington, DC, acoustic blues, because that's the only way that the true story is going to be told.

The blues are an essential and integral part of my life. On a good night of playing music, all the songs and feelings of the people that came before me and all the expressions of my culture and history pass through me, and it's not under my control. That's what I strive for. I don't worry that much about how it's understood or how it's analyzed or accepted by other people. As long as I feel that for me, on that particular night, or that moment, that I'm open to the best that can happen, and letting it happen and helping make it happen, then the audience will understand it one way or the other. I love this music. I do it because I don't have any other choice. It's what I'm drawn to. I could have taken my life in a different direction and done something else where maybe I would have lived more comfortably or maybe I'd be considered more of a success. For me to be able to express myself musically and artistically in the way that I do when I make music has become my life's priority.

I'm lucky that I've been able to know, play with, and learn from some real master musicians, some of the greatest of my time. I feel really fortunate in that way. This book is not about marking my place in history. That remains to be seen. That's not up to me to say. This book is about the wonderful music, the amazing musicians, and the thriving regional scene of which I was also a part. I am telling the story, but it's about all of that, not just me. This is not an autobiography with personal details. It's about the music and the music scene and all of my friends in it.

If I try to think in terms of how I'm going to impact the history of the music, am I really being honest or am I just trying to tailor what I'm doing to this end result? It would be great if people consider me to be a half-decent musician, but other than that I just want to reach in as many directions as possible and just be honest and true to myself and to be open to whatever it is that passes through me; and of course, a lot of it is my own culture, my own history, my own ancestors flowing through me. At the same time, there are lots of other influences too that get in there. I want to be open to that because that's how the music evolves.

Some people who talk about traditional music often take folks like Charley Patton or Robert Johnson, or Blind Blake, or whoever—back in the days—and nail them down, isolate them, freeze them in time, and then call that "tradition." The fact is that the music evolved and keeps evolving. All those guys like Robert Johnson, their ears were wide open and everything that was available to them at the time they put in their music. It's just that now I live in a time when I have a lot more available to me. To me, when you talk about tradition, that process is the tradition, the process of taking—of keeping your ears wide open, creating, wanting to express yourself, and taking influences from whatever is available and putting them through your own spirit and heart and having them come out.

For me, what I love about lots of different types and styles of music and musical traditions is to find the similarities and the common ground and the connections, because it's human beings making the music and we all experience similar emotions. To me it's fascinating to discover similarities cross-culturally to music and people. Musicians have always played the music they like, without caring about terms or delineations. Black and white musicians in my time played together and shared many of the same musical traditions, especially here in the region of the music they now call "Piedmont Blues." The only time there were issues is when it came down to the economics of the music business, when white musicians were being highly paid for the music they copied from African Americans. Whenever black musicians complained about so-called cultural appropriation, you'd need to follow the money. It's about who originated the music and who cashed in on it. We didn't have those issues here in the DC music community, because we were not making too much money anyway. That was more in the electric and rocking blues. Our community was about sharing and carrying on traditions. Even the creation of terms like "Piedmont Blues" is problematic. I'm sure there's somewhat of a regional style. But I've been to Appalachia, I've been to the Piedmont foothills, and to the Tidewater of the Atlantic and I've never had to clear customs or show my passport for going through. The culture flowed freely across those supposed regional boundaries. Appalachian blues, Piedmont blues, Tidewater blues—those boundaries didn't really exist. To me, those words and phrases don't mean that much. The music either touches you or moves you and you can either dance to it or you can't. It's either good and it's rejuvenating and inspiring and nourishing, or it isn't. That's what matters to me, not the categories.

I toured with Robert Lockwood. We got along great. I loved him and admired him greatly. He didn't take any shit off people, but he was a real gentleman and he carried himself and had this class that our generation doesn't have anymore, this gravitas. We were somewhere in Germany and had just finished a show and were walking along the street late at night and this young kid runs up to him, "Please, would you sign my scrapbook." Robert Lockwood says, "Sure." As he's signing it the kid said, "Yes, and you are the stepson of Robert Johnson?" He replies, "No, no. I'm not Robert Johnson's stepson." And the kid started arguing with him—"Yes, you are. I've read this." He's actually telling Robert Lockwood who he is, which is crazy. So, Robert signed the book and closed it and gives it back, and the kid goes on insisting that Robert Lockwood is Robert Johnson's stepson. Robert said, "Just because some motherfucker was shacking with my mother doesn't make him my stepfather."

I am not saying that a person outside of the African American culture cannot be trusted to write about the blues, but I think that there are very few people that come at it from the perspective of respect, who just purely want to spread an understanding of it and an appreciation of it. It's not a matter of ethnicity, skin color, or national origin. (After all, my friend and writing partner Frank Matheis is a German American.) It comes down to truly loving, respecting, and appreciating the music, culture, and people of the blues.

Often declarations are made about the blues and blues musicians, such as, "This is the last (of this)," or "This is the first (of that)" or "The best (of this or that)"—but I don't believe that. Things don't happen like that. They start and evolve and change and they continue to change. If you look at things closely and carefully or honestly enough, you find connections, or continuities. The people who make those pronouncements are too often only serving their own careers. It adds value to what that person has done to say, "Well, I was here with the last of this," or "I was here when this started," or "I discovered the first of this," or whatever. But to me as a musician, and to most musicians, that doesn't mean shit. Good musicians don't think in those terms, because those are obstacles to becoming the best that you can be at something, reaching the height of your art and craft. If you feel like, "Okay, I'm the best," or "I'm the first," or "I'm the most important," or whatever.

I don't think that blues happened because of Jim Crow or slavery; I think that blues happened in spite of it. All these people, my people, were brutally yanked from their homeland, and they had their own sense of aesthetics and creativity, their own desire to invent. They did that in spite of oppression. Because of the suffering, the human spirit was under attack and the people needed something to bolster, to sustain their spirit. Blues is that sustenance that people can get from music created during that time, of the brutal Jim Crow post-slavery oppression and violence. The blues is alive and well and is still being created because even though we don't have slavery or segregation per se, people still struggle through hard times and need that nourishment for the spirit. That's what the blues does. People need it. Life is hard, work is hard, and then you celebrate your life. That gives you the strength and the ability to keep moving forward. That to me is what the blues is about. It's the relationship to blues lyrics and tonal languages of Africa. It's the singing, the music, the way the singing and the instrumentation evoke the emotions, the way that instruments are manipulated to imitate the human voice, the rhythm, the dance of it. In Africa, dance is a big part of everything and music is a part of life. Part of what was brought here from Africa is the sensibility that there is not a separation between performer and audience. Music is played at every event. There's music for work, there's music for birth, there's music for death. There's music for every aspect of life.

The blues is my music, our music, for every aspect of life.

Chapter One

THE EARLY YEARS

I was born May 8, 1954, in Washington, DC, Washington Hospital Center, on the eve of Mother's Day. My mother Willa Mae Wiggins, who is now called Vicci, still says that I was born on Mother's Day. It's an interesting story that I hear every year, at least once a year, and twice a year when May 8th doesn't fall on Mother's Day. My mother and I both had a rough time at my birth and they didn't expect either one of us to survive, and especially not my mother. She is 91 years old now in 2017; her birthday is in August. Every year on my birthday and on Mother's Day she tells the same story about how we were both in such bad shape and how my father had given her an organdy nightgown—it's a type of cotton—soft, sheer cotton. It was a long nightgown with hundreds of pleats, all the way from the neck down, and up to the collar. The nurse said, "With such a pretty nightgown, she has to wear it." She put it on her right after I was born, and my mother says she could hear the people talking as they passed by the room, and they said—"That girl in there is gonna die." I was born very premature. At that time people that were born that premature usually didn't make it. It's different now. Something happened and she hemorrhaged badly and she almost bled to death. We almost both lost our lives but, as you can see, we both made it.

My father George L. Wiggins was a cartographer for the U.S. government—the Department of the Interior. My mom was a housewife, but she worked sometimes at secretarial work. She was also a substitute teacher. With my natural father and mother, I had two brothers and one sister. My father had heart trouble. The story that I was told was that he had rheumatic fever when he was young, when he was a teenager, and that it scarred his heart badly and eventually it just wore out. My father was in his thirties when he died.

My musical background started at home with my mother and natural father. They were music lovers, and record collectors—a lot of jazz—not so much blues. My father played the piano. This I learned later in life, and I don't have a memory of him playing piano. I do remember him singing in the choir at church.

He played the piano, and they loved piano music. Most of the records I remember them having when I was a kid were jazz albums. On Saturdays or Sunday evenings we would all gather around the record player and listen. I remember thumbing through all these great piano records, looking at the sleeves of artists like Meade "Lux" Lewis, Earl "Fatha" Hines, "Little Brother" Montgomery, and "Fats" Waller. Of course, the records had all these musicians' photos on them—and they were flashy. I looked at them and to me, as a kid, they were like superhumans. I remember Earl Fatha Hines—there was a record of him sitting there in a blue suit that matched the piano he was playing. That's one of my earliest memories about music.

Another musical inspiration was in elementary school, Rudolph Elementary in Northwest Washington, DC. When I was in the fourth grade, I had a teacher named Mrs. Brooks. She was a tall black woman who played the acoustic guitar, Odetta songs and "folk songs" popular at that time, Pete Seeger and all that. She would play a tune or two for us. I remember "I know an old lady who swallowed a fly. I don't know why she swallowed a fly"—and stuff like that. "Puff the Magic Dragon" and "Blowin' in the Wind"—songs like that. She did quite a bit of Odetta songs.

We lived on Gallatin Street in Northwest Washington, a close-knit community of people that were originally from the Deep South, folks that moved to Washington as part of the Great Migration of African Americans from the southern states. People did right by their neighbors and had a way of sharing and supporting and taking care of each other. For example, when we were kids growing up, we would get home from school and neither one of my parents would be home from work. We would be there for a couple of hours all by ourselves. The families had a plan worked out. If someone came to the front door with bad intentions, our instruction was to go out the back door and jump over the fence and then enter by the backdoor of our neighbor, Miss Hattie. This cooperation, as well as our celebrations, the culture and the way of life were essentially a continuation of the customs and traditions from the Deep South that were brought to Washington. My parents were from Alabama and I think my neighbors Miss Hattie and the others were probably from South Carolina. We often had celebrations, parties, barbecues or whatever. Everybody in the neighborhood gathered, especially in the summer or the spring when the weather was nice. The neighbors would be outside in the backyards having a whole block party. In every backyard, there were cooks barbecuing food and they'd have all their favorite dishes of potato salad and greens, barbecue ribs, chicken and pound cake, and we would all share, passing stuff right and left over the fence. Somebody might have just got back from being home, out in the country, and they would bring home a fresh load of blueberries and they would pass them over the fence. I remember these things very well and fondly.

Sure enough, there would always be the one troublemaker that would show up, rooting around, seeing what trouble they could stir up. Before you know it, all hell would break loose and there'd be arguing, pushing and shoving and people getting their feelings hurt. Sometimes it even came to blows, with people drinking and all. Somebody would get a lip busted or an eye blackened. Before you know it, they were fighting right and left. Chairs got knocked over, glasses and bottles broken, people screaming—and of course a whole bunch of people laughing at all the commotion. Finally, people would wear each other out and there would be some calm renewed. I wrote a song about that "No Fools No Fun," based on that scene, but fictionalized to a degree. I say in the song that the police would come and take away the bad people, but we never saw the police in my neighborhood. My uncles actually took care of that. Ambulances took away the hurt people. The blood got mopped up and the broken glass got swept up. When things calmed back down and my mother would look at my father and laugh and say, "You know what they say, 'No fools no fun.'" My mother often said that phrase. To be honest, Uncle Oscar was known for stirring up trouble and hurting people's feelings. Someone would wind up crying and then you'd have to calm them down. Usually when my mother used the phrase "No fools no fun," it was mostly about my Uncle Oscar, the psychologist. He was a lot of fun but he was also a real troublemaker who was fascinated with people's minds, and after he drank a little he was good at playing mind games, on finding people's weak spots and attacking them on it.

The world changed, of course, after my father died. My uncles helped my mother raise us for a while, but my mother got remarried not that long after my father passed. My new stepfather, Elliot M. Johnson, was a lieutenant colonel in the military. He had a daughter, my stepsister Cynthia Johnson. Later my mother and stepfather had two sons, Elliot M. Johnson Jr. and William C. Johnson. I never thought of them as half-brothers. I just accepted them as my brothers. My stepfather was the opposite of musical, if there is such a thing. He was so nonmusical that during the time that we lived in Germany, at Christmas time, for example, he would play Christmas carols on a reel-to-reel tape. Because of the difference in the electric current, the American appliances had to use a transformer, which made the reels run faster. Listening to these carols was like the Chipmunks, but he didn't even realize it. That's how nonmusical he was. He was totally regimental and military minded, a true career soldier. My stepfather spent a lot of his adult life living in war zones.

We had no business being father and son and I surely did not get along with him. He died in 2013, and all those years we had our problems. Eventually, as I became an adult, I realized what a good man he was and how much he did for us and how, in a way, I was pretty selfish as a teenager; but, in another way, we were just not destined to get along. He served in three wars—World War II, Korea, and Vietnam—a warrior with a stepson who lived in the hope and expectation that warriors would be obsolete one day. We never understood each other very well. I went to see him in the hospital the day before he died but he wasn't aware that I was there.

As much as I have come to understand how well he took care of us and how good he was, there is one thing that he did that to this day I can't seem to forgive. He drew a gun on me and my brothers. It was late one summer evening. We were summoned for one of his bedside lectures where we were expected to stand with our mouths shut, to listen to him tell us what was what. To my surprise and shock, I noticed that he had a pistol in his hand. He gestured with it and said, "You have gotten too old for me to whip you anymore. So, from now on this is how it is going to be." I don't think I will ever forget that or forgive him for that. I wrote a song about it.

German Luger Blues

There once was a Colonel, had three stepsons
He drew down an old German Luger gun
And he said, Any more upbringing you need done
This is how it is going to be
I mean this is how it is going to be
    It was not the eldest
Nor the middle son
Action was taken by the youngest one
He stole that old German Luger gun
And he threw it in the deep blue sea
I mean he threw it in the deep blue sea
    From that day on
The sons were done
They were done with being Colonel Johnson's sons
And two of the three fell in love with guns
And the one that didn't was me
I mean, the one that didn't was me.

We lived in Germany for four years from 1965 to '69, when my new stepfather was transferred to the military base in Mannheim. In Germany, I attended the Department of Defense School, where I was introduced to my first serious musical instrument, the saxophone, which I played in seventh grade in junior high school—now they call middle school. My two youngest brothers, Elliot and William, went to a German kindergarten and at the time they both spoke as much German as English.

When we came back to the States, we didn't move back into Washington, DC, as my parents tried to give us a better way of life. We settled in suburban Northern Virginia and I attended a predominantly white school. It seemed to me, as a young black kid, that the folks there were still trying to fight the Civil War, given the attitudes of some people. We lived in Fairfax County, off of Fort Hunt Road—right down the road from Mount Vernon, where George Washington lived. I never liked it there, and I still hate Alexandria and Northern Virginia in general. When my family moved back from Germany in 1968, it was right before the race riots after the assassination of Dr. Martin Luther King. By then I was in Stephen Foster Junior High School. If you know anything about Stephen Foster, words like "darkies" were often in his lyrics, with racist undertones. Right from the get-go that was alienating and indicative of the broader cultural attitude. I didn't like Northern Virginia.

In my school in Virginia they didn't supply you an instrument. You either had to buy one or rent one. My parents were not interested in helping me to pursue that, and so I could not afford a saxophone. Instead, when I was in high school, in the ninth grade, I bought a harmonica with my paper route money, a much more affordable instrument. I used to sit around Fort Hunt Park trying to figure out how to play it. One day I hit a note by accident and realized, "Oh, that sounds like something I heard before." Then I started trying to do that on purpose, figuring out the riffs and learning to make it talk. That's how I figured out how that worked.

Though when we came back from overseas and moved to Virginia, we still attended church in DC. My oldest sister, Cheryl Anne Wiggins, who converted to Islam and is now Rabyah Khaliq, often took me shopping in DC on the weekends. Basically, my parents sent me along with her as a "chaperon" to keep her away from the boys. She was friendly with street evangelist Flora Molton, and that's how I also befriended Flora. My sister regularly stopped by where Flora was sitting and playing music. In the hot summer days, my sister always brought Flora a cold drink. She would always make a point, whenever we were in DC together, to stop and spend a little time just talking to Flora. That's how I would hear Flora play slide guitar and sing. We would stand there and talk to Flora and listen to her for a while. That made a great impression on me and reminded me of the music I heard in the church in my grandmother's town in Titusville, Alabama.

My overall school years were split between the predominantly black elementary school in DC when my father was still alive, and later the Department of Defense schools in Germany, and then the white suburban school in Northern Virginia. I was lucky that I had some good, conscientious teachers in the DC elementary school before we went overseas. They were supportive and nurturing and I believe that they did their best to give us a good education. That school was mostly black and it wasn't until the last year before I left that I had white classmates and a white teacher, because even after "integration" many of the white kids went to private schools; it wasn't like all of a sudden there were a lot of white kids in our school. On the last day before my family went to Europe, I went around to all the teachers and said goodbye. One teacher bent over to hear me better and, almost instinctively, I kissed her on the cheek. It wasn't planned. All the kids screamed and laughed, because that was such an unexpected action. The teacher turned red as a tomato, but she thought it was sweet.

It's interesting how people perceive both the separate but equal and the integration issues. Often, it's a myth. Truly, integrated education was a mixed blessing. Of course, it was good to bring people together, while trying to guarantee people that were discriminated against a good chance at a quality education. At the same time, a lot of black traditions were lost because of it. People went from going to school in a place where there was family and community, where people loved them and respected them and wanted them to do their best, and be the best they could be, to schools that had been previously all white where no one gave a shit about them and no one respected them. No one even wanted them there. A lot of our holidays and rituals and celebrations were lost because in the schools that we got sent to, they didn't carry those on.

When I got back home from living overseas, attending school in suburban Virginia, there was a very small minority of black students. There was a loss of community and the support system that we had in the mostly black school. There were cultural assumptions about everything from art and music to history, about what's beautiful and what's art, and what's good—basically everything was based on a white European-centered standpoint. People had no qualms about saying nappy hair is ugly, big lips are ugly, things like that. That type of racism was the accepted thing. Once I was in the so-called integrated schools, many times I was the only black person in a classroom, or maybe only one or two of us. That was not easy and sometimes alienating.

In school, they didn't teach anything about African American or Native American history. They basically left it alone, swept it under the rug until fairly recently. When I was in high school we had all this African American history. It was one of the things that we protested about in my schooldays. We fought to include black history. The response of the folks in power was to create "Black History Month." To me that was bullshit, because if you were able to pick one month out of the year and segregate that and call that "Black History Month," then you could still continue to teach the same wrong, untrue bullshit the rest of the eleven months of the year. I wasn't down with Black History Month. I wanted to tell the truth and we were never taught the truth. Just the other day I saw a documentary about all the broken treaties between the Native Americans, and I didn't realize that Andrew Jackson signed into law the Indian Removal Act. They didn't teach us that. There was a certain amount of African American history that I learned on my own just out of curiosity and desire to learn from sources other than what they were feeding us.

Where I went to high school most of the black students lived in a neighborhood called Gum Springs. My family and maybe two others were the exception. The Gum Springs families were direct descendants of George Washington's slaves. They all lived there and had never been anywhere else in their life. The vast majority of them, at a certain point in the day, after lunch, were bused to vocational training. At the time, they tracked those black kids that way habitually. When I was in junior high the school counselor called my mother to the office one day, and she said, "Well, we have a problem." My mother asked, "What's the problem?" The counselor said, "Well, your two daughters and your son have all registered for college preparatory classes." My mother said, "And what's the problem with that?" The counselor said, "Well, we've found that most of our colored students are not college material." Of course, my mother tore her a new one. That was what we faced there.

I have always felt that it is important in life to leave it better than I found it. Being well aware of my history, there are a lot of good reasons for someone who looks like me to walk with constant anger, bitterness, and hatred. I feel like I need to be stronger than that. I need not to give my life and my spirit over to people who seek to demean me or suppress me. I want to have a loving, kind, empathetic, generous, and gracious spirit. To me that is the definition of a healthy spirit. To let someone else change my nature, to make me instead of being a person with an open heart to be suspicious and scared—I think those are weaknesses. People think if somebody walks with a scowl on their face or a hard look and won't give anybody the time of day, that's tough. But to me that's not tough. That's just protecting yourself and that's letting the fear rule how you behave. I think it's much stronger and tougher to walk with an open heart and to take each person as they come until they show you who they are. I feel like that served me well. I've made good friends all over the world and I've been treated well and have been well respected, because I take each person as they come and I try to treat each person with respect and generosity and openness and, sure, sometimes it backfires.

When I was a teenager living in a predominantly white neighborhood, my house was down on the cul-de-sac. One day a car was coming along slowly and pulled up in front of me, and the guy in the driver seat rolled the window down—and I thought, well, he's lost, maybe he needs directions. With the spirit that I try to keep, I walked up to the car, stuck my face in the window and I smiled at him, trying to help him. And he spits in my face. I remember that to this day because of the fact that I was smiling when he spat on me. It made me feel stupid, but in a way, if I had walked up to him, afraid and hateful, then he would have won. Sometimes I wish I had a brick or something that I could have chucked through his back window as he pulled off. What a coward. He spat in my face, he laughed and rolled his window up, and took off. If he stayed there, who knows, I might not be sitting here right now. I might be sitting in Lorton Penitentiary somewhere, because I might have yanked him out of the car and beat him to within an inch of his life. But you can't let cowards and hateful people change your essence.

I have my nature and what I consider to be a healthy spirit, and I feel like everyone needs that. It's hard and not easy. Knowing the history, it's hard for black people to maintain a healthy spirit with all the reasons why and all the things that happen day to day that work against that. And at the same time that's what we're stuck with. We can't let all those outside forces change us or destroy our spirit or sicken our spirit.

I got involved in school politics because I was outspoken. When I was a high school sophomore they started a Student Advisory Council, which had two elected students from each school to attend school board meetings and to give their two cents' worth on policy and the quality of education. I ran for that council and that was one of my first crowning accomplishments. I remember once the student council wanted to have some nationally known rock band play at the prom. Then someone asked, "Why do we never have any black entertainment?" The school disciplinarian got up and said, "Well, you know, it's majority rules." I was sitting way in the back, and it just pissed me off, so I said, "Okay, so fuck the minority then, right?" He barked, "Who said that?" It doesn't take much nerve to sit in the back and shout something out, so I stood up and everybody cheered. I said, "Well, you have a whole segment of your population that you're leaving out, that you're cheating out of their education just by saying they don't have a say just because majority rules. That's not democracy. That's de facto segregation." From that point on I was in trouble constantly, branded as a troublemaker.

Nonetheless, it was a personal achievement for me to be elected. I remember how proud I was when I found out. The student government and Student Advisory Council had elections at the same time, and all the results were on the blackboard. I walked into the room, and they were supposed to have erased all that off before all of us candidates walked in there, and one of the people pointed to this one name that had a vast majority of the votes. It was me.

It was a struggle to get a good education and to be represented. But as much as I knock Northern Virginia and as much as I hated that school, and fought them at every turn, I feel like I got a lot of mileage out of that education. I actually got a good education. Maybe it was better because I had to fight for it.

One of my main musical influences and inspirations in my youth was my older brother Skip, a great guitar player and singer. My two brothers, Charles J. Wiggins and George L. Wiggins Jr., who we call Skip, both live in California now.

He is very talented, and he is definitely one of the reasons why I play music now. As far back as I can remember Skip had a natural talent. Any instrument that you put in his hands he would fool with, and within about an hour he would get music out of it. When we were growing up, he played some piano, a lot of guitar, and woodwind instruments. You name it. The one thing he couldn't figure out was the harmonica, which was good for me. He's just such a great player and made me always want to be able to express myself musically. Skip attracted all the best musicians in the neighborhood and they were always hanging around my house to play with him, and naturally I always wanted to join in.

My brother Skip was named after my father: George L. Wiggins. He got the nickname Skip after my father passed when I was seven. One of my father's dear friends was visiting my family and giving his condolences, and he looked at my brother, who was the oldest male in the family, and said, "Well, now you're skipper of the ship." We started out calling him Skipper when he was still little and by the time we were in high school the name had evolved into Skip. That was his name ever since. Skip has been writing songs as far back as I can remember. As we were growing up there was always music in my house. Once I picked up the harmonica I would sneak in on the outskirts of the jam sessions and noodle along until they got tired of me. Then, after a while, I noticed that it took them longer to get tired of me. My brother kept a journal. One time I found his journal was laying on the bathtub and I picked it up and looked at it, and I saw in there where he had written "Phil is starting to get pretty good on the harmonica." That was acceptance. All through high school I was lucky to have all those kids hanging around to play with my brother because I got to jam with them, to practice with other musicians, to play live music, and that's how I learned.

Later, I joined the folk club in high school because that was the closest thing to the music that I liked. Also, from the time that we moved back to DC, I discovered the Smithsonian Folklife Festival. By about 1970, I attended the Smithsonian Festival in DC in the summertime, where I could hear all these guys from the Deep South sitting down on the Mall just like it was their own back porch, playing and singing. It was a realization deep down inside, "Hell, yeah, I recognize that and I love it." I connected with that music on a deep level, with the songs and with the musicians as if it had always been a part of me. I somehow believed that I felt how they felt, and I connected with the acoustic country blues, recognizing that the blues were very close to me, a very intimate and integral part of me. That's how I knew that I wanted to play blues. I trace that back to the feeling I had in my grandmother's neighborhood in Titusville, Alabama. I was very influenced by the church music at my grandmother's place. She was a very special person in my life. I was always drawn to my grandmother, Effie Mae Carter, and I loved her very much. I always felt close and connected to her and to the time that she represented. She understood me and I understood her.

On Wednesday nights, they had prayer meetings at her Green Liberty Baptist Church, which she always attended. She did not like to go alone because she disliked walking back home in the dark by herself, so she always enlisted one of us to walk with her. My brothers got hip to that and would make themselves scarce on Wednesdays, so it was usually me who ended up walking with her. I remember standing outside of the church and hearing the elderly women sing prayers and praises. They would do what's called "lining hymns," which is when one woman sings a line and the rest of the congregation answers in unison in call-and-response. The content of the lyrics was deeply religious, but the sound was pure deep blues. To me the spirituals and blues were musically the same. It was the most direct and powerful expression of emotion that I have ever heard and it took a deep hold of me. The music connected it all. I have told that story so many times that I sometimes wonder if it actually happened. So, I made a song that I call "Prayers and Praises" to keep that memory sharp in my mind's eye. I like that the song tells a story, although there are no words.

As a teenager, I loved all kinds of music: Motown, soul music, psychedelic music and all that, like Jimi Hendrix, but I wanted to play country blues. That's what drew me to the folk club. Nonetheless, I put together a band that I considered to be at the time electric blues, similar to Chicago blues, but it wasn't. We didn't know that much about what we were trying to do. Then, also in high school, I had my first acoustic guitar-harmonica ensemble experience. I met an acoustic guitarist, Robin Borum, in school. He was a great guitarist, an Arlo Guthrie fan. I also sometimes played with Tom Rivers, a great Merle Travis-style fingerpicker. I didn't realize at the time, but they both played very similar to Piedmont blues style, because it incorporated the same fingerpicking techniques. Robin and I considered ourselves as a duo for a while and we actually played at the folk club at school. He is still in the Northern Virginia area, as far as I know. I think he's a salesman. I don't think he plays music at all anymore. Tom Rivers still plays as far as I know. He's a great guitar player. It was unusual that he played that straight-up Merle Travis style fingerpicking.

When I was in the tenth grade, I met a harmonica player in Alexandria named Skip Matthews who turned me on to Chicago harp players. He was a few years older than me and he lived in the attic of the house of an elderly couple. He had a cot, an old cheap stereo, and stacks and stacks of records. At the time, he was bad-ass on the harmonica and he had studied all the styles. That's where I was exposed to the history of the blues harmonica. He had them all—Little Walter, Big Walter, Sonny Boy Williamson, Sonny Terry, Junior Wells—all the greats. Of course, I was fascinated and totally focused on hearing all of them and soaking it in. Hammie Nixon was one of my favorites.

One day I was in the kitchen and my mother was listening to twanging country music on the radio. It was the Grand Ole Opry broadcast from Tennessee.

Perplexed, I asked her, "Mom, why do you listen to that?" She said without the slightest hesitation, "I just love to hear white people sing about their troubles." That was good enough for me.

I graduated from high school in 1973. While in high school, during the summers I performed at the Smithsonian Festival backing up Flora Molton on harmonica for two years in a row in 1972 and '73. Then I went off to college.

During that period, I also spent time with Flora's guitarist Ed Morris. He had been around Washington for a long time as a performer, and had even taken a few lessons from Skip James when he lived in DC. At the time, nobody I knew had as much knowledge about blues history and the various blues styles as Ed. He also had a tremendous collection of all kinds of rural blues records from the 1930s. He took the role of teacher who was keen on sharing the history with me, and I was eager to soak it all up. He turned me on to Skip James, Son House, Mance Lipscomb, and so many others. It was the equivalent of having my own private blues tutor—a true aficionado. My interest was piqued and I started to seriously delve into the blues history, collecting records and deeply listening to the old blues. I picked up country blues albums from reissue labels like Yazoo, Blue Goose, Arhoolie Records, and all that—not knowing that eventually I would get to meet Chris Strachwitz, who owned Arhoolie. Ed Morris was an interesting guy and a superb musician, but a complex soul. Today, in looking back, I think that maybe he might have been bipolar or something, because he was very moody and eccentric. At the time, I was in high school and he was in his late thirties or early forties. He was not a professional musician and he played music on the side while holding a day job at a record store, Records and Tapes, Limited. I think he went through some long periods of unemployment too. Ed had no training, no education, no college, and he was totally immersed in music.

He lived with his wife and two sons in the public housing projects off of Route 7 in Alexandria—a rough area. I used to hitchhike to his house and spend hours and hours listening to music and jamming. Then I had to leave late at night through that dangerous neighborhood. I would go there anyway and put up with all that because I was drawn to playing music with him and listening to his huge collection.

There I was, a teenager who by all rights should be hanging out at the 7-11 and chasing girls, but I was spending my time in the apartment of this guy who was probably fifteen years older than me, smoking pot and learning all about the blues. It was a huge gift and he had a tremendous impact on me. Ed was a great instrumentalist, with good taste, but he also had well-tuned ears for the music and he listened and absorbed deeply. His interests were much broader than just being fixated on one particular person and trying to emulate that style. He was a true musician but was also a pot addict who smoked an immense amount of marijuana; but he didn't ever get the good pot, because he didn't have much money. He was constantly puffing pot in a bong but he thought that putting water in the bong detracted from the potency, so my throat would be on fire, the room would be so thick with smoke that I couldn't see the hand in front of my face, but I wouldn't be stoned at all. All I would have for my effort was a sore throat and a bad headache, trying to play harmonica.

As crazy as it was, I played some great music with him, and it was a real gift to be with him, because he was a brilliant fingerstyle guitar player and I got to hear his amazing music collection—and not only stuff that was on labels, but live performances that he had recorded of Flora Molton, Skip James, and John Hurt, and a local guy named Ed Green. He had a little music room with an old reel-to-reel and a bunch of microphones set up in this convoluted way—some were hanging from the ceiling with pieces of cardboard taped to them. He recorded everything and he had tons of reels of music that he had recorded of me and Flora Molton, sitting in that room.

Ed Morris played a particular guitar fingerpicking style that he said was a reaction to and rejection of the Gary Davis school of guitar that was so popular at the time. Ed was a protagonist of the Skip James style and he loved Mance Lipscomb and Blind Boy Fuller. He figured out how to accompany Flora and to help give her music some more form and shape. The way he created music around Flora's singing and playing was just genius. He played a song Flora wrote, for example, called "The Sun is Going to Shine in Vietnam Some Day," an antiwar song. Eleanor Ellis still plays Ed's guitar part note for note. That song remains a strong example of his guitar playing. It's cool, but it's not symmetrical. You've got to pay attention when you're playing it, it's so idiosyncratic, but it's beautiful. He had a good way to play behind Flora Molton because Flora's playing was raw and modal, and the only clue that you had about chord progression was from her singing. Ed was good at creating lines and building progressions that gave structure and motion to Flora's playing.

Ed Morris died very young from an aneurysm. I wish I knew what happened to his family and where they are, so they could know what a great musician their father was. Today, Ed Morris is almost forgotten, an obscure sideman, but he was a brilliant musician who deserves a place in the regional music history. He gave me the foundation of my blues education, and he was very kind and good to Flora Molton. He brought Flora into the coffeehouse circuit and was a steady support and facilitator for her until he died.

At the time, Ed was the only white musician I knew that paid any attention to the black blues musicians in the DC area. The blues fire had been lit on college campuses, but seemingly they were mostly interested in the musicians from the old 78-rpm recordings. Ed was one of the few people in that scene that spent time with people like Flora and Ed Green and the local black musicians.

Ed was able to get Flora a certain amount of recognition and elevate her from playing on the streets of Washington to other venues, like the Smithsonian Festival—even though Ed never played at the Smithsonian Festival with her. There were a couple of events that were offshoots of the festival, indoor events where he was invited to join me and Flora—and there's a photo of me and Flora and Bernice Reagon with Ed Morris there. I'm certain that those people would not have known or connected with Flora if it weren't for Ed's efforts. He also was an important guitar teacher, but for some reason Ed was not accepted by the white blues establishment. They did include one of his quotes once about Skip James on a record that was released by one of the local labels, but they never recorded him or took him seriously as a performer. That may be in part because when I first met Ed he had recently quit performing in public, and he restricted himself to backing Flora. I suggested several times that Ed and I should play as a duo, but he no longer wanted to get out before the coffeehouse crowd. He said he was performing at one of the coffeehouses and some girl in the audience shouted out something like, "Oh, you're just faking" and he got so humiliated that it turned him against playing in public. That one experience shut him down—it's funny how that will do it, but he felt humiliated and ended his career, because one stupid person said that he wasn't authentic. That voice coming out of the dark struck him down.

When I was in high school I met John Jackson. There was an old guy in Alexandria, Virginia, named Philip Roberts, who had an art shop where he refurbished paintings. They called him the Mayor of Cameron Street. He ran a concert series right there in Alexandria. Roberts hired my band to play a concert on Tavern Square. He invited John Jackson to play before us—almost like he was opening for us, which was ridiculous. John Jackson was just an amazing musician from Virginia. If you listened to John Jackson talk, to his Virginia dialect from the mountains of Western Virginia, in Rappahannock, you'd almost need to do musical notation to get it, his language right, because his accent and his voice were so lyrical. We were a bunch of young guys, and here came this amazing older gentleman, John Jackson and his wife. He opened the show and I was amazed and astonished. "That's who is opening for us?" Our band sucked, basically. But, I got to meet John and Cora Jackson that night. John was one of the greatest regional musicians ever.

They say opposites attract—I think that John and Cora Jackson were like that in a lot of ways. John Jackson was not that tall, but stout, and you could tell that he had powerful hands—that he worked with his hands all of his life. He wasn't real imposing but you could tell he was a powerfully built man. Cora was tall and thin—almost with a severe facial expression. When you saw John, when listening to him talk and seeing him interact with people, you would think butter wouldn't melt in his mouth. Cora on the other hand you would think that if you chucked a teaspoonful of butter in her mouth it would burst into flames. She was just as feisty as he was mild-mannered. They showed up and were dressed out nice, but very country. They definitely had country sensibilities and aesthetics. I loved it and loved meeting them. They sat down and relaxed and she opened up her bag and they had some brown liquor, I think it was bourbon, in these nice aluminum collapsible cups. They had a portable ashtray and they made themselves at home. There was this environment that spread out around them as they were sitting there relaxing. They smoked Pall Malls, non-filter cigarettes. You got a coupon with every pack and you could save those up and get merchandise with them, and that's what they smoked.

I remember hearing John Jackson play and I was just blown away by his singing and his guitar. I was glad to have met him, but I was almost embarrassed to go on a stage after him and play. I knew, "These are my people." I completely ignored my bandmates and spent the whole time hanging with them. John and Cora stuck around and they listened to the band and we talked all evening. At the end of that night John said, "Well, you have to come to Glen Echo and play with me next weekend." That was the Glen Echo Folk Festival. I thought, "This old man, he's just being nice—he doesn't mean that." I didn't go. The next time I saw him he said, "You know, I looked for you all day that day. Why didn't you show up?" He was actually angry with me because I didn't show up. That's when I realized that John Jackson didn't say anything he didn't mean, and that he was that generous and that sincere about wanting me to come and play with him.

For some reason when I first met him he thought my name was Robert. Every time I'd come up to him to greet him, I'd say, "Hey, John, how are you?" And he'd say, "Hey, Robert. Good to see you." Then after a while he would start calling me Phil—or Philip, because he knew my name, but I want to say for about the first half a year that I knew him he went back and forth between calling me Robert and then calling me by my real name. Then Robert got phased out.

That's how I got to play with John Jackson.

He wasn't that easy to play with, as he had his own sense of timing. You had to pay attention in order to play with him. Plus, he was a master of the fingerstyle guitar, and his playing was very intricate. He was a songster, and it seemed like every song that he played was picked out because it was special to him: it either told a story that he liked or it had a cool lick or was challenging on the guitar. He seemed to enjoy playing songs that were technically difficult because he had amazing skills. There wasn't a lot of space. He didn't need harmonica or anything else, because of the intricate way he played, but he enjoyed playing with other people and he enjoyed playing with me. Of course, I felt fortunate and grateful that he did, because I loved playing with him, and loved hearing him play.

When I was just out of high school I took my first road trip playing music with Archie Edwards, Mother Scott, and this couple named Elsa Hayes and

Terry Phillips, who was nicknamed Vigo. It was before I started to play with John Cephas and Big Chief Ellis. There was this girl named Meg Bowman who was just about my best friend in high school. When she got out of high school she went to Kenyon College in Gambier, Ohio, and she became president of the folk music club there. Kenyon College put on an annual festival. Since I had been telling her about Archie and Mother Scott she talked the school into hiring them for the festival. Me and Elsa and Vigo, and Mother Scott and Archie Edwards, we all hopped in a car and drove from DC to Gambier, Ohio, for my first road trip. All the way there and back was a long trip and a lot of driving. Mother Scott kept everyone awake and jazzed up by telling stories and jokes and laughing and helping people keep their eye on the road. By then Mother Scott was in her mid-eighties, if not nineties. I remember walking around the campus with my friend Meg and Mother Scott, who walked very slowly, and we all just got in the habit of walking slow. Once, after we walked her to her room, we realized we were all still walking at her slow pace. I never will forget that.

Mother Scott kept Archie in line. She said, "That Archie, if we're playing together and he starts that old braggadocio, I just reach over with my foot and mash him." Yeah, she kept Archie Edwards in line and she kept us all going, and it was great—my first music travel.

Mother Scott was from Mississippi. She ran away from home when she was very young and she wound up in the Rabbit's Foot Minstrel Show. She told me that Bessie Smith taught her how to play the guitar.[1] The first time I met her, she came to the Childe Harold one night with some friends of hers. It was her eighty-second birthday when we met. She invited me to play a tune with her, and then she said, "I want you to come and have lunch with me next week." She lived around 16th and O Street, which was not that far from where I was living on 16th and S. I went to her house, and again, it was like being at my grandmother's house. It was spotless. We hung out in her kitchen and everything was in its place and it had that grandma smell to it. She made us a nice lunch. A funny thing happened when she was talking to me: Being southern and all, she had some friends—some white friends that were wealthy Virginians. At the time, I wasn't exactly a hippie, but I was in my raggedy blue jeans and just letting my hair grow wild and stuff. Mother Scott, she said, "Some of these ladies that I was sitting with, they offered to buy you some clothes." I thought that was funny. They didn't get it. I was just being comfortable wearing rags. Of course, that was the look back then. I finally grew out of it. But I'll never forget that. She said, "My friends want to buy you some clothes." I remember just loving spending that day with her, because she reminded me of my grandmother. We did a lot of playing together, and we traveled some more together.

Vigo was a hustler in a way. He was a folk musician who played the guitar and sang, a talented guy—but he always had a couple of angles that he was trying to work on Mother Scott. When he saw how she trusted me and how we hit it off, he was trying to colonize me to help him to get information out of her that he wasn't able to get. I didn't even respond. I think that he was maybe thinking about writing a book about her. He had an inkling of some personal information and he wanted to get more of it—about her and her family history—and he wasn't able to get it. He felt like I would be able to get it because he could tell that she trusted me. She was very private and I don't think she wanted a book written, so I let it go in one ear and out the other.

I had some great songs. There was an old gospel song, "I Am the Great I Am." I used to love to play that song with her. I played at the Smithsonian Folklife Festival from about 1971 on all the way up and beyond '76. For a time, I moved to New Jersey to live with an aunt when I first went off to college. I started out going to this little community college in Vineland, New Jersey, called Cumberland Community College. Initially, I had no plans to go to college and I had decided when I graduated from high school that I was going to get a job, find a place to live and just work for a while to figure out what I wanted to do with my life. My parents insisted, however: "No, you're not. You're going to college." Because I hadn't done anything in terms of preparing to get into a college, I wound up going to live with my aunt and go to that community college, because she was a professor there and she could get me in easily.

That was in 1974. I spent my summers back at home, and that's how I wound up being at the Smithsonian Festival during those summers. After I earned my associate's degree, I came back home to DC and continued going to college at Howard University while living back at home with my folks. My stepfather by this time had retired from the military and he was working for Howard University as the dean of the school of nursing, even though he didn't have a medical background. It was purely an administrative job that he had but it allowed me to attend tuition free. I studied political science for maybe a year before I dropped out.

I loved church gospel music because I grew up with gospel and spirituals in the church, especially in my grandmother's neighborhood during childhood summer visits in Titusville, Alabama. My blues epiphany came at the Smithsonian Folklife Festival at the National Mall where I heard these guys sit and play acoustic blues—Johnny Shines, Sam Chatmon, Robert Lockwood, and Howard Armstrong. They were getting down, playing like it was their own back porch. That's when I knew—the way they feel is the way I feel. I want to play the blues.

In 1976, I was at the Smithsonian Folklife Festival playing with Flora. There I met and got to be very good friends with Johnny Shines. He was playing at that festival, and we ended up hanging out a lot together talking, and for some reason we just connected. The festival never presented us together. We were playing separately on the different stages. I remember talking to him about how I was digging playing gospel with Flora, while what I wanted to play was a lot more blues. He said, "Just hang in there—you'll get your chance." I remember one thing he said: a lot of these record producers who he was trying to get to record him complained that he sounded too much like Robert Johnson, which is ridiculous because he played the same songs that he and Robert Johnson had played together. He had a beautiful falsetto voice. Johnny Shines was very encouraging and supportive of me. He was a real inspiration to me, a guy who was too often underrated. He was one of the originals, an itinerant musician, but somehow, he didn't get the true respect he deserved, and because he was a companion and partner with Robert Johnson, the entire music establishment wanted to place him in the shadow of Robert Johnson. He told me that the record producer Nick Perls (Yazoo and Blue Goose Records) told him that he sounded too much like Robert Johnson, and so he didn't want to record him. That hurt Johnny. Other than that, we didn't talk about that. It seemed to me he didn't want to dwell on the past, or maybe that he was tired of people asking him about, or wanting to talk about, Robert Johnson rather than to talk to him about himself. He told me that when he played with Robert Johnson, who had a bigger name then, they went busking in towns all over the South, and to maximize their take they would go to different parts of town, both claiming to be Robert Johnson and then get back together.

Johnny Shines was a real serious person. I don't remember him joking or laughing much. Maybe he was a little bitter about the recording industry. I wanted to hook up and play with him, to be his harmonica player, and I asked him if we could play together, but he said, "No, you need to go and finish college. I don't want to play with you until after you go and get your college degree." Then, after I finished my associate's degree and then dropped out of Howard University, I actually ran into Johnny Shines. I was in my late twenties, almost thirty years old, and feeling like I was grown. I walked up to him, and said, "Hey, Johnny, How you doin'?" He looked at me and said, "Well, you're near about a man." I thought, "What do you mean—'near about'?" Of course, I didn't tell him that I had dropped out of college, but he felt like education was important and getting my college degree was important, and he was encouraging me to do that rather than to just go on the road to play music. I had dropped out of college believing that, ultimately, I wanted to play music, even if I had to work at whatever crap job I could get to support my music habit.

When I knew Johnny Shines, at first, I honestly didn't know anything about him being one of the originals. I was just a teenager who loved to play music and I was meeting all of these great players, older guys. I didn't know anything about Johnny Shines, for example, about him having spent time traveling with Robert Johnson. I just knew that he was this nice man from the Deep South who came to Washington who played beautiful guitar and had this beautiful high, powerful voice that was almost like superhuman sounding, with so much feeling and emotion. He just had a beautiful voice—the likes of which I had never heard. I was able to get to know that person and be a friend to him, and most of all get to sit next to him and play music with him and add what I do on the harmonica to his sound. In those years, I was just a kid who was not yet aware of the history and tradition, but I didn't look at these guys as blues icons. I was just loving playing music and hearing these amazing people that could play and sing well. The music was the impact on me, not the legend of Johnny Shines or whatever—it was just the sheer beauty and power of the music that he made, and that I could sit next to him and hear this incredible music come right out of that body. I knew that these guys were important, but because they played very good. I didn't know what an icon Henry Townsend was—I just knew he was a man who played incredible piano and guitar and he reminded me a lot of my family, because he and his wife would show up there and Johnny Shines would be there and Big Chief Ellis and his wife and they just treated me well. They shared everything they had. I would eat food with them and hang with them. They were great and wonderful and amazing musicians and they felt like home to me.

I was on stage playing with Robert Lockwood and Johnny Shines. Now, years later, I can look back at it and be amazed that I was able to play with such blues masters. It's an eye-opener for me at this point in my life that it was my dumb luck and my blundering and my wandering around, just pursuing what I loved at such a young age, that took me to people that were the pinnacle of that music. In hindsight, I was a young man who was encouraged and mentored by the true originals, by the guys who carried that music from the 1930s on. The musicians who had played with Robert Johnson accepted and encouraged me. These guys were legendary and to me they were just like kin.

A lot of people feel that Robert Lockwood was unfriendly and unapproachable. I always felt that he was a perfect gentleman who had old-school gravitas and dignity. I can remember the day that he actually accepted me as a friend. We were in the Green Room at the K-Wood Theater in Washington, DC, with several of the local acoustic blues players, along with Dr. Barry Lee Pearson of the University of Maryland. We were all talking and laughing about Archie Edwards and how braggadocio he was. In a pause, Barry Lee interjected, "Well, we all have to get along with Archie." For some reason that rubbed me the wrong way, and I said, "Fuck that. The only person I have to get along with is Wendy Chick." Wendy and I were living together and we eventually got married and had a family. Robert looked at me, at first shocked and surprised; that then changed into a smile of approval. We were friends ever since.

The Smithsonian recognized the importance of bringing these musicians up from the Deep South and putting them on the National Mall as if they were in their backyard playing music. Somebody like me could just walk right up to them and talk to them and get to know them, and eventually play music with them. That's an amazing gift that the Smithsonian Festival has given me. That was the beginning of it all, when I first met these amazing musicians. All of this happened because Dr. Bernice Johnson Reagon, one of the important organizers of the festival, did not kick me out of the Smithsonian Folklife Festival. I am forever grateful to her. Bernice Johnson Reagon, the gospel singer with Sweet Honey in the Rock and an important civil rights activist, was a cultural historian in music history at the Smithsonian Institution, where she directed a program called Black American Culture in 1976. Bernice Johnson Reagon is an amazing singer and scholar, a Folkways artist who issued *Folk Songs: The South*, with Folkways Records in 1965. She is a profound voice in the arts community of Washington, DC, and the nation. In the 1960s, she was a member of the Student Nonviolent Coordinating Committee Freedom Singers, at the forefront of the African American Civil Rights Movement. She got me into playing at the Smithsonian Folklife Festivals and I am grateful to her to this day for taking a chance on a ragged kid with an Afro way back then. When Flora brought me there and Bernice agreed to hire me to play with Flora, she facilitated my first break. I don't know if she thought much of me as a player, but I think that she probably thought—well, he's helpful to Flora, and it seems like she appreciates the help, so I'll keep him around and he can help her get around and stuff. Because I think she saw how I looked out for Flora and that's why she let me stay around. If it hadn't been for Bernice accepting me there, who knows if I would have ever met Big Chief Ellis and John Cephas. I met them at the Smithsonian Folklife Festival, almost on an equal footing, because I was also a hired musician at that festival. They just accepted me right from the beginning as one of them, along with everybody else. In a way, it definitely was a milestone life changer for me, my association with the Smithsonian Folklife Festival.

I met John Cephas for the first time at the festival in 1976. John came with Big Chief Ellis, who was the bandleader of the group that John was in, the Barrelhouse Rockers. I always thought his name was Wilbur Ellis, but his real name is Wilbert. I think maybe John Cephas put the bug in Chief's ear, but Chief was the one that asked me if I wanted to join his band. I remember meeting Chief. When we first met, I did not even know he was from Alabama—but I knew he was from the South. I knew that he had spent a lot of time in New York and that he was a sought-after sideman for years. He wrote a song called "Dices" that someone else got credit for, and it was a popular song, "Dices oh dices, please don't crap on me." I remember going to his house. It's funny, because it smelled like my grandmother's house. I experienced that several times in my life, a smell and a home environment that brought back memories of my youth in Alabama, like the first time I went to Mother Scott's house. I remember sitting in her kitchen while she was preparing us lunch, and it smelled like my grandmother's house—I don't know what it was, maybe it was pork or something similar that was cooking, and all of my senses pointed me home to my grandmother—the cooking smells, the décor, the neatness with everything in its place, everything spotless clean. The people took their time to be orderly and clean, to wash things and put them back in their place before they moved on to the next thing. I felt like that was a real Southern custom or sensibility. Getting to know Chief, it felt like family to me, just like Mother Scott and just like my own grandmother.

The Chief was a great musician with a beautiful thick voice, like honey. He could sing high, but he had a real deep resonance to his voice. He was a fantastic piano player, a barrelhouse style pianist, with a great left hand, very strongly influenced by Walter Davis, who he would often talk about. I think he may have known him. Big Chief Ellis was the bandleader and they had a bass player named James Bellamy, a hard-core funk player who learned how to walk the bass from Chief. He had never played that walking bass before he met Chief. Bellamy was a short guy who always wore dark colored clothes and dark shades. He always had a joint in his hand. He was a person who loved to share his pot, but he did not like to pass a joint. Back then no one smoked in public that much. We would be standing there at the Smithsonian Festival—or, I remember we were in a room at the Library of Congress about to play a gig, and he was smoking a joint. He wouldn't share and pass you his joint—he would make you your own and light it for you. He wouldn't pass it back and forth. That was James Bellamy. It was those three—Chief, John Cephas, and Bellamy—they were called Chief Ellis and the Barrelhouse Rockers.

From what I gathered, at the time it was John Cephas's first experience playing in public. He was very, very nervous about it. I was in the audience at the Smithsonian Folklife Festival to hear them play, of course fell in love with their music, and I liked hanging around with them. They hooked up with the famed pianist Sunnyland Slim, who played with Muddy Waters, the Howlin' Wolf, Robert Lockwood, and the great harmonica player Little Walter. Sunnyland happened to be there at the same time, and so was the lap steel player Sonny Rhodes. We were just hanging around in a crowd, walking, talking, and laughing after everything had shut down at the festival—everyone was leaving, going home. Sunnyland passed by a stage and jumped up and went to tinker on the piano. We realized that the PA system had been left on. They all said, "Well, cool, let's play. Let's have a jam." They all got out their instruments and started playing, amazing a few stragglers that were walking by. Johnny Shines came over to me and said, "This is your chance. I'm going to go up there, I'm going to play, and then I'm going to call you up there, right? Here is what I want you to do—I'm going to sing a phrase in your ear, and then I want you to play it right after I sing it." That's what he did, and that's how I met all those guys—Johnny Shines, John Cephas, and Chief and Sunnyland Slim and all them. It was really something.

There was this guy who ran a club called the Childe Harold. He would come to the Smithsonian Folklife Festival in the afternoon just to snoop around to see who the blues players were. He would get whoever they had brought from the Deep South or Chicago, or wherever, to come in the evening and play at the Childe Harold club. He came that day and he asked Sunnyland Slim and Chief and the Barrelhouse Rockers if they would come play and they said sure. I always went there anyway after the festival so I wound up there, too. That night they asked me to come along and sit in with them. At the end of that night Chief and John asked me if I wanted to join the Barrelhouse Rockers. That was 1976.

The Childe Harold club on Connecticut Avenue just north of Dupont Circle was my home away from home, and there were several milestones that happened for me in that place. I lived right around the corner from there. One late afternoon Johnny Shines was there and Big Walter Horton with his band from Chicago. They were sitting around having lunch, getting ready for the evening gig, but Big Walter was already drinking heavily with all of his guys. The owner of the club said to Johnny Shines, "Boy, I sure am glad that Big Walter and them flew in, because, I mean, as drunk as he is I'm glad he doesn't have his pistol on him." Johnny Shines looked at him and said, "No, they drove." The owner turned white as a ghost. Big Walter had gone to the men's room. I had to go, so I went and I walked into the men's room and he was standing there at a stall, and I said, "I just want to say what an honor it is to meet you. I always loved your playing." He turned around and he looked at me and he threw up all over my shoes. I had these summer shoes of woven material, almost like straw, and what he threw up was almost pure alcohol. It went right through my shoes. That was a bad omen for the evening. That night was also the first barroom brawl I had ever been to in my life. Big Walter was playing his ass off. The mic had a bunch of yards of cord, and he was roaming through the audience with it blowing harp, playing to the women and stuff. There was some redneck guy there who had sat down at my table, this guy with a cowboy hat. He had a drink and when it was empty he took it and he knocked the glass on the floor and broke it and then he set it down in front of him. I looked at it, and I looked at him, and he said, "Getting ready for a bout with a black man," and he was drunk. When the waitress came by and he wasn't looking I just took it and passed it to her. Then I thought the threat was over. But the rowdy guy got up and he was stumbling around the room like a fool and he stepped over this young black woman's feet. Her boyfriend stood up and dumped a pitcher of beer on his head and all hell broke loose in the room. There was all this fighting and somebody came out of the kitchen with a brass pipe. Everybody was just rolling from the front to the back fighting. Finally, the cops and ambulances came and they took people away. Me and Big Walter were standing on the front porch of the place. He looked at me and said, "You know, there ain't no way in hell to have a good time on a Saturday night." I went home and I had been wearing some jeans and this white cotton Mexican wedding shirt, and it had blood all over it. I thought it was ruined. Later I talked to a girlfriend of mine, who said, "You know, if you soak it in cold water the blood will come right out." "Really?" I went and fished it out of the trash and soaked it, and sure enough blood came out. I wore that shirt for probably another five years after that.

Shortly after the night at the Childe Harold, Big Chief Ellis and the Barrelhouse Rockers asked me to play with them at the National Folk Festival over at Wolf Trap. Henry Townsend was there with his wife, Chief Ellis and his wife. John Cephas was there with his fiancée. I remember that all those people were like a family. They had a lot in common on a real deep level culturally, a real southern thing. Chief had owned a liquor store in DC, and he liked to drink a bit and he surely liked his moonshine. He taught me the way you test moonshine for purity: you pour a little bit in the cap and light it. If you get a steady blue flame that means it's pure. If it has flecks of yellow or orange in the flame then you know it's not very good quality.

When Jimmy Carter was elected president and they had the big inaugural celebrations and festivities downtown, and we were invited to perform on a float. They had a big parade with a float from each state. The Chief was on the Alabama float. That was when I found out that he was from Alabama. We played on that float—me and John Cephas, the Chief and James Bellamy, riding along with a famous football player from Alabama. It was freezing cold that day, and Chief was passing around a flask of moonshine for us all to warm up with. The cool part of that parade was that the floats left out of some warehouse in Southeast Washington and had to go through some neighborhoods before getting to the parade route, and then again through those neighborhoods on the way back. The sound system was on and all along the route people were enjoying our music, passing by apartments. The people were sticking their heads out the window and listening, bopping along having a good time. Another big part of it was later that evening there was an event at Union Station. My mother had come to town and I invited her to come and hear me play and spend time with me. I never will forget two funny things that happened. The first one was John Cephas had his girlfriend there and she walked over to my sister and shook her hand and said, "My name is so-and-so, I'm John's fiancée-wife." We laughed about that for years. The other amazing thing that happened is my mother walked into the room, and she saw Big Chief Ellis, and said, "Wilbert, what are you doing here?" It turned out they were from the same little town of Titusville, Alabama. The Chief was my father's classmate growing up from grade school. At that point, I hadn't met very many people that actually ever knew my father, because he passed away when I was so young. It turned out that I was playing in a band, and the bandleader was a friend of my father from childhood. The next time I was at the Chief's house he broke out the moonshine, and he said, "I can't pass this to you anymore. I know your people." From that point on he looked out for me like family. It was no longer "just anything goes." After that he kept his eye on me like kin. For me it was great, because it was another affirmation that I was in the right place at the right time, with the right people, musically and in every other way I was at home.

Chief was a great man who projected that greatness. The piano players, especially the barrelhouse piano players, they're a breed to themselves with a common gravitas. They all, to some extent or another, presented themselves as people to be reckoned with. I will never forget Memphis Slim in Paris. He had it in spades. Of course, by then he had become wealthy and quite famous and ran one of the biggest concert halls in Paris. The Olympia Theatre was his home venue. People looked up to him and to Chief Ellis the same way. I don't know what it is about piano players but there's a similar sense of dignity, the way they carry themselves; be they from New Orleans or Mississippi, they all seem to have that in common.

I played with Big Chief Ellis for just a couple of years. Not that long after we met and started playing together he decided that he wanted to retire and move back down to Titusville, near Birmingham, Alabama. He sold his store and went home. Not long after that he passed away from a heart attack.

During the time of the Barrelhouse Rockers, we mostly played at the Childe Harold and festivals like the National Festival at Wolf Trap and the Smithsonian Festival. John and I partnered up and played the Glen Echo Festival. The Big Chief never played that festival because they weren't paying. We traveled on short road trips together. The one thing Chief did that was funny musically was we'd be playing together doing these tunes that would go from the one-chord to the four-chord to the five-chord. Sometimes when Chief would get to the four-chord he would shift—if you're playing in G, so G is the one-chord, and then you go to the four-chord, which is C—and then halfway through the four-chord he would forget that he was playing in G and he would just carry on in C, and all of a sudden, the four-chord becomes the one-chord. I'd have to adjust on the fly. There are different positions on the harmonica. You can play a chorus or two in that key, and I would switch to the first position actually playing straight harp in the first position until I had a chance to switch them out. It would take me a minute to figure out what's going on, and then to switch, and by the time I switched Chief would have shifted back. It was the one funny thing.

It wasn't that there were great exciting stories taking place in that time, as much as that these people felt like home to me. Being around Chief and being around his wife, when they were together it felt like home, my sense of "home" that comes from my mother and the way she used that word. To her it was where we all came from in Alabama at my grandmother's house in Titusville.

All of us musicians, and also at home, we were insulated. We dealt with each other and within the black community. It's funny—and in a way, that's the story of my life growing up. In my grandmother's neighborhood, and even in my neighborhood in DC, we didn't encounter white people that much at all. When we were traveling together we were focused on who we were with. One thing is, we didn't stop at restaurants. Chief's wife—and Henry Townsend and his wife too—no one bought food. People got hungry and one of the wives would go into their bag and they'd pull out roast beef sandwiches that they had made from the leftovers or fried chicken. It wasn't like we had to stop at restaurants or get food from people that we didn't know that might mistreat us. Everything was self-sufficient. That comes from growing up in the time of segregation. The folks got so that they didn't trust eating fast food—that was sort of new at that time. Not only did they not want to face being mistreated; they didn't trust the food unless they had prepared it themselves. They knew their level of cleanliness and they knew that that food was prepared the way they liked it, seasoned the way they like it. I remember just being the lucky beneficiary of that because Henry Townsend's wife would pull some delicious things out of bags and pass them around, and the same with Chief's wife. They could cook and the stuff was seasoned perfectly and southern, the way I grew up with.

Of course, the racism was there. I'm aware, for example, that my uncles, my Uncle Oscar and Ted, they delivered groceries on a store bicycle. One day they decided to go joy riding out of the neighborhood. A sheriff or a policeman pulled them over and got them and took them in the woods and pistol whipped them and left them there. They were very beat up and they made their way back home, but they didn't want to tell their mother, my grandmother, at the time. They were almost programmed not to want to tell anything bad because someone might want to seek justice and then there would be retaliation. I don't think they ever told my grandmother that that happened.

Uncle Ted, for example, he wanted to be in the FBI. That was his dream when he was going to college, and he studied criminology and he excelled in his classes. He graduated at the top of his class and went to register to apply for a job at the FBI. The first person that he came in contact with was a clerk typist receptionist that sat in the front lobby. She said, "It's not our policy to hire colored people." That's as far as he got. That was in the 1950s. He wound up being a successful attorney and he had a good life, but a clerk typist receptionist thwarted his dream. In my family, no one dwelt on any bitterness. When they talked about that whole subject of racism and trying to make it in that environment, the way it was expressed in my family was with a lot of humor and with a lot of confidence on how we would succeed. My parents were smart about that in terms of sheltering us from racism. They never wanted us to feel like anyone was treating us less than we should be treated. I came in contact with it when I was out in the world on my own. There were things we did by habit, like whenever we were going home to Alabama we would leave DC at four o'clock in the morning so by the time we got Deep South it would be daylight, plenty of daylight to burn to get to my grandmother's house before dark. We would never have to travel after dark and never have to worry about having to find a place to stay. We wouldn't stop—we might stop to have lunch at some overlook or something, but we would eat our own food that we had packed and we'd keep going until we got to our destination. We would plan it so that by the time the sun was down we were there. Those habits started under the Jim Crow segregation time as a matter of safety.

Those were my formative years, and after Big Chief Ellis went back to Alabama, John Cephas and I formed a duo . . . and that changed my life forever.

Ed Morris, Phil Wiggins, Flora Molton, circa 1978–80. From archives of the Travellin' Blues
Workshop. Courtesy of Paddy Bowman.

Flora Molton busking in front to Woodward & Lothrop department store on Street in Washington,
DC, 1980. Photo by Axel Küstner.

John Cephas jamming with Tim Lewis at John's carpentry workshop at the National Armory in Washington, D.C., 1978. Photo by Axel Küstner.

John Jackson at the D.C. Blues Fest, 1990. Photo by Fernando Sandoval.

Archie Edwards, circa 1987. Photo by Dexter Hodges.

Phil Wiggins and Archie Edwards backstage at the DC Blues Fest, 1990. Photo by Fernando Sandoval.

Mother Scott with adoring friends, circa 1978–80. Back row L to R: Paddy Bowman, Ed Morris, Larry Wise, Willie Gaines, Archie Edwards. Front row L to R: Flora Molton, Tim Lewis, Mother Scott, and Phil Wiggins. From archives of the Travellin' Blues Workshop. Courtesy of Paddy Bowman.

Phil Wiggins (holding talking drum) with Dr. Barry Lee Pearson (r) next to John Cephas (with hat) on tour for the U.S. State Department in 1982, performing for children in Accra, Ghana.

At the Oxon Hill Festival 1982 or '83. Front row: Eleanor Ellis, John Jackson, Roy Dunn, Flora Molton. Back row: John Cephas, Roger Gregory, James Jackson, Larry Wise, Phil Wiggins. Photo by Myron Samuels.

Leroy Gaines in his living room, 1978. Photo by Axel Küstner.

One of the first meetings of the DC Blues Society, circa 1987. Top row L to R: Rick Franklin, Neil Harpe, Ben Andrews, John Jackson, Eleanor Ellis, Archie Edwards, Phil Wiggins. Middle row L to R: Dr. Barry Lee Pearson, John Cephas. Front row L to R: Flora Molton, Mark Wenner, Bill Harris, DJ Joe "Bama" Washington of WPFW-FM. Photo by Dexter Hodges.

John Jackson, c. 1982. Photo by Myron Samuels. Courtesy of
Josh Samuels.

Archie Edwards and his wife on their front porch, 1980. Photo by Axel Küstner.

Chapter Two

THE CEPHAS AND WIGGINS YEARS

John Cephas was my senior by twenty-four years. He was born September 4, 1930, in the Foggy Bottom section of Washington, DC. His father was a Baptist minister and he started singing as a child in church. Before John Cephas and I started playing professionally we used to sit around the living room and play the blues, never expecting to get famous, to tour the world or to make it a career that would extend over more than three decades. We made music for the love of it and never imagined that this roots music of black people would have any perceived value outside of our own enjoyment. Even in the black community, the blues had somewhat of a lowly reputation, something unsavory rather than cultured. The blues was culturally diminished; but that was not unusual to me. When you grow up African American in America everything you see and hear on television is that your culture doesn't matter. The voices that speak for or about us are not always the way we would refer to ourselves, the way we would define our own culture. We value our own music, our own art, and we cele-brated the blues, but we did not perceive it as culturally significant. John Cephas and I went from playing locally and in our own backyards to having the good fortune to perform on every continent—except Antarctica—and everywhere in the world.

Music crosses all boundaries and brings understanding and harmony. I have found that no matter who you are, for human beings, laughter always sounds the same, crying sounds the same, and when someone is in pain it sounds the same, when someone is happy it sounds the same. Those basic things transcend differences, and that's what's in the blues—laughter, crying, moaning, wailing, shouting, celebrating, arguing—that's all right there in the blues, and that's all just real basic human expression, and I feel like that transcends any lan-guage and any culture. I like honesty in a song, something that is real. I don't like pretense, fakery, or false voices. If you listen to a song and say to yourself, "Man, that person has been through hell and back and they survived it and they thrived, and I have a little bit of shit that's going on in my life"—I can handle it. If they can handle it, I can handle it. Or man, I'm feeling bad, but this music makes me want to dance. All of a sudden, I feel so much better. That, to me, that's worth listening to.

The acoustic blues scene in Washington, DC, was and is a thriving, creative, and wonderful blues community, maybe one of the most giving, most supportive of them all. It was also just dumb luck that people of the personality of John Jackson, John Cephas, and Archie Edwards, who were by nature very generous people, happened to be in Washington, DC, at that moment in time. What happened in DC to form the acoustic blues community didn't happen in other cities. No place had the spirit of community that we had. Archie's Barbershop was a central meeting point, but it was more than just a place to go. There was a cohesiveness of community, and there were generations after generations joining the scene. That's how it evolved over more than forty years.

The blues in this region is different from that of the Mississippi Delta. Mississippi was a hell of a place to be from for a black man. It was dangerous and violent and the musicians reflected that. This permeated the songs. When we talk about blues being sad, this is an expression of the people's lives. Sometimes you hear people say "If I'm feeling bad, if I'm feeling down, I'm feeling sad, I don't want to listen to something that's going to make me feel worse. I want to listen to something that's going to make me feel better." The blues tell a story not to make you sad, but to make it sound happy. It's a form of catharsis. When you write a song, it's going to tell a story. What's the story that you have in your head? What's the story that you have in your life? If you're going to write songs, you've got to write about what you know. If what you know is danger and violence—that's what's going to come out. That's what the words are going to be about, because that's been your experience. Blues songs are about so many different subjects and they carry so many different emotions, and the so-called Piedmont blues is the same way. It's about life.

You had wonderful musicians who made their homes here. Archie Edwards, John Cephas, John Jackson, Chief Ellis, Flora Molton, Mother Scott—all these people were here just doing what they have always done: making their music in their own homes, and in their own community, for their own celebrations. Having those people in close proximity with people like Joe Wilson from the National Council for the Traditional Arts (NCTA) and folklorists like Ralph Rinzler[1] and Bess Lomax Hawes, and others who were involved in the National Endowment for the Arts and the Smithsonian, created a special relationship of mutual support and recognition. The folklorists and traditional music establishment became close personal friends with the local musicians because they loved the music and the culture. They shined a light on these important African American musicians who up to a certain point just carried on their music almost in spite of the culture around them. I think that these traditional blues artists had never imagined or thought about that music and culture having any value other than the immediate cultural value within the African American community. I don't think that they ever considered that it would be important for future generations to know how they lived and how they survived and thrived. History has proven otherwise. The mere fact that people worldwide are interested in the acoustic blues to this day shows the importance of this music. The players I knew started to understand that the world was very curious about them and their music, and that there was very high regard for it. They recognized that their own blues culture, the music they played on a Saturday night, was something of value. I am sure that John Cephas never looked at himself as a cultural ambassador until he became friends with Joe Wilson, the director of the NCTA.[2] Before that John was just a guy who played the blues, who didn't give a shit about much of anything, and had never played in public that much. With his relationship with Joe he grew into a blues ambassador, a person who realized the value of what he had and the importance of passing it on. When I first met John, he thought that blues was just party music, which I think is still the most important role of it. I think Archie was probably the same way. John Jackson had caught on to it much earlier.

The true blues, the way we play it, is not very high-browed. You have some drinks and play some music, have a good time, get the folks dancing. It's the soundtrack for card games, drinking, arguments, and sharing food. It is also a culture that came out of the post-slavery Jim Crow segregation era, with the musical precedents of spirituals and work songs coming out of slavery times. It's the music of the poorest, most oppressed and suffering people, a form of entertainment during a very difficult time. It helped sustain people, helped them survive and to flourish. It was music with an incredible amount of tenacity and creativity, played by people equally tenacious. Finally, people see the value in that, but we, as African Americans, had to reach the realization ourselves, to see it first. Once the local players recognized that they themselves were important musicians and artists who should take pride in the music and culture they knew, they recognized the value and the need to pass it on to younger generations. It was cultural validation.

The center of the DC blues scene was Archie's barbershop at 2007 Bunker Hill Road, NE. The first time I went to the barbershop I was with Archie, who I had met through Mother Scott at her eighty-second birthday party. We played a little bit together that day and he got excited about wanting to make music with me. I went to the barbershop with him and we were hanging around and visiting different places around town in DC where he was performing. We made the rounds and stopped in and played at this place and that place, just for friends. I wound up at the barbershop with him and the Gaines Brothers, Leroy and Willie. It's funny, but I still know these guys by their drinking habits. Archie, for example, liked to drink cognac and milk when we were jamming together. It was after hours and he knew that some folks were going to show up to play. It was Archie and his buddies—the Gaines Brothers and a bunch of other people. The Gaines Brothers from Virginia were big lanky guys and great players. You could see a real strong family resemblance. They looked a little bit like they had some Native American in their blood, but I found out in later years that most African Americans that think that they have Native American blood don't. They both had freckles, which was unusual for black people. They had big but gentle personalities and they were badass players. I don't remember ever going to a concert and hearing them play; and the only time that I ran into them was probably twice at Archie's Barbershop.

There was always a real strong sense of celebration. The barber shears were put away and bottles of drink were put out, and people were just relaxing and enjoying themselves playing music. There was also a real strong sense of competition. Of course, Archie ruled the roost, although there were some guitar players there that were his equal if not better, but they all deferred to him because they were on his turf. It was an older generation of men that had a lot of style and class and gravitas. They all just had a great sense of self and carried themselves with dignity—because in a way they already realized that they were important people. I think that was a generational thing, that people carried themselves with more self-respect back then.

Archie Edwards was a special guy. People who knew Archie would think that he was a little tough guy with a Napoleon complex, trying to compensate for his small size by projecting a big personality—but the truth is he was all that and the linchpin of the community. There are others—John Jackson and John Cephas—who received more notoriety. John Cephas traveled a lot more. But if you wanted to know what was going on in our community, you would talk to Archie and he would know the score. He was the glue of the community. He made a point of staying in touch more so than any of the others, calling and checking in to see what you're doing, how you're doing and what's going on—what's going on in the scene. He was like the clearinghouse of information about the blues scene. It was hard for anyone to help Archie to advance his career because he was distrustful of people. As everybody knew, there was always a real strong sense of competition between him and John Cephas. For example, John recommended Archie to tour with us on the American Folk Blues Festival. At the end of that tour Archie wrote Horst Lippmann a long letter trashing John. I don't know if he thought somehow that Lippmann and Rau would pick him to tour instead of us, or what, but for some reason he felt like writing that letter. I don't remember exactly the details of what that letter said, but it wasn't nice. I remember John telling me that Horst Lippmann wrote him and said, "What's wrong with this guy Archie? Why is he so jealous?" I don't know what was in the letter word for word, but it made Archie seem paranoid and jealous. Yet, as in all those guys, Archie was all right, he was just being Archie.

The local musicians all had day jobs where they worked very hard. They did hard, physical labor. Archie ran his barbershop and was a security guard at the National Guard Armory. John Cephas was a carpenter. John Jackson dug graves. After their day work they worked hard playing music. Music was their form of fun, a relief from their hard day jobs. But they were used to working hard and they didn't mind it. They had very strong work ethics and took pride in everything they did, great pride in their work. They each put a lot of effort and energy into their work, and equally into their own enjoyment. As a young man, I liked playing music with them and eventually it got to a point with us all . . . and with me, when we wanted to make a living playing our blues. Those guys, that generation, they had an unbelievable energy. John Cephas worked hard all day and played music until late into the night, but he also loved fishing. Early mornings, after a long gig, I would be tired, "I'm going to bed"—and John would be, "Well, I'm going to get my fishing tackle together. I'm going out, going to go fishing." He would get up early and drive all the way to the Eastern Shore. I couldn't even keep up with him. But it was his joy to do that.

I think that when those guys came up and had to work as hard as they did just to have food on the table and a roof over their head, they had a lot more energy than what we have now. Most musicians in my generation haven't had the experience of playing for dances and parties. My generation of professional musicians play where people are just sitting on their butts listening, and in a way, that's now the measurement of a good gig: "It's a great listening audience— you could hear a pin drop." That's not what this music was made for. It was to cut through people arguing with each other, people cleaning up their last bit of greens and potato salad, or people arguing over a card game. It was music for people dancing, getting up and moving around. I consider myself lucky for having known people who were born and raised and came up in that environment and to witness that myself. Your energy level is like a muscle and if it gets used a lot then you have it; if you don't use it, then you lose it. When I tired after a long gig, and was thinking, "Let's pack up and get out of here. Man, we can go relax, have a beer, go to bed, whatever." Then some kid would come along to ask John a question, and he'd have the guitar packed up and he'd unpack it. The next thing you know an hour later we were still sitting there and he's showing someone something, and I'm like, man, I'm so tired, but he wasn't.

Our acoustic blues scene in DC was different from anyplace. When you think about someone trying to make a living playing blues in Chicago or Philadelphia, or wherever, it's nightclubs, and anybody that comes in with a guitar it is like competition. When you're on stage you're either cutting it or you're not, and when not then you get kicked off the stage. I don't know if it's true or not, but I had always heard that Hound Dog Taylor once shot his bass player in the butt for not playing right. That atmosphere didn't exist in DC and Northern Virginia as we had a strong festival scene, which was a way of making money playing music, but also a totally different atmosphere than playing in nightclubs or for house parties. It was a peaceful, safe and open relaxed environment more conducive to cultural exchange. For one thing, part of your performance was answering questions, was talking about what you do and why you do it and where it came from. They were open to people walking up to them and asking them questions, "Can you show me how to do this?" I think it goes back again to having the right personalities in the right places at the right time, because the festivals had a lot to do with taking the edge off of some of these guys, whose life experiences maybe taught them to not be as trustful. I saw that a lot with Archie Edwards. He was torn between being a respected teacher and performer at festivals and also keeping one eye open all the time to not be ripped off again. He was still a bit suspicious. All of the musicians I played with had the self-preservation instinct of being mistrustful to a certain extent, but they sort of overcame it. John Cephas—he had it to a great extent, and at the same time he was just wide open and generous. Those two opposing realities came together to form the dynamic. They were used to being ripped off by people who took advantage of the fact that their music wasn't valued. "Come play for us and we'll give you free drinks. We'll charge admission at the door and you can have half of that or whatever." Making recordings and people coming to them, saying, "Oh, we love what you do. We want to get it on record," and this is the deal. Then you make the recording and you don't ever see a penny back from it. Then, the record executives say, "Oh, well, we haven't made back what we spent to make it yet." Everybody knew the word-of-mouth stories from other black musicians, reports about being ripped off by the industry in lots of different ways. It's very common knowledge—so that people were leery that maybe it didn't happen to them. The festivals were different. Here we were respected, honored, and revered and well taken care of.

The DC musicians were very generous. John Jackson, John Cephas—they were such powerful mentors, with a real strong desire to see the music carried on. Those were just incredibly strong roots established by those people. They were good stewards of carrying the music and culture on, and they did not define that by race or gender. They passed it on to Mike Baytop, Eleanor Ellis, Michael Roach, and Rick Franklin—and of course to me. Those of us who were the "younger generation" were exposed to these wonderful players with this incredible talent and ability, and also the strong desire to pass it on. There were enough of us that we were fortunate enough to spend time with these masters that we not only learned what we could in terms of music skills; we also learned that there's no place for ego, there's no place for star complexes. If a person like

John Jackson is going to be so open and welcome you into his home, how can I do any less?—because he is the beginning of it. He came from the roots of it. He was there during the hard times that created this music and he can invite and welcome anyone, of any ethnicity or description, into his home, have them sit on his couch as long as they want to, and give them everything he can possibly give them in terms of sharing his music. If a person like that can do it, how can I do any less? I think there were enough of us of the younger generation that benefitted from that in our music community.

I was performing in Belize, in Central America, recently. Just about every night the owner of the place where I was living and playing, Captain Ron, and I, we were up on the second-floor balcony looking up at the sky because on a clear night you could see billions of stars. It was just beautiful and then I was thinking about that blue midnight sky and came up with the term "pistol blue"—"it's pistol blue, a sky shot full of holes." It's a whole different way of looking at it than the way we were looking at it in that paradise. I'm always playing with and experimenting with words and imagery as a musician and songwriter. I've always loved poetry and literature. Whenever I hear a phrase, I'm playing with words in the back of my mind seeing what's in there—what rhythm is here or repetition—just taking words apart, listening to them, hearing them in lots of different contexts. I have been doing that for all of my life, contemplating words and lyrics to see if there are other meanings in it or other ways to work with it. Like, "I'm the person that put the 'harm' in harmonica." That sounds good, and I wish I could use it for marketing. "Phil Wiggins—*he put the harm in the harmonica.*" Except, well, it's not true. I try to play well, to play sweetly and passionately with feeling, but it's not harmful no matter how tempting the wordplay. When I hear a word, I feel like automatically working it, as a songwriter and lyricist as much as a harmonica player. Songs and music have always been an integral part of me. The blues is part of my heart and soul, not just aurally, but also lyrically. I have found amazingly beautiful phrases and lyrics in blues songs. To understand American or Western poetry requires a certain knowledge of the culture and the history that it was created in. The same goes for the blues. In poetry, allusion is one of the most commonly used devices where in a few words a person will provoke you to think of a whole body of literature, or at least a particular novel. Within a couple of phrases, they can have you thinking. In America, occasionally those who write about and analyze poetry, and are accepted as authorities, will sometimes read a poem by someone like Etheridge Knight, or any of the black poets—and not have full understanding or knowledge of that culture required to comprehend what the poet is alluding to. They sometimes don't even see the craft and the beauty in some of the blues lyrics, which are often degraded as crude and primitive. They miss it because they don't know the culture and they often don't truly respect the power and beauty in the simplicity of blues lyrics. They just take everything at face value because it's blues, "just poor, oppressed black people's writing" and they assume that we are not sophisticated thinkers, and blues lyrics are judged to be simple. That happens a lot.

I don't like a lot of fat in lyrics. I like lyrics when they're honed down to just the essence, the most potent. To me lyrics are like poetry, it happens when you have something that's extremely important to communicate—your life depends on you being able to communicate this to someone and have them understand it exactly the way you mean it. At that point, when the stakes are that high, that to me is when poetry happens. There can be poetry that's clever or that's flowery, but to me when it's crystal clear in the simplest way, that to me is the best way. I feel like a lot of that happens in everyday speech, when you're just talking to people it can be poetic. My ears are always wide open and I deliberately listen for poetry in what people say.

The poetry happened when I played with John Cephas.

We played together in a duo for more than three decades as Cephas & Wiggins. That's a lifetime career together, a true partnership. We made it last and we were internationally successful. Any partnership like that takes work and effort on both sides. We managed it. John was an amazing musician—probably the best I've ever known in my life. That's the main reason how we made good music together. When I first started playing with John he hadn't played in public that much and he didn't think of his music as being stageworthy or being important. John was a great musician and a wild guy. Over the years as we were playing together he gained more self-respect, more understanding of the value of his music and artistry, and he embraced the idea of being a musical ambassador and a tradition bearer for the roots blues.

In the early days, all through 1976–77, John Cephas and I played local gigs wherever we could get them, while we both had day jobs. We played at the Cellar Door, the Childe Harold, Wolf Trap Farm Park, and other regional venues. During the time when John and I first started out together, I was doing things with different people at every opportunity, exploring all musical angles. I realized that we had the potential to make good music together. For one thing, no one could sing like John. He had the most warm, soft, and beautiful voice. His timing, rhythm, and chord changes were very strong and consistent. He was a person that I could play my best with, whereas some of the others—as great as they were, there were times that I would be lost because they played very idiosyncratically, individualistically, with weird shifts that would sometimes throw me off. John Cephas wasn't a better guitar player than John Jackson, who was wonderful, but he paid a lot of attention to details when he was playing. John Cephas was smooth and he made each song unique and fit to what he was good at. He probably had more experience than any of the others playing house parties and dances, so he understood that part of his job was to provide dance rhythm for people. So, rather than saying that he was the best musician that I ever knew—although on a certain level I still believe that's true—he brought out the best in me as a player.

To play with John Cephas, I tried as a rule to be as out of the way as possible and to help support the rhythm. John's voice was so pretty and soft, so I used the harmonica as percussion whenever he was singing. I refrained from playing countermelody because it wouldn't work, because it would overpower his voice. Learning to play as an ensemble as a guitar and harmonica duo took time. It was a learning process, something I had to go through as a maturing musician. Looking back, in the early days there were moments when I definitely overplayed. Once John and I found our stride, we learned our parts, learned to listen to each other, to hear and communicate, to become in perfect harmony with each other. Like many young players, part of my growth process was learning how to give space, how to accompany instead of playing over others. That's what every harmonica player has to learn, when to lay back and when to get up front. Sometimes John would be critical of me, pointing out when I soloed too much or when I was overpowering.

When I first met John Cephas in 1976, the big joke among all those musicians was how nervous he was about playing in public in front of people and that he couldn't stand still because he was nervous. That was my first impression of John—aside from the fact that, of course, he was a great guitar player and had a beautiful, warm voice—but he hadn't had much experience playing in front of people. At the time I had met him I probably played in public more than he had. He played mostly house parties in his own close-knit community down in Virginia and also in the Foggy Bottom neighborhood of Washington, DC.

Everybody thought of John as being from the country and a lot of people think he was born down in Bowling Green, although he was actually born and raised in Washington, DC. His family spent a lot of time down in Virginia where they owned some land. John spent some time down there when he was growing up, the same way I spent time in Alabama when I was growing up. John built himself a house and he also built his mother and father a house right next to his. He was a carpenter and a shop foreman at the National Guard Armory. He built his own house brick by brick. He did it all, the bricklaying, the carpentry, the electrical work—all that because he was very enterprising, a very hardworking person, the foreman of his shop. He took care of business, and he had great pride of his carpentry skills and electrical skills. He was very well respected at the National Guard Armory and RFK Stadium. There were military people wandering around there that had rank that thought they were this and that— there were all these power games. John was a strong character who fit right in there. None of them challenged him because he got stuff done. They'd tell him what they needed done and leave him alone because they knew that if they tried to screw with him it wasn't going to serve them well. Everybody knew that. In a way, it was almost like plantation mentality. To survive you had to be strong, but get along. That was John.

We were musical soulmates, but as people we disagreed on things like politics. For example, John was fiscally and socially conservative. At the same time, he had a heart of gold, and he was a very generous and hospitable host. Hospitality meant a lot to him. He was a man who had worked hard all of his life, and he managed to build a good life for himself, and no one gave it to him. He earned every bit of it.

John loved living in the country, but he was not into rusticity. He liked the latest, most modern things. He's the first person I knew that had a desktop computer. When I first met him, he had two or three typewriters. He was always into the latest trend. When he bought a car, he would keep it a year and then trade it in for the newest model. He wasn't into antiques, or collecting old stuff, and he wasn't into roughing it. No woodstoves! John wanted the height of comfort and the best that technology could provide. The same with his musical gear. Today there are many blues musicians who try to emulate the old blues players by using the same old instruments and amp setups as used decades ago. Not John! He was not into old guitars or amps, but he had the newest and the best.

He also had a bad hearing problem, I think as a result of working as a carpenter for so many years around power tools and never wearing ear protection. He lost a good bit of his hearing. To compensate, he liked to plug his guitar into an amplifier and crank it high. To me, it wasn't a good tone because it didn't sound anything like an acoustic guitar. When we started out, the electric pickups for acoustic guitars were quite primitive. He would try whatever the latest thing was, always looking for the newest gadget. He tried everything. Finally, as the technology progressed and others were installing pickups into the guitars, he would take these beautiful guitars, like his Taylors and the Wayne Henderson guitar, he would send them to Fishman to install a pickup in there for him. John would plug his guitars directly into an amplifier that he had sitting right there next to him on the stage. A good soundman would figure out that he used it as his monitor, and take two lines out and have one going through the PA and one going through that amp just so John could hear it. It wasn't optimal in terms of sound quality, but it was best for him and he cranked it up loud. I remember sitting on stage playing with the Blue Rhythm Boys, with two guitars, a violin, and trumpet—and then sitting next to John—and he was way louder than all those people together. It was just because he couldn't hear that well.

When John first invited me to play, just the two of us, it was in that neighborhood in Bowling Green and Woodford, Virginia. I remember going to meet John in Chinatown on a Friday night after work. The plan was to stop in Chinatown and have a meal and then go on down to Virginia to spend the weekend. John came rolling up in a pickup truck that smelled like you wouldn't believe to high heaven. I said, "John, what the hell is that smell?" He said, "I've got a truckload of elephant shit in the back." John worked at the National Guard Armory and, when the Ringling Brothers Circus came to town, that's where they performed. John's carpenter shop was there and he made a deal with the elephant handler that he would clean up the elephant shit if he let him have it. He put it in barrels and then he would dump it in the back of his truck, and take it down to Virginia to put it on his garden. He told me, "Man, that stuff, that fertilizer is so good, when you throw that on the garden then you've got to jump back so that you won't get knocked over by the vegetables jumping out of the ground."

I met him and we had dinner in Chinatown and we went on down to Bowling Green. We got up early the next morning and started going around the community working—sorting potatoes at one place where there was a guy who raised chickens. We sorted his potatoes and he gave us eggs. John did some repair work on the freezer of this other guy. All these things were happening, and money never changed hands. It was all barter—you do this for me and I'll do this for you. We spent the whole day doing that. Somewhere along the way we stopped and John bought a big bushel of crabs that had been steamed in Old Bay. I knew I wasn't supposed to eat them, because I have an allergy to shellfish, but it smelled good, so I was popping the little claws off and munching on them. We wound up drinking and playing music half the night, and I was still eating on those things, and all of a sudden, my eyes started swelling up. It was dumb luck, because I was having trouble breathing and I passed out. After I passed out my breathing relaxed and I wasn't panicking and when I woke up in the morning it was okay. I think passing out saved me because otherwise I would have panicked for not getting enough air.

We had some of the best times down home with his whole family. His father was bedridden. I don't remember what was wrong with him, but from the time I had met him he was in bed all the time. He was a very smart, well-educated, and well-spoken man. John and his mother, Sylvia, would always tell me to go and speak to John's father. I would go and hang with him, and I used to enjoy talking to him.

That was the first time that I went down to Virginia with him. At that point, I had known him for a while. We had done a couple little coffeehouse gigs together. After Chief Ellis died, John called me up one day, said, "You know, people have been calling me, bugging me to come play here and there, and I don't like going by myself to do that. Would you like to come and do some of these things with me?" That's how we started as a duo. I said, "Well, you know, we should spend some time playing together so I can learn some of these tunes that you've been playing." He said, "Well, come on down to the country with me."

We would do that—on a lot of weekends I would go down to spend a weekend at John's house in the country. Sometimes his family would go with him and we would play house parties down there where people were drinking, gambling, listening to music, and all John's crazy neighbors would come.

John embraced this rural persona, with bad grammar and all that, but I know he wasn't raised that way. His father was well educated and spoke English with perfect diction. He was an interesting man and fun to talk to. That's how I know that John liked to almost be in character in a way, a smart guy being a rural fellow. John was a jitterbug too. He liked to be a badass. When I first met John, he liked to drink and be rowdy and loud.

We met in the Ruby, a Chinese restaurant in Washington, DC, on the way down to Bowling Green. John loved Chinese food to the point where I don't eat it much anymore because I got sick of eating the same thing all the time. Whenever we went into the Ruby, the owners of the restaurant treated John as he was the mayor of Washington. Everybody from the owner to the dishwasher would come out and greet him and shake his hand and welcome him to that restaurant. At first I thought it was because they liked his music and thought that he was famous, but they actually didn't know anything about that. The reason why John was such a celebrity was because of an incident at the restaurant. John came in late one night because in Chinatown in DC, they stay open into the crazy wee hours. It was two o'clock in the morning and John went in there to get something to eat after a gig. In walked a young guy pointing a gun at the owner. John got mad. He wasn't going to take that while he was enjoying his meal. He just went up to the kid and grabbed the gun away from him, and got in the startled robber's face. "I don't know what you think you are doing here, but you're not going to do this in my restaurant." John was a big strong guy, and he grabbed this guy by the seat of his pants and the scruff of his neck and shook him and chucked him down the stairs. The bewildered kid beat it out the front door. John picked up the gun off the floor, said, "I think I'll keep it." He still had that gun when I met him. That's why they gave John the royal treatment because he saved their butts one night.

John Cephas was a very strong-willed guy. Besides being a great musician and a hard-working craftsman, he would always take very strong stands on different issues. He wasn't a person who compromised at all. I remember late one night, probably two o'clock in the morning, we stopped at a gas station. There was a couple of big old burly guys working there, and one guy filled the tank up while John went to the bathroom. I was sitting in the car waiting. When John came back the guy had cleared the gas pump meter, and he told John how much he owed him. John looked at the meter, at the gas pump, and there wasn't a figure there because the guy had cleared it. John said, "Well, I don't know how much you put in there. I'm not going to pay you that. The meter is clear. It doesn't say how much." The guy said, "Well, I'm not trying to rob you. I'm just telling you I just cleared it. I thought you were done. I just cleared it." John said, "Well, I'm not paying you. I know it was on empty. I'll give you what I know is about half a tank full. I'll pay you that much." They argued for a good 20 minutes. John paid him what he wanted to pay him and wouldn't pay a penny more. I said, "Well, John, what if the guy had wanted to fight you?" He said, "Well, so be it." He wasn't going to get ripped off. He had learned to overcome by being strong.

He was a tough character, a good man but a complex human being. He would always surprise you. Just when you thought you had him figured, when you thought you knew what he would do next, he would surprise you. On one level, he was kind and generous, on the other hand he could be hard-nosed. When it came to homeless street people and panhandlers and beggars he could be harsh. John would not even tolerate talking to anybody who came up to him begging. He would just call them a sack of motherfuckers and tell them to get out of his face. I've seen that several times. It seemed cold, but I can't blame him. He didn't beg anyone for anything, and he didn't like to owe anyone anything, and he didn't like the idea of me owing anyone anything. He wouldn't loan anyone money and he wouldn't borrow any. He was conservative, but he earned his own living. He was very generous.

John was absolutely at his best and his happiest when he was in his garden down at his house in Woodford—they called it Bowling Green because that's where the county seat was. The biggest joy of John's life was to put a seed in the ground and watch it come up and watch it bear fruit. John seemed to almost in a childlike way go for the greatest degree of intensity in life—you know, always trying to get the best out of every moment in life. One time when we were heading back from a gig in Charlottesville, Virginia, and we were coming down the road at about two o'clock in the morning, we hit a deer that came out of nowhere. The next thing we know, the Dodge Caravan was totaled and we were stranded at the side of the road until someone came by. Eventually, the AAA towed the vehicle and they dropped us at John's house maybe about five in the morning. We had a gig coming up that day, and given how late it was we could only expect a few hours of sleep because we had to hit the road early in the day. I was so tired I just wanted John to show me to a bed. When we got out of the guy's car, John turned to me and said, "Man, we've got to go and pick some of that corn!" I said, "What are you talking about?" He insisted, "That corn, I can smell it, man—it's ripe right now. We've got to go pick some." We went out there at five o'clock in the morning picking corn. Finally, I said, "Okay, cool. Now I'll go to bed." He goes, "No, we've got to sit down and eat some." So, we did. We cooked some corn, sat down and ate it and it was so sweet. Then we had to get up so early. By the time we got in bed it was probably eight in the morning. At noontime, we cooked some more of that corn and ate it; it already was not as sweet as it had been at five in the morning when we ate it. He was right. That was life with John.

At that time, as a young guy, I was working at a law office in the mailroom. I delivered packages in downtown Washington, and did court filings. I took documents down to the district court and to the Federal court and filed claims. That's how I supported myself, while I got closer to the point of playing music for a living and getting to the point where I knew that I had to sink or swim with music.

When John Cephas and I first started playing together, I, along with my ex-wife who at the time was my girlfriend, we created a good promo package. Back in those days it was different than it is now. There were no Internet websites. We had one of those old-school promo packages that included photos and news articles and quotes from people. The reason I know that it was good is because just about every agent that John and I ended up with after that point used a lot of that material in their promo. They just took it and put their name on it, which pissed off my wife Wendy, because a lot of it was her work. Before that I was arranging the bookings, making phone calls and setting dates, but that did not work out. Once in a while something would happen where we would be double-booked or some other screw-up would happen—and rather than John being able to say, "Okay, this went wrong—let's figure it out and figure out how to fix it"—he would get nasty about it personally—name calling and all. Finally, I realized that it was not worth it to me to be doing this and having to go through these kinds of conflicts with John. I'd rather have someone else do that and I'll just make music with him, which was why I associated with him to begin with, just for the music. Our first agent was John Ullman. I turned all the promo materials that Wendy and I had put together over to him, and he took them and put his name on them. Rather than having to have fights with John about stuff that there's no real point in fighting about, I'll let him fight with John Ullman and I'll just go make music with him, and that will be that.

From the beginning, we split the money 50/50. Then, after a while, John came up with this idea, well, because we would use his car and he did all the driving he would take 10 percent additional. Then he formed a company, John Cephas, Inc., and he blindsided me with that. We were on our way home from a road tour, and on the way through town we stopped at this lawyer's house that John was friends with and that he had done business with, and this guy had helped him set up his corporation. And he said, "Well, from now on John Cephas Inc. is going to be the company we do all the business for Cephas & Wiggins through. When we get paid the company gets 10 percent and the agent gets whatever the agent gets—like 15 percent—and then we split the rest." That's how we did it. John signed the contracts with the record labels. Any royalty payments that might be coming, went to him and now go to his estate. I only own the publishing rights to my own songs. I was not good at the business end of things and maybe I should have been.

To my knowledge, we actually never made much money from our recordings. It's something that I never dwelled on or talked about—I guess it's stupid on my part, but I never was that curious about that. Of course, you hear stories all the time about artists getting ripped off by labels, and I don't know of anybody that made recordings and got wealthy off them or could go and buy a house or whatever. In my experience and in the experience of most of the people I know, the best thing that you can do is try to get a lump sum in advance and then, unless you stay on the record companies like a hawk, after a while the royalties just sort of peter out and you never get much. The biggest check I ever got from royalty payments was when someone else recorded one of my original songs and I got songwriter royalties. I got a nice fat check one time because Saffire the Uppity Blues Women recorded my song "Fools Night Out." That was the biggest check I had ever got, and even that wasn't that much.

It was around those early years that I met Dr. Barry Lee Pearson of the University of Maryland; Joe Wilson, the director of the NCTA; and Dick Spottswood, the local radio host, producer, and folklorist. They were movers and shakers of the local music establishment, friends and associates of the more senior blues players in the community, like John Cephas and Archie Edwards.

I first met Barry Lee Pearson not long after I got to know John Cephas, right around 1977, at some event where Archie Edwards was playing, because at the time he was tight with Archie Edwards. I think it was around the time that he was doing research for a book that he eventually wrote that was about Archie and John Cephas. He and Archie used to go to Colonel Brooks Tavern and play together. My first real clear memory of him was that I got invited to perform at the Takoma Park Folk Festival one time. I went there to perform and they actually wanted to charge me admission. I said, "Well, I'm here to perform." They insisted, "Yeah, but everybody pays admission." That seemed absurd to me. I said, "Well, but I wouldn't be here if they didn't ask me to come to perform. I don't see why I should have to pay to get in to play." Right while I was having that argument with whoever was at the door, Barry Lee walked up and I recognized him. He said, "What's the problem, guys?" I said, "Well, they want me to pay to come in and play." He talked to them and fixed the whole thing where they didn't charge me and everybody calmed down and cooled. That's my first memory of Barry Lee. He deserves a lot of credit as one of the first folklorists that respected and took an interest in the local musicians, more so than anyone. We toured with Barry Lee on the State Department tours. He also helped to set up a West Coast tour for us of California in 1983; first the African tours and then the West Coast tour. Barry Lee was included as a musician and as a de facto road manager. He definitely helped in setting up that tour. In the African tour, he was included to be the road manager and musician for that, and I don't know how he handled this, but at that time he and John both were drinking too much.

Honestly, when reflecting on those early times, Barry Lee and I didn't get along that well; but over the years we reached a better understanding and had more respect for each other to the point where we wound up being good friends. I don't mind saying that when I first met Barry Lee, I thought he was an arrogant, difficult white guy that felt like he had the right to define and evaluate my music. Over the years, I learned that part of that had to do with my own ego and my own prejudices. Over time I could see the way he would talk about me, and my music, and I came to understand that he did appreciate my playing. I learned to respect him and I think it was the same for him. It just happened gradually over the years. Now we are good friends. Dr. Barry Lee Pearson is a great writer. He has a fine-tuned ear and a talent for writing down what people tell him—for capturing the story as it was told by a particular person. Even though he told stories exactly the way he heard them, they were still being filtered through his sense of humor and his sensibilities. What came out is what that person said. Barry Lee respected that person and he appreciated that person's personality. He got the sense of humor, he got the anger, and he understood it. When you read the books that Barry Lee wrote, you get a sense of the person. Too often music authors make the book more about themselves. When his book *Virginia Piedmont Blues* came out with the biographies of Archie Edwards and John Cephas, I saw how meticulous and caring he was. I think that book changed my attitude about him. I realized that he wrote from a position of respect and that he was a good listener and he wrote basically what people said. Barry Lee has proven to be a person that approaches that job and that duty with a lot of integrity, respect, and reverence, and also with a good open ear to hear what the person says, how they say it, and to understand what they mean by it, and then to record that without it being colored by his own personal preconceptions. By getting to know him better and by his work I got to appreciate who he is.

All those guys—Barry Lee, Joe Wilson, and Dick Spottswood—in the beginning I think that they didn't think much of me. Joe Wilson and I also ended up as friends over time, but in the beginning, it seemed like they thought and wanted that I would just eventually go away; but I never did. They definitely gave me the feeling of disapproval and that they didn't like me by the way they treated me. I don't know what they thought, but I guess I didn't fit their definition of a bluesman. They weren't very friendly, or very respectful. They made it obvious what their preconceptions of me were by the things they would say. I remember one of my first impressions of Joe Wilson—I think I was at a NCTA cookout, they were having a barbeque—and what he said to me, "You know Adam couldn't have been a black man, because no black man would have gave up a rib." That was a joke, I guess.

Joe Wilson was the only person on the planet that John would listen to. Joe was a really unique person—it's like a cliché, but he was really like a force of nature. He was a really special brilliant person and he and John were best of friends. Joe just liked everything about John and he felt like John had strong character and he just loved him—best friends all the way. He was a folklorist and journalist who served as the executive director of the National Council for the Traditional Arts (NCTA) and he became our most important career catalyst.

Barry Lee, Joe Wilson, and Dick Spottswood all loved John Cephas. He fit their image of what a traditional bluesman should be. Joe immediately took to John Cephas and vice versa. Those two became fast friends right away. To a large extent I can understand why. John was very independent, self-made, hard-working, a beautiful singer, a good guitar player, and at the same time just a real character with a lot of integrity. Here I was, just a teenager, a beer-drinking, pot-smoking, Afro-wearing, raggedy-jeans teenager that expected them to just automatically respect and like me. For me, at the time it didn't matter what they felt or thought or how they treated me. What mattered to me was that I was welcomed and included in the black blues community. John Cephas, Archie Edwards, John Jackson, Flora Molton, Mother Scott, they all welcomed me. Those were the people that I admired and those were the people that I was there to spend my time with, so I didn't care that those other people didn't think much of me. I think it was because I was young, but also because at the time they didn't know anything about me, my family history, and things like that. My parents were black people from the Deep South and they stressed good education and good grammar and good diction and I had a good upbringing. I know that it took me a while to learn to play well with John Cephas. None of the heavy hitters of the local music establishment openly criticized me, but I know now, in hindsight, that when I first started playing with John I was terrible. I played too much, too fast, too loud. But I learned. I spent time with John Cephas and with John Jackson and with Archie, and I learned how to play better, or how to play together with someone and accompany better. Now, upon reflection, these folklorists, the white music establishment, they were older academics in a close-knit group with similar attitudes. I was just a wild teenager with a big Afro, just full of vinegar. I had my own ego and sense of entitlement and all that, and I just assumed that I would show up and everybody would love me and love my playing. They didn't know me and I basically didn't know shit. But we all got over it in time, and I think that's how we wound up gaining some respect for each other.

All the local musicians regularly met at Archie Edwards' barbershop for jam sessions and we all knew each other and were friends, but we were never united under one umbrella until the editor of the local newspaper the *Unicorn Times* and Paddy Bowman founded the Travellin' Blues Workshop. They recognized that there was a vibrant local blues scene still somewhat under the radar of the local white music fans, which had all but ignored us up to that point. All those people were looking elsewhere for the authentic roots blues, and all along we were right there under their noses. The Travellin' Blues Workshop was a non-profit organization set up by genuine music lovers with the mission of promoting us and giving us a greater platform, a bit of recognition. Mother Scott, Elizabeth Cotten, John Jackson, Archie Edwards, Flora Molton, John Cephas, Ed Morris, Larry Wise, and Tim Lewis were part of that, with Paddy Bowman and Elliot Ryan, the editor of the local alternative newspaper the *Unicorn Times* setting up concerts and gigs. The way that I learned that I was part of it was a bit unusual. I was walking along one day and saw a poster up on a telephone pole that said, "Appearing (here and there)," and it listed all these people, my music friends, including me. At that point in time I was actually playing with every single one of them, and none of them had mentioned it to me. I called up a few of the others, and asked, "Do we have this gig coming up?" It turned out that none of them knew anything about it, that there was this concert being advertised involving all of them and I was the first person to actually mention it to the people. It was all good, because we knew that they were coming from a good place with the best of intentions. Paddy Bowman, who did most of the work related to the Workshop, and Elliot Ryan were true music lovers. Paddy is very down to earth, very smart—a quick woman—good at dealing with people, and lots of different personalities, very calm. I always had the impression that she was a strong woman, a real navigator and quick thinking on her feet. Most of all just a real lover of the local music and she was very close with the musicians. We played for the kick-off of the Travellin' Blues Workshop at the Martin Luther King Jr. Library, where Bess Lomax Hawes[3] came to the performance. Aside from a few local events, John and I never went on the road to perform on behalf of the Travellin' Blues Workshop, but they were significant because they led to bigger things for many us, and for Cephas & Wiggins it brought us to our first LP on the German L+R (Lippmann and Rau) label.

Tim Lewis, the filmmaker and musician, was a good friend of mine. He was very intense, a very small wiry person, animated and passionate. When we first met, he wasn't much of a musician, but he picked up the guitar and was a quick learner on the instrument. He met Flora Molton and learned quickly how to get in there and help back her up. During part of this time I was in and out of DC, because I was going to college, so Tim and Flora were playing together with Larry Wise on harmonica as the Truth Band. Tim had a voracious curiosity about everything. He wanted to learn more about Flora and wanted to learn more about the music.

The harmonica player Larry Wise was also a frequent member of the Truth Band. I first met him at a gig John and I had, where Larry just came up and

introduced himself. He lives in Philadelphia now where he is a well-established
street busker. He is very smart, very graciously humored, and an excellent musician who recorded some fine songs with Flora. He was married when I met him,
to his beautiful wife, Neecie. I also met his brother. Larry told me a story that
he had another brother who had gotten into some trouble. They got involved in
sticking up a store, but something happened and they ran. From what I recall
of the story, the person pursuing them had a butcher knife and stabbed Larry's
brother who died as a result of the puncture wound. It seems to me that if there
was a demon in his life, it was the loss of his brother. That was my feeling being
around him. He was very energetic with good ideas and energy for moving
forward with music. He was the one behind the idea of him and Flora and Tim
Lewis going down to New Orleans and trying to get gigs down there. He was a
very good player and singer with a great singing voice and a cool style. I think he
had some disagreements with Ed Morris and a falling out. I was off at school at
the time and I had introduced him to Flora. I turned him on to her. By the time I
was back home from school after those two years, I think he had already moved
to Philadelphia. Then someone whose name I'm not going to mention, because
that person feels bad about it, told me that Larry had died. Later, I found out
that that wasn't true.

In 1978, by Larry's suggestion, the Truth Band did a road trip together down
to New Orleans where they wanted to play the Jazz and Heritage Festival. The
only problem was that they weren't booked. But they went anyway to see if they
could meet the folks and work their way into a gig there—and miraculously
they actually ended up playing the event. I don't know how they did that. You
can't do that anymore. After playing in New Orleans they went on to Texas,
where I met up with them. I got on a Greyhound bus and went to Dallas, and
then we went to Houston, Austin, and San Antonio together. Shortly after that
trip Tim Lewis got into filmmaking. We all went and did some cameo appearances in a film that he was working on.

While they were in New Orleans at the Jazz and Heritage Festival, Tim Lewis
met German blues enthusiast Axel Küstner, who had been sent to the U.S. to
make so-called "field recordings," to scout out American roots and blues musicians. The trip was funded by the German concert and record producers Horst
Lippmann and Fritz Rau. Tim Lewis told him all about the DC scene and the
musicians in the Travellin' Blues Workshop. Photographer and amateur musicologist Axel Küstner and sound engineer Siegfried "Ziggy" Christmann subsequently toured all over the South to photograph and record the country blues,
and that's how they ended up in Washington. They came up and recorded Flora
Molton, Archie Edwards, and us. Because of Tim Lewis's recommendation, and
apparently supported by the publicity material issued by the Travellin' Blues
Workshop, which Axel and Ziggy knew all about, they came specifically looking

to meet Archie Edwards and John Cephas and to record some of the Piedmont style blues. They met John at his carpenter shop at the National Guard Armory. He called me up and said, "Hey Phil, there's these guys from Germany here who want to record me, and you should come and play on these recordings." We did a session right there in John's shop at night, and then we recorded in John's living room down in Virginia. That was our first recording. They took those tapes back to Germany, to Lippmann and Rau, and issued our debut album, *U.S. Field Recordings, Volume 1. Living Country Blues USA—Bowling Green John & Harmonica Phil Wiggins from Virginia, USA. 1980.*[4] We performed songs that we knew well, our standard repertoire of songs we had played for a long time: "Black Rat Swing," Eyesight to the Blind," "Guitar and Harmonica Rag," "Rising River Blues," "I'm a Pilgrim," "Chicken Can't Roost Too High for Me," "I Ain't Got No Loving Baby Now," "West Carey Street Blues," "Richmond Blues," "Pony Blues," "Goin' Down the Road Feelin' Bad." They gave us those stage names, which we had never used before, and which we eventually dropped in favor of Cephas & Wiggins. We went along with it at the time, but we of course realized that this was a marketing ploy. Somehow people did not yet acknowledge DC as a center of the acoustic blues, and perhaps that's why they felt compelled to give us these "blues names" to make us sound more authentic, as if we needed it. Axel and Ziggy were good guys who we liked well. We were happy to get an album out and we knew that it came with good intentions. John had actually used the stage name "Bowling Green" once in a while prior to that. I thought my assigned name "Harmonica Phil Wiggins" lacked imagination, but I went along with it. Upon reflection, I should have insisted on my actual nickname, which was "Mojo."[5] When I was growing up I did have the nickname of "Mojo," which my Uncle Oscar gave me, and he called me that most of my childhood— but I didn't like it because the reason they called me that was I had punched my brother in the nose for messing with me and had bloodied his nose. They thought that was funny and they said, "He put the Mojo on him." I didn't like it because it was me being mean to my brother, and I wasn't proud of that. I didn't embrace that name, but that's what I got called. But the thing I thought about later, though, was when they were talking about that "Harmonica Phil" maybe I should have gone with Mojo, but I didn't. I didn't much like the idea of a stage name to begin with, and didn't feel like investing any energy and trying to think of one. I just went along with it, because it didn't matter to me as it wouldn't do any harm, and I just let it go.

John eventually also came to understand that "Bowling Green John" was simply pretentious. Of course, over time it became clear that this was yet another case where well-meaning outsiders think they understand the blues and blues musicians, but in actuality try to shape the music or the musicians according to their own perceptions and imagination. For a while I was "Harmonica Phil

Wiggins" and John was "Bowling Green John." It was our first major break as a duo and a fine album, recorded in true blues format, like the field recordings done by people like Alan Lomax decades earlier. I am still proud of that record today, as we recorded the songs that we were practiced in performing at that time, songs from our standard repertoire that we had played at house parties and local gigs around Virginia and DC.

A lot has been said over the years about that first recording and people believing that they were responsible for everything that happened subsequently. We were happy to do the album and it led to good things, but *U.S. Field Recordings, Volume 1. Living Country Blues USA* was not well distributed in the United States and gained us very little attention locally and nationally. Basically, nobody was able to buy it, and most blues-focused people didn't know the record existed. We sold the albums at gigs and that was about the extent of it. There was no radio or press marketing, so in that sense the album was obscure. It was inevitable that someone would have made our first recording soon around that period, because we were already on the radar of people like Joe Wilson, the director of the NCTA, who would later become an important career catalyst. We were grateful for the opportunity to make this record with Axel and Ziggy. We liked everything about it, but claims beyond that are perhaps far-fetched. Joe Wilson, who became our de facto manager, advocate, and career catalyst, didn't connect with us because we had a record in Germany. As proud and happy as we were with it, it did not help us locally. Those developments were separate and in large part the result of John Cephas's friendship with Joe Wilson. The album did lead to a great tour to Europe, and 1980 and '81 were major breakthrough years for us. We played the Hudson Clearwater Revival Festival in the Hudson Valley, New York, a festival that was organized by Pete Seeger, where we appeared as solo performers and in conjunction with Leon Redbone, John Hammond, and the Paula Lockheart Trio. We also played the Towne Crier Café, a roots and folk venue in the Hudson Valley of New York, at the time in Lagrangeville. We also had several performances at the University of Maryland Black Student Union arranged by Otis Williams. Things also picked up at concert halls and nightclubs in the DC area, including the Cellar Door, Childe Harold, Wolf Trap Farm Park, the Kennedy Center, and Crampton Auditorium at Howard University, plus numerous concerts sponsored by the Smithsonian Institution and the National Park Service.

When Axel and Ziggy took those tapes back to Horst Lippmann over in Germany, he invited us to be part of the American Folk Blues Tours, which got us quite a bit of recognition in a twenty-six-city European Tour during March 1981. We were also included in the album made of the now famous American Folk Blues Tour '81, along with a series of American blues musicians. That was our first major international tour, mostly in Germany and Scandinavia, and suddenly we were in the company of some of the best names in the blues. We shared the stage with Sunnyland Slim, Margie Evans, Louisiana Red, Hubert Sumlin, Lurrie Bell, Odie Payne, and Bob Stroger. Carey Bell and I were the harmonica players. Together we played concert halls in Germany and in Paris. When the album of this tour was released, the author in the album liner notes described us as follows: "One can feel their shyness when thousands of hands show appreciation of their excellent performance."

It was very exciting for me to tour Europe at the time. For a while we were better known over there than we were in the States. The audience in Europe was very excited to have us. It was amazing. We would be on the stage and people would throw bouquets of flowers. It was unbelievable. To me, as our careers were getting launched over in Europe, I felt that the audience appreciated the blues, and us, and they were giving our music the status that it deserved at home. It was wonderful. I have always loved to travel and it was a great experience. Having lived in Germany for four years and traveled all over Europe when I was a child, traveling got in my blood. It was great to be able to go back to some of the places I had visited before, and being able to understand the language. For me, as a young man, it was just like a dream, because we were being treated with the respect and recognition that I felt the blues deserved and that we were not yet getting at home. Plus, we were able to go to all these amazing, beautiful places. It was funny because John almost immediately started looking to me whenever someone would speak to him, to interpret what they were saying—even if they were speaking English with a German accent. He would look at me, "Okay, what did he just say?" I fell into that role, and that began on that first tour and set up the dynamic that lasted pretty much until John passed on, that in a way I took care of him. It was funny, because even back at home people would speak to him and he'd look at me and like almost expect me to translate or interpret. That's what that was like. It was just an unbelievable dream.

That excitement in Europe went on for at least a few more years. After a while the audiences started to become jaded. I think there were some German promoters that figured out that as long as they could say this person was from the U.S. and from the South, people would come out to see them. They started bringing people that simply weren't very good, and I think the German audience felt like they'd been burned a few times. But, I had great memories of those trips. I remember in a small town in Scandinavia where we're walking around after hours at night and we went into a cozy pub with amber light and dark wood everywhere. The people were sitting there just completely relaxed, and we walked in and the guy sitting there says, "There's a gentleman sitting at this table over here that wants to meet you." We went over there and they invited us to sit down and we're talking about this and that, and the guy reaches in his inside jacket pocket and pulls out a leather pouch of tobacco and two pipes and fills them both up and passes me one and we sit there and smoke pipes together and drink some brown liquor together. I was thousands of miles from home and yet I felt right at home.

John Cephas never liked to travel. He was like a bundle of contradictions because on one level he liked the prestige, the attention, but he was not comfortable traveling. He enjoyed seeing faraway places and historical sites, but at the same time a half hour from his house he was out of his element and very uncomfortable. In Europe, he liked getting the recognition, he liked the audiences and all, but he hated, for example, getting up in the morning and not getting what he liked to eat for breakfast. It was a constant struggle and this went on for years for John to get his eggs cooked the way he wanted them. For me, I had lived in Germany for four years. I loved those one-minute soft-boiled eggs. You knock the top off and you take your little spoon and scoop it out. I love that. John hated it. He demanded, "I want my egg cooked hard. I don't want nothing runny on my egg." We would be in a restaurant and John would try to get these jokers to cook him an egg hard or to scramble it. For a while I tried to say, "This is the way they do it here." And he said, "You know, if these motherfuckers came to my house and were a guest in my home, if they asked me to paint the egg blue, I would paint the fucking egg blue for them." At that point, it became clear to me what it was all about. It was about hospitality. I've seen him figuratively paint the egg blue, like bend over backwards to make people feel welcomed and comfortable in his home. That's all it was about. It wasn't that he was just some idiot from the country or some ugly American that just didn't know how things worked. I learned an important lesson about hospitality from him from that. He also didn't like the hard rolls you get with German breakfast, with cured meats and brötchen. John hated that stuff. He complained, "You go into breakfast and they give you a whole bunch of lunch meat and hard rolls!" Of course, the rolls weren't hard, just crispy on the outside and tender on the inside, but to John they were hard rolls. He was open-minded about learning about history and culture, and visiting places, but he didn't like to be even in somebody else's house rather than his own house. He liked being where he was in control of everything, where he knew where everything was. That's where he was comfortable. If his level of comfort went down, and the further away from home he was, the worse it was. He didn't like these great old historical hotels all over Europe right in the cities where the heat sometimes didn't work—they were big and drafty and all that. I loved them because they had personality—plus, you could walk out the front door and you could walk anywhere you wanted to go. John wanted to be in hotels that were almost like Holiday Inns way out on the highway where there was nothing else. They were chain hotels that were all exactly the same from one place to another. John liked them because in the summertime they had air conditioning, and in the winter they had very efficient heat. I hated them.

In 1981 we also toured Paris with the American Folk Blues Festival. The famous pianist Memphis Slim had a regular club gig there. Sunnyland Slim, who was touring with us, knew Memphis Slim and all the Chicago players that were with us knew Memphis Slim very well and had very much respect for him. To them he was blues piano royalty. All they could talk about is how much they looked forward to visiting him and jamming in his club. They played up things like, "Yeah, he has got a gold-plated Rolls Royce," and this and that. We all went and met him—Margie Evans of course was snuggled up to him the whole time, and we played the gig with him and it was great. At the gig, there were a bunch of American expatriates living in Paris. There was a young guy, a young white jazz guitar player, and we got to be friends in the course of the night, just hanging out backstage talking. We decided to go barhopping after the gig. First, we went to see a great barrelhouse piano player, Booker T. Laury, who was a childhood friend of Memphis Slim, who was playing in the lobby of a fancy hotel. We stayed and watched him play and then we went to a couple of other bars, and as we went from place to place some of the guys we were hanging out with would peel off and go home, one by one. Finally, at the last place it was just me and the guitar player, and he said, "Well, I got to go, but there's this place called the Chevalier du Temps—you should probably go there because they play until eight in the morning." I got on the subway and I got off and I wound up at this jazz bar, and the hostess was a transvestite named Malicia Battlefield. I came in and she said, "You're new here." I said, "Yeah, I'm from the States." She said, "Well, what are you doing here?" And I said, "Well, I'm on a tour with the American Folk Blues Festival." She said, "Oh, you're a player?" I said, "I play the harmonica, but I don't have them on me." I don't remember if I actually had them on me or not, but I wasn't feeling like putting myself out there. Then she started to search my person saying, "I know you have them on you somewhere," while patting me down. People were jamming music like a bat out of hell and I did join in and blow some harp. There was this guy I will never forget, a light-skinned black guy in a white zoot jacket, navy blue pants, a red shirt, and a big old gold tie. He was blowing a clarinet like I never heard. I was thinking, "Wow, this is amazing." I stayed there until they kicked us all out—at probably about 8:30 in the morning. Then I realized I didn't have any money in my pockets and I had to get back to the hotel, and I hopped over the turnstiles, which the guitar player warned me not to do, to never get caught on the Paris subway without your subway card, because they'll take you straight to jail—it's very serious. I was nervous about that, having to hop off over the turnstiles to get back home. When I got off the subway unscathed there was a young girl standing there with a backpack on. I heard her say something in English to somebody so I just asked, "Hey, you're from the States." She said, "Yeah. I'm just hanging here. I don't have anywhere to go right now." I invited her to come have hotel breakfast. She went back to the hotel with me and we were sitting there and I told her, "Look over there, that's Sunnyland Slim and that's Hubert Sumlin, and that's Bob Stroger, and that's Odie Payne." She had no idea who all those people were. That's a night that I will never forget on that first tour.

Here we were, me and John, two people who loved to play the blues, and now we were out in the world. It was a special feeling, going into different venues and playing blues for people who seemed to truly know and love the music. People treated us with respect, like celebrities. The musical profession in Europe comes with a certain amount of respect and status more so than in the States and we experienced that in a positive way. Also, it seemed that they honored our heritage. Being black blues musicians from America in Europe carried a certain amount of moral authority. European people know that you come from a place that you've had to struggle and they seem to understand and respect that and they treat you accordingly.

After we got back from Europe in 1981, we received more local coverage. That year we played the Blues Alley music club in DC and we were featured on *Art Beat* on WETA-TV Channel 26. The American Folklife Center featured us in an outdoor concert at the Library of Congress and we played the Summer Concert at Fort Dupont Park as well as the Bear Mountain World Music Festival in New York. Things were picking up, and we could see that our career was ascending.

In 1981 I got married. I met my wife when I was maybe nineteen years old or so. I had been at Cumberland Community College in New Jersey for two years, came back home and I was living at home, continuing my studies at Howard University. I met Wendy Chick, who had just moved to DC and was with a couple of other people and they were looking for another housemate to share the rent in a group house. We got to be good friends, and after a while we grew to love each other. We lived together for a long time and then we split up for a while. She moved to Boston and I would go up there and visit her. That's when I used to go over to Berklee School of Music and hang out in the practice rooms and meet people that were studying music there and jam. At that time in Boston they had live blues bands playing all over. Every night of the week there was blues. There was this guy Little Joe Cook who was an institution in Boston. He worked at a restaurant—basically he was like a dishwasher and busboy. I went to see him many times. He was one of the best unknown blues singers out there.

After we got married, Wendy and I lived at 18th and Kalorama Road, Adams Morgan, in DC. Things were just picking up for Cephas & Wiggins and we had another tour over in Germany and other European spots with the American Folk Blues Festival, this time with Sunnyland Slim and Louisiana Red. At that time, as we were building a music career, I was still working a day job in a law firm mailroom delivering packages and doing court filings and things like that. John was working as a carpenter and I was getting by the best way I could while playing music at night. I'd play at the Childe Harold in the house band. Every Thursday night they had a jam session, almost like an open mic, except they had the house rhythm section. I had a Twin Reverb amplifier and used to drag that thing over there, because I lived about five blocks from there. After a while I would get there early to set my amp up on the stage and people would use it all night, and then I'd go up and play my two or three songs and get off. One night I went down there and I didn't take the amp, and all the guys in the room were like, "Phil, where's your amp, man?" I said, "Well, I didn't bring it. I got tired of dragging that thing down there and just getting up and playing a couple of songs, and then, you know, it's not worth it for me to drag it down here." They said, "Why don't you join the house band?" They hired me because I had equipment.

One time two famous musicians came around: the Texas singer/songwriter Townes Van Zandt and Doug Sahm. They had equipment problems so I went home to get my amp so they could borrow it. They were happy for it and I was glad to help.

Our oldest daughter Eliza was born in 1983 while I was very far away from home touring in Europe. The tour was organized by the German promoter Rolf Schubert. It wasn't the Lippmann & Rau American Folk Blues Festival tour, which we played in 1981 and '82. There was a big group of us traveling together— John and me, Louisiana Red, Sunnyland Slim, Bob Stroger and Hubert Sumlin, Odie Payne playing drums, plus the Chicago guys—Billy Branch, Carey Bell, and Lurrie Bell. When we started touring for Rolf it was just the two of us, and we would have these German blues guys opening for us, which I used to get a kick out of hearing people singing blues with a German accent.

My daughter Eliza was about a week old when I met her. It was hard to be that far from home when my wife was having our first child. The birth went okay, but right after that Wendy was having trouble. I got a communication from her—"You need to come home"—but I didn't. I knew that my sister was with her, so she was in good hands; but was also thinking about the money part of it, because if I bailed on the tour I wouldn't get paid and we couldn't afford that. That's why I did it—when that was our livelihood, and I was worried about that. For whatever reason, I chose not to drop what I was doing and go home. That's a big regret.

When my daughter was born, we were in a fishing village on the North Sea coast of Germany and we went into a pub to celebrate with our host Helmut for a celebratory toast. There were about eight old guys sitting around there and they had a bell hanging over the bar. I go, "Huh, I wonder what that sounds like?" And I rang it. Suddenly, all those eight guys stood up and started walking toward me, and said, "Danke schön, danke schön." They shook my hand and patted me on the back. I thought I was celebrating the birth of my daughter and instead I unwittingly rang the bell to buy a round for everybody in the pub. That cost me a pretty penny, almost everything I earned from the gig that night. That tour was during the German veterans' celebration, and they celebrate for at least a week. It was more than Veterans Day, because the way that we found out was that a lot of the hotels that we had booked to stay in we had gotten bumped out of because all the veterans were in town for the celebrations. We were thinking—well, you know, when you're thinking of German veterans a lot of times you think of Nazis. Then, this old guy came up to me and said, "I want to shake your hand. You know, at the end of World War II we had to walk across Europe back to Berlin and the only people that treated me like a human being were the black GIs. They would give me water, they would give me food and cigarettes. I want to shake your hand and thank you." That touched me.

John got a back injury on the job at the DC Armory and retired on a disability. He gave them a lifetime of hard work, but at a certain point he couldn't stand that job anymore. That injury prevented him from doing that hard work, with heavy lifting, and gave him his freedom. He used to be on that job pretty much twenty-four hours a day. A lot of times he would stay overnight at the Armory, spend the night there. He had a room in the back where he would stay. He'd be in there at three o'clock in the morning sawing boards and working when there was a job to be done. But he just reached a certain point where he looked at his life and he said, "I don't want to give them any more of this life. I want my life." After the injury, he was no longer willing to sacrifice himself. He worked it out and got an early retirement from the Armory with a disability pension.

In a way that made it difficult for us, because he had that steady income and I did not. I had a young family to support and I needed to work a lot more than he needed. He was twenty-four years older than me, established, economically stable with a steady income, and he had built a house that was paid for, whereas I was paying rent. I was working and trying to support a family with a day job and with what I made playing music, and John essentially wasn't dependent on his music income, because he had enough of a pension. Not to say anything against John, but we both needed different things out of the whole music scene.

Barry Lee helped us get booked on overseas cultural tours sponsored through the U.S. State Department United States Information Agency. We traveled as the American Blues Trio to Africa in 1982. We played in Botswana, Zimbabwe, Mauritius, Madagascar, Ghana, Mali, and as the Bowling Green Blues Trio to the Caribbean and South America in 1983 and again in 1984. He had connections with Sandy Rouse, a State Department official, and her husband Don Rouse, a good clarinet player who would later join us to play on the 1993 album *Flip, Flop and Fly*. We did tours of Central and South America and the Caribbean and Africa. Barry Lee played guitar with us and we were billed as the Bowling Green Blues Trio.

I loved traveling all over the world—going to Africa, that was a milestone for me. We were in Botswana and Zimbabwe just after independence, a young country where I met many amazing young people that were very smart and strong and optimistic about their future. I remember being in the amazing country, the island of Madagascar, where they have a long tradition of harmonica there with strong crazy rhythm. I was fascinated by the African music, by the relation to blues and blues lyrics and the tonal languages of Africa. I think it's the singing, the music, the way the singing and the instrumentation evoke the emotions, the way that instruments are manipulated to imitate the human voice, the rhythm, and the danceability.

Travel is just one of the greatest gifts I've been given in this life; but these tours were even harder for John, because Europe is in many ways similar to the U.S. in terms of economic systems and culture, with America derived from European cultures. Being in Africa and Central and South America and the Caribbean, the cultures were even more foreign to John. John liked having his personal comforts and conveniences. In those places, you just didn't have that. In lots of places that I just loved and embraced I would say, "Wow, this is so different from home. It's beautiful." John would say, "No, it's dirty and the air conditioning doesn't work. The heat doesn't work. Nothing works on time. There's not a set price for anything. You've got to haggle for everything. Everything is a struggle. It's a big mess." He didn't dig it. At the same time, he had a sense of history; he had a curiosity about other cultures. He definitely did not like the challenges of traveling in places like Central and South America, the Caribbean, and Africa.

Traveling with these two guys was interesting and fun, and it was comical, and at times it was frustrating. Both Barry Lee and John liked to drink a lot during that time—and a lot of times that impeded Barry Lee's ability to do his job as the manager. My whole outlook on things was very different from both of theirs. They were more similar to each other than either one of them with me. We would go places, and I would be excited: "Wow, this is incredible. This is great. I can't believe we're experiencing this." Their reaction: "Man, this place is filthy. I can't wait to just get to the hotel and sit down and just play some cards and drink." I couldn't wait to get out and walk around and take a look at what's going on and meet people—and they didn't trust anyone and weren't that curious about meeting people. When we came home from these trips, it was as if we had taken two different trips because what they knew and remembered and their overall impressions were different from mine. I often wondered if we were all on the same trip. It was definitely interesting and exciting.

We were in Honduras one time and we had three hotel rooms. My room was down on the end of the hall and John and Barry Lee's rooms were way down at the other end. I got up in the morning, and I could hear a bunch of military people talking. The first impression I had was that there were two GIs that came out in their civilian dress uniforms. One guy had on his uniform. The other two guys said to him, "Didn't you get the word? The order of the day is civvies." He responded, "No, I didn't. What's going on?" The two guys say, "Well, one of our GIs was out last night partying in a Jeep and he hit a civilian and ran over him and there's some anger in the town. Today we're not supposed to wear our uniforms so that we are inconspicuous." That was my first impression of Honduras. I walked down the hallway to John's room. The door was open and every piece of furniture in the room was busted up. I walked down to Barry Lee's room and the door was not open but not locked, I opened it and I walked in, and there's John wrapped in a blanket sleeping in a chair in Barry Lee's room, with Barry Lee lying on the bed. I was baffled, "What is going on?" It turns out that when John was sleeping in his room the night before, about a foot-long giant centipede crawled across his neck in the middle of the night, and he jumped up and hit that centipede with everything that was in the room. He hit it with the dresser, he hit it with a night table—everything that wasn't nailed to the floor he picked up and hit that centipede with it. That's how he destroyed all the furniture.

Once, John, Barry Lee, and I were riding somewhere out in the country of Botswana in Africa and all of a sudden, some soldiers ran right up to our van and ducked down behind it and then started shooting off into a field on the other side of us. Of course, we all got down shouting, "What the hell is going on?" It was the Botswana Defense Force. No one was shooting at us. They were just hiding behind us and shooting at other people. Also in Africa, in Mali, I remember that we had left the capital city and we were going somewhere out in the country to do a performance and meet some musicians. As we were driving along the road we suddenly slowed down and we came upon this procession of people with a lot of screaming, shouting, and moaning. There was a big old flatbed truck decorated predominantly with red color. All the people were wearing red and had red streamers on. Some of them just had red paint all over them. Right in front of our van, at the end of the line, there were several young teenage boys. Each of those boys had one boxing glove and they were hitting each other hard. I asked the driver what was going on and he said it was a funeral procession for a very popular boxer from Bamako, Mali, who has passed away. This is the funeral procession. I asked him, "So the funeral color is not black—it's red?" He said, "Yeah, you are right." I asked, "Well, and those young boys they're boxers and that's why they have boxing gloves?" He said, "Yeah, that's right." And I said, "Well, why are they each only wearing one glove?" He replied, "Because we don't have enough to give each one two gloves. Boxing gloves are hard to get in Bamako." As that was happening, I remember the John Hurt song "Louis Collins":

The angels laid him away
Oh, when they heard that Louis was dead

All the people they dressed in red
The angels laid him away.

That line "All the people they dressed in red" showed to me a direct link between West African culture and African American culture. That was an exciting revelation.

We were in Kenya with Barry Lee Pearson. Neither one of them wanted to leave the hotel. I was climbing the wall and couldn't stand to stay sitting in the hotel any longer so I went on my own and I ran into this this guy—I can't remember his name now. He started talking to me and he said, "You're not from around here. Would you like to go to a Masai village?" We got in a cab and went to the outskirts of Nairobi to a place called Gonehill. There we got in another taxi that didn't have any floor in it and we went riding way out, to this traditional Masai village where there were huts. They looked small, but it was crazy because when you got inside they were spacious. All the men were away with the cattle. The guy who brought me there had some relatives there—we went in and sat down, talking to the woman of the house. The woman didn't speak English and she looked at me and asked my host, "What kind of black man is he? I don't recognize his tribe." We sat and talked and sipped tea for quite a while. When we came back to the hotel, I introduced my new friend to John and Barry Lee and we had dinner together. But it was often when we would travel I would spend my days wandering on my own because John didn't want to leave the hotel.

In Belize, in Central America, we were playing an outdoor U.S. embassy party and right at five o'clock on the dot we just got swarmed by a huge number of mosquitoes. They came down on us like a biblical plague. It was indescribable how many descended upon us, actually like a fast-moving dark cloud. They got to me in particular—my arms swelled up from being bitten so much. We went inside and they brought me rubbing alcohol and washed my arms with it and the swelling finally went back down. It was inconceivably cruel. Someplace in Africa we played at another embassy reception. When we were done playing we noticed all the leftover food at the buffet. The food looked good and we didn't want to waste it, so we wrapped it up with the idea of taking it back to the hotel for later. We get back to the hotel and we're drinking and playing cards. John got this bag of food and opened it up and I reached in there to get one of the little party sandwiches or whatever. John said, "That will be one dollar." "One dollar? Are you kidding me?" He said, "Yeah, yeah, that's what I'm charging for that." "But John, it's not yours," and he said, "Well, I brought it back." Barry Lee thought that was brilliant, thought it was good. "John, how can you sell me something that we brought home for free?" Barry Lee thought that was a stroke of genius for John and his business acumen to sell us back the food that we brought. I didn't give him a dollar and I wouldn't eat it. Did he want the dollar? We were all drunk, playing cards and being pretty stupid in general. That was the environment. He definitely wanted the dollar. That's one thing about John—I have never ever gotten the upper hand on him in any financial arrangement—any bet or anything like that. I have never ever won a bet with John, and I've never seen anyone else ever win a bet with John.

He would sometimes say things just to piss people off, to piss me off, to be the opposite of politically correct. One of the things John said that I will never forget was on the way back from the African tour. Sometime after the tour we were at the Puget Sound Guitar Workshop talking to some guys who were into African-style music, and they were curious about our impressions of the Africa trip, knowing we had just finished our tour. I answered, "Man it was beautiful. I never imagined I would ever be there—and just three inches of steel and wood got me all the way to Africa." John's response was, "Man, if I could find the people that went down there and got my people out of there I would run up to them and kiss them." My jaw was like on the floor. I was raised with a sense of history and knew about slavery and how Africans were kidnapped, taken in chains and how they suffered, a terrible part of African American history. But John, after having spent that month in Africa, he was fed up, tired, and irritated. I couldn't believe that came out of his mouth, but I can understand why he felt like that. Because he built his house, he lived very comfortably, everything was under his control, and his heat worked in the wintertime and his AC worked in the summertime, and life was good for John. I can't knock it. I can't argue with it, but I know it wasn't right.

By the time we returned from the United States Information Agency tours, our audiences stateside changed very gradually. We were well-known to the point where we were making more money here than we would make in Europe. I think it had a lot to do with people wanting to hear more of what we were doing. At the time, we were the only guitar-harmonica duo on the acoustic blues scene, a spot that was previously held by Sonny Terry and Brownie McGhee. Not to say that we copied them or played like them, but we had similar musical, cultural, and geographical traditions and we respected them, but did not emulate them.

John was an amazingly talented, wonderful, and complex person. In our performances, he liked to educate people as well as entertain them, and he talked a lot about the different styles of blues. Some of this stuff was based on reality and some of it was based on his impressions and his logic. One of the things that he got in the habit of saying for a while was that in the Delta blues, down in Mississippi, life was hard, it was hot, the slave masters were mean—and that was reflected in the music. He claimed that in the Piedmont region it was lush, green, and the slave masters weren't that bad and the slavery wasn't as harsh and that was reflected in the music. After a while of hearing him say that, I said, "You know, John, you've got to stop saying that because slavery is slavery. Chattel slavery is chattel slavery. If someone is using you as livestock, that is not a good situation by any stretch of the imagination. You've got to quit saying that." He actually rethought it and quit saying that. But, he said that for a long time, and I think that on some level he believed that.

John loved being at home. The place where I saw John at his absolute best, most beautiful, most relaxed, most open—and most generous—was walking around in his vegetable garden. Nothing excited John more than planting a seed in the ground and then after a time seeing what came of that. He was almost childlike to see plants growing out of the ground, "Look, there it comes, there it comes. Wow, look, it looks like the field cress is getting about ripe. Go get a bag and a sharp knife and come out and get some." Later in life, in my eulogy at his funeral, I made the analogy of him planting another garden as he traveled all over the country and all over the world planting seeds of traditional country blues, being able to see that garden flourish—to take root and bear fruit and flourish; and the fruit drops down and those seeds from that fruit take root and it goes on and on, and how that garden will continue forever, because the fruit—the seeds that John planted will continue to bear fruit, and that fruit will drop seeds and they will bear fruit, and on and on.

The hardest thing about my relationship as John Cephas's musical partner was that he had a very serious drinking problem, and that would manifest in some pretty crazy ways. Those are my worst memories, even though he was a great man and a good friend. I'm reluctant to say some of the things that I experienced because once in a blue moon John would be so drunk that he couldn't play well—or he couldn't play at all. John was a person who should not have had a drink in all his life, because he was an alcoholic who had been in St. Elizabeth's for treatment of alcoholism, but he never actually managed to quit drinking. When he got drunk he would be totally unwilling to compromise. That got to be a problem. That's the reason why to this day when I play a gig I don't have a drink until after I'm done, because I know things can happen—and things often did with me and John, where one of us needed to have a clear head to sort things out. If I had been drinking at all, I was in for a long and miserable evening trying to sort out messes.

Those nights being on stage with him were horrible for me, knowing that that audience was getting robbed because he got so drunk that he couldn't perform at his best. As our career ascended we went through some pretty hard times. I felt bad that people spent their little bit of money to come out because they needed to hear good music, and they left their home and they paid their money, and they basically got robbed. I had a hard time with that. Some nights it would be late, we'd put on a show and then it was time to pack up and get out and John was getting in a fight with the hosts, because he got drunk and he just lost track of CDs. No matter whose fault it is, it doesn't require getting angry and calling people a sack of motherfuckers and having blood feuds with people. That doesn't solve anything. If the money count is not right, let's look at it, figure out what went wrong, and then make it right. If everybody stays calm and doesn't get personal and doesn't make enemies, generally you can work that stuff out. When you add alcohol to the mix and someone's ability to reason goes out the window, and instead they just want to fight and be hateful—then you're not solving anything and you're just making it a long, miserable night.

John may have been a hard-drinking man, but that did not define who he was as a musician or as a person. He was hard working and a little crazy. He was a thinker and a student of history and at the same time, at a certain point in his life, he was an alcoholic to the point where he spent some time in rehab. I understand where he was at because I am no angel and had my own ins and outs with drugs and I probably still drink too much. I've had my bouts and probably spent most of my high school career stoned. I had my bout with cocaine and all that stuff.

I have seen the best and the worst of John Cephas. We were like any good friends that had a deep, close relationship, like family. We saw each other's good and bad sides. John was a good man who wasn't judgmental. John didn't suffer fools, and he didn't put up with people that were foolish. He was just this whole bundle of contradictions. He could be gentle and also one of the worst bullies that you'd ever want to meet. Bullies act out of fear and insecurity, and I think John had a lot of that. Any situation he had to deal with, in terms of business or anything—was easily adversarial, and unnecessarily so. Because of it, people would let John get away with so much that they wouldn't let anybody else get away with. Sometimes he treated people like shit. I asked myself why people gave him a pass, and I think that for a lot of white people it was guilt. Most people that came to our performances would speak highly of John. "He was the sweetest man I ever met." "He was such a gentleman." He was. But he was also the opposite: a complex, beautiful human being. Some people would witness his bad side and ask me, "Oh, man, you really put up with a lot of shit. Why don't you stand up to John?" But the thing that they didn't know is that John didn't get away with anything where I'm concerned. He was smart about choosing his battles, and when I was pushed to a certain point I would kick his ass. No one saw it but me and him. People didn't know. They accepted that in some rare occasions in public I would just put my foot down and say, you know, "John. You're fucking up—knock it off." Like most bullies, when you do that you see a whole different person.

In 1983, I taught for the first time at the Augusta Heritage Center Blues Week, in Elkins, West Virginia, a weeklong music workshop retreat. That was the start of my teaching experience and a relationship with the center that lasted all these years. Blues Week was started by musician Joan Fenton, who had at that time lived somewhere down in western Virginia. She had become aware of the Augusta Heritage Workshop, in Elkins, West Virginia at Davis & Elkins College, which at that time was a celebration of mainly Appalachian culture, but also branched out over the years into Cajun, Irish, and lots of different styles of music. Joan had the idea of having a week devoted to the music of the black people that settled in the region of Appalachia and the nearby regions of the Piedmont and Tidewater—essentially the regional blues now called Piedmont. I remember that she introduced the Center to some friends of mine that are excellent musicians, the Harris Brothers from North Carolina. They play everything—Delta blues, Piedmont blues, swing music, and more. Joan decided that the black culture in that region also needed to be represented, and she reached out to John Jackson and Sparky Rucker from Tennessee, about starting Blues Week with acoustic blues. They asked John Jackson if he knew a good harmonica player or anyone else that would be good to have, and he recommended me. That's how I wound up there. Talk about Br'er Rabbit being thrown in the briar patch—I landed right in that beautiful location, in the hills of West Virginia at this college campus. The people there were so fired up and so excited that we came that they made us feel like royalty. I remember the first night I was hanging out in front of this place called the Ice House, a little bar that was actually once an icehouse, where they used to store ice before there were refrigerators to keep things cool. They turned it into a bar. I was there late at night, partying hard, and some guy came up to me and said, "Man, this is great. You know, people have come from all over the country and all over the world. I just met someone from Europe, and they all came here. I was talking to a guy who quit his job so he could come to this." I got a hard feeling all of a sudden, like, whoa, this is serious. I'm standing here, partying, high as a kite, and I have no plan for what I'm going to do tomorrow, and there's somebody who quit his job to be here. At that moment I got serious, put down my beer, and went straight to my room, got out a notebook and some paper, and started figuring out how to teach harmonica. Let's see, I guess I could do numbers and arrows. I made up my own version of harmonica tab, and listed out some songs. Of course, the next day had a life of its own. In the course of it I realized that I was ready to teach.

It was incredibly rewarding and fun. I taught there again this year, in 2016. From that very first one, over the years Blues Week at Augusta kept getting better. For the next year, I was able to convince them to bring my partner John Cephas, so you had John Cephas and John Jackson. The students would come from all over to be completely immersed in the culture of the blues and the music, all day and all night. People literally sat up and jammed and played until the sun came up. Then they would go sleep for a few hours and get up and spend all day in classes. During the first couple of years I taught classes all day and then a "mini class," and the local people could come after work and participate. I spent all day playing music and all night jamming. John Jackson would sit on Hallie Hurst's porch 'til the sun came up playing and singing, just talking to people and telling stories. People came from all over, and caught the blues fire there. They took that fire back home to their own communities—and we, as teachers, never had any qualms about passing it on to all people, no matter who and where they were from. DC is pretty close proximity to Elkins, West Virginia, so the immediate impact of this teaching center was profound. There are professional musicians that have made a career playing blues who got started and inspired by being at Augusta Heritage Workshop. When people asked me what it is like, I told them that it was a vacation in the true sense of the word: it's where I go to get rejuvenated, to get fired up, to get reenergized. Also, from the very first year I was there, I had already started fooling with writing songs. It seemed that in this nourishing environment I had the creative spark to finish songs that I had started. Here they would see the light of day because in all-night jams I'd pull those songs out, with people playing and singing with me, and I could try out a song to see if it worked out good. I was encouraged if people would be happy playing songs that I made up. So that was a big thing for me and it definitely helped me in my songwriting process—although "writing" has very little to do with the process, but building songs, making up songs—that's where they got finished and tried out and revamped.

Some of my greatest memories were those all-night-long celebrations, jam sessions at Augusta, with these amazing musicians, black and white, just playing, being friends and having fun. There was John Jackson, John Cephas, Etta Baker, Howard Armstrong and his guitarist Ted Bogan. The great Cajun fiddler and singer Dewey Balfa was there and horn player Rusty Mason. I loved Dewey Balfa and he loved John Cephas. He was crazy about John and his music. I never met a musician with so much humility. He and his family can be pretty much credited with the whole Cajun music scene as it exists now. I remember when he got his National Heritage "Living legends" award[6] he was talking about the whole experience of having people discover his culture, and hold him up as an ambassador of his traditional music. He said, "You know, I remember a time when being a Cajun was something you wouldn't say out loud. It wasn't something that was considered to be something to be proud of. You call somebody a Cajun it was almost like an insult." He said, "I remember people started coming down here to Louisiana and wanting to learn about my culture and wanted to hear the music and wanted to know about it . . . You know, I feel like a little dog barking in the dark: I can't see what I'm barking at, but I'm still barking." I loved him. I guess he probably drank too much, but he was that wonderful person. He would never turn down a drink and he would always welcome you. When I was playing the "Eunice Two-Step" he got excited when he heard me playing that, so he just welcomed me right into their music circle and encouraged me to play along with them and learn other Cajun songs. He was one of the people that would be up all night long playing music until the sun came up.

It was wonderful. We were outdoors, totally immersed in music. Those are some of the best memories of my life. Thinking of great memories, but not at Augusta, I loved meeting and playing with bluesman Henry Townsend, the piano and guitar player. The last time I was with Henry Townsend he was in his nineties, but he was still, even at that age, one of the most open-minded and think-on-your-feet people. I remember sitting and having a conversation with him, and he was 100 percent in the present—his ears and his mind wide open. He was coming up with fresh perspectives on our conversation even at the age of ninety. I also loved playing with the Holmes Brothers. We just lost Wendell and Popsy of the Holmes Brothers, and even now I often play with Sherman. Wendell Holmes was someone that I admired as a person. I always enjoyed running into him. He had a catchphrase for me. Whenever he saw me he would always say, "Man, you've got a winning hand. If I had your hand, I would throw mine in." I never knew what it meant, but it always made me feel good when he said that. He was just real friendly. Those were some of my best memories.

In 1983 we also released our second album, *Sweet Bitter Blues.*[7] "Dog Days of August" was an original of mine. Margie Evans was on one of the vocals, from the American Folk Blues Concerts live recording. "Big Boss Man" and "Bye, Bye, Baby" from the American Folk Blues Festival. "Sweet Bitter Blues" is a good song and written by Otis Williams from the University of Maryland. Mike Rivers had this big yellow school bus and he would take it on the road and do recordings at festivals and other places. And then when he was home he would pull that school bus up behind his house—and he had rooms in his house that he used as studio rooms—but all the equipment, the board and all that was in that school bus. And he had lines running out of the house into the school bus, and that was where the control booth was, in the school bus. That's why he called it Gypsy Studio, because it traveled a lot.

I remember when we did those sessions, the feeling was good in the studio. John was happy being there and it was good. We played songs we had down well and we were well prepared to make a good recording. We had been touring and playing a lot and we knew all the songs down pat. So, that was a joyful and pleasurable experience, in such an unorthodox studio where the booth was in the school bus out in the backyard. Some studios can be claustrophobic, but Mike Rivers's house was comfortable and welcoming. It was a good feeling at that session. In later years, John got difficult to do recordings with. He just hated the process and he didn't like rehearsing. The way John and I learned songs was to perform them. That's how we got good at playing songs. When we came up with new songs to add to our repertoire, he wouldn't want to play them in public, because he was afraid someone else would hear them and record them before we had a chance to. He wanted to record them before we played them in public. In the meantime, he wouldn't want to practice them until when we recorded them—we didn't know them that well, and then after we recorded them we started performing them.

When we ran out of our regular material and had to learn new material in order to make albums, it was difficult because we recorded songs that we didn't know that well. We learned them in the studio. With many sessions I was personally unhappy, and don't have real fond memories of these recordings, but the albums were well received to critical acclaim and, when I hear them today, I like them much better than I did when we made them.

As we were traveling the world and playing different venues, I often grappled with how the acoustic blues music is presented now—in some ways in a way that I think it never was intended. When we played house parties it could be noisy, but people would be able to hear well enough to dance to the music and to have a good time. As we started to play larger concert halls we of course needed sound reinforcement. That technology changes the music in a way. For example, I was sitting next to John, who was the primary singer, and he was a natural without formal training. I realized that he never belted out a song. The reason he sang so pretty was that he didn't strain his voice; he always sang softly. But you wouldn't be able to do that in a larger auditorium without some good microphones. And that's why back in the day you had these shouters that would belt out the blues—Howlin' Wolf, whoever—would have these big booming voices that could project across a room, to be able to be heard like at the party. I still prefer putting on an event where people are in a smaller, more intimate gathering, different places, instead of having like these big concert hall rooms and trying to fill it with acoustic music. I just prefer natural sound quality and for people to be totally present in the experience. I feel like when people are dependent on the technology to preserve the experience and time, then the people cease to be completely present.

As in any vibrant music community, there are the resident players and the extended family, people who passed through often or rarely, but were very much part of the cultural fabric of the scene, even if they lived elsewhere. When they showed up there was joy and musical celebration, and they were always welcomed as integral members of the music community. The fabric of the regional East Coast blues extends north to New York, where the Reverend Gary Davis was reigning as the teacher to many down south through the Carolinas. Major players from around the country—the roots, blues, country blues players—they were considered part of our scene, the barbershop scene, the DC scene. When they came through they were important friends, musical compatriots, and family, part of our community. Some of these guys were among the best:

Philadelphia Jerry Ricks

Jerry Ricks used to come to DC before he went to Europe in 1971, back in the days when John Hurt lived here. I think he came down to meet with John Hurt and was introduced to Archie and the barbershop way back then. He did more on the guitar with dynamics and motion than just about any other player I can think of. It was always exciting to hear him play. A lot of times when he would start a set, I would find a place to go where I was away from people so no one would come up and start talking to me while he was playing. I could just listen and get transported by what he was doing, because he did move me. The audience was mesmerized by his playing, and what he would do with motion and dynamics. He had a way of just pulling you along with him.

I jammed with him a good bit when he would come to DC, and also, we were together at Augusta Blues Week a few times and we spent some time jamming there, especially after he returned from a long spell in Europe in 1990. He would come to my house to my New Year's Day party and it was just incredible. We would start playing music in the afternoon and go until the next day. And we did that. Jerry was a welcomed visitor whose playing was well respected and whose style fit right in.

We ran into him frequently on the concert circuit all over the country. He is often referred to as a Delta blues musician, which seems incorrect. He could surely play some Delta blues, as we all could, but he was generally an East Coast picker from the same tradition as all of us in DC. He had played with Mississippi John Hurt, Lightnin' Hopkins, Mance Lipscomb, Jesse Fuller, Skip James, Lonnie Johnson, and Doc Watson, and locally with John Cephas, Archie Edwards, and John Jackson.

Moses Rascoe

Moses was a truck driver from York, Pennsylvania. He always kept his guitar in his truck and whenever he passed through DC, he would stop in at Archie's barbershop and jam. He was a wonderful player and he fit right in. He was accepted as a welcomed friend and a member of our community whenever he came through town. He had a great repertoire and fine skills. He was a wonderful guy—big and muscular and big hearted to fit his size—just a good person, a real nice guy. We got to be good friends. He was straightforward and I liked him a lot, and he seemed to like my music, and we got along great. I don't know what else I can say about him. Most of the playing I did with him was with the Travellin' Blues Workshop events for fundraisers and things like that. I never played in a club with him, and only played with him maybe once or twice. John Cephas and I did a few festivals where he was also at in the late 1980s.

He was originally from North Carolina and he had an album, *Blues*, in 1990 produced by the Philadelphia Radio DJ Gene Shay on Flying Fish, the same label that John and I were on. Later people said that it was Bruce Kaplan of Flying Fish Records who first introduced Moses to the blues scene in DC; but he had been coming there for many years before, going back to the late 1970s, so I doubt if that is true. Maybe he was introduced by Philadelphia Jerry Ricks, another frequent visitor and friend, or maybe it was the other way around, but even though people claim once again to have "discovered" him, that is simply not true. Moses Rascoe was considered part of our music community, as a friend, and he had been playing with us for many years before the white music establishment finally caught on to him in 1983. It's just that those folks didn't know it. He was one of the unsung players in the East Coast tradition, a guy that I liked very much and had hoped to do something with, but that never worked out.

Frank Hovington

I remember when we first met Frank Hovington, the great Piedmont-style picker and singer with a wide reputation. He was a farm worker and not a professional musician, but he had a reputation as one of the best. He was very much within the same musical genre that we played. Although he kept to himself and did not venture out to join in the DC music community, he belonged musically in every way. Because he was way out in Delaware and never ventured out, John and I drove out with Dick Spottswood to Delaware where Frank Hovington lived. They picked me up in DC, and we drove out to Delaware and we got close to the area where Spottswood thought Frank Hovington might live. Spottswood had been to his house before to record an album with Bruce Bastin, but that day he got lost on the country roads in the lowlands of Delaware. We stopped to get directions and Spottswood asked in this weird archaic way, "I understand there's a colored settlement somewhere along here." Nobody said that in like a hundred years and I was thinking, "Damn, what are you talking about?" But he got directions until we found Frank Hovington. He was living in a trailer way out in the country and he had like twenty-five little nasty dogs living under his trailer and they all had names of Republican politicians and presidents. There was Lincoln, Eisenhower, and Nixon. Apparently, Frank Hovington and his father were staunch Republicans because their family ancestors were slaves, and that memory was fresh in the collective family history, and because Lincoln had freed the slaves.

Frank Hovington was an amazing player and John's equal, playing similar music and coming from the same tradition. We spent the whole afternoon playing, as he and John were figuring out a way to tune their guitars to complement each other. I think they used drop D tuning. It seemed like one of them was an octave lower so he'd have more bottom and wouldn't conflict with the other one being more on the treble range. But we had a great afternoon and evening playing music and talking. It was a great session.

Rumor has it that DC guitarist and record label executive John Fahey stumbled upon him when he was collecting records out in Delaware. He played the 1971 Smithsonian Folk Festival, recorded one album *Gone with the Wind* on the Flyright Label. Otherwise he was very obscure, but we considered him as one of us.

Michael Roach

Michael Roach is a Washington, DC, native son who is now an expatriate living in England. He used to go around with us. Michael did whatever he had to do to put in time with the people that he wanted to learn from, and he worked hard at music and he learned it well. He was a student of both John Cephas's and John Jackson's since the mid-1980s. They met Michael at the Augusta Blues Week in West Virginia and he hooked up with them back in Washington for lessons. He also learned from Archie Edwards, Bill Harris, Jerry Ricks, Turner Foddrell and his brother Marvin, and from the performers at the concerts and festivals. He was president of the DC Blues Society between 1988 and 1992.

I worked with Michael after John Cephas was president of the Blues Society, and then I became the president after him, but I was more of a figurehead. Michael Roach was the work force. He was the one who got stuff done.

He is now the resident Piedmont-style player in Britain, where he is actively touring, recording, and teaching that tradition to enthusiastic local audiences. After he emigrated to England he started a blues workshop based on the Augusta Workshop. He brought John Jackson out just about every year until he passed away. He is very successful and it has to do a lot with his work ethic. He's a hard worker, both in working on his music and also working on the music business.

Howard Armstrong

I remember Howard Armstrong coming and spending a few days hanging out with us all. He came to my house and had a meal. I used to have a nice poster of Carl Martin, and when he walked into my apartment the first thing he said was, "There's Brother Martin." He recognized the poster. He spent time with us, I think when he came to DC. Rich DelGrosso was with him, who was a longtime student of his. Sunnyland Slim I remember came through. I mean, you know, they would come for an event, for like a concert or whatever, and would just hang out with the community of players: John Cephas, John Jackson, Archie Edwards, and all of us. I remember a story about Howard Armstrong. It didn't happen in DC—it happened at the Augusta Heritage Center in Elkins, West Virginia, which turned out to be an extension of the DC community, because all those DC folks would convene there in the summer. At that time, we stayed in the dorm that's called Gribble, a straight-up, hard-core dormitory, and we stayed on the top floor where it's as hot as hell. One morning we woke up early—John Cephas and Rich DelGrosso and I are going to the men's room to get our showers. We were walking down the hall—John was wearing his bathrobe and cowboy boots and cowboy hat. We walk into the bathroom and there was Howard Armstrong standing in front of the mirror, like close, with one of those old double-edged razor blades, the naked razor blade in his hand. He was holding it next to his face, looking in the mirror with a serious look on his face. John walked through there and he said, "Howard, what are you going to do?" with this very worried and concerned tone, implying that Howard might be contemplating suicide by slashing his own throat. It turned out that was the way Howard shaved. He would take a naked razor blade, and he would shave his beard, no foam, no handle. He was very clean-shaven below the lip and his pencil moustache was a work of art. He did all that with a naked razor blade. That was Howard. He was a real Renaissance man. He was a visual artist, a musician—he had all these things going for him. He made amazing drawings and paintings, as well as calligraphy. Mandolin player Rich DelGrosso used to say, "You don't want to be behind Howard Armstrong at the bank when you have to sign a check. He's standing there and it takes him—his signature is like a work of art." I remember him coming into one of the classrooms at Augusta, and there was a chalkboard. He put a piece of chalk in each hand, and he drew—simultaneously with both hands—a picture of a man and a woman looking at each other with lust in their hearts—left hand and right hand at the same time.

He claimed to be able to speak a dozen languages. But what that meant was he could say hello and order a drink in about six different languages. All those guys—Martin, Bogan, and Armstrong—they were itinerant musicians who traveled to all the different coal camps. They could sing German, Polish, and Italian songs, tailored to the audience. They knew how to make a living going from one to the other, and they basically would play whatever people at that particular camp wanted to hear. When they came to a Polish coal camp, or the Italian coal camp, or to "the Natives"—which was the hillbilly coal camp, or the black coal camp, they had the songs ready to make the people happy and earn good tips. That's why they knew such a wide variety of music. I remember Ted Bogan being at Augusta and they had him playing the afternoon session, and he started playing "Coming in on a Wing and a Prayer" and then he followed with "You Will Never Find Another Kanaka Like Me." They all had a real fascination with Hawaii and Hawaiian music. They truly played everything. That was common with all of us. John Cephas was the same way. He didn't play Polish songs or anything like that, but even though they pegged him as Piedmont,

John played torch songs, pop songs, gospel songs, and country songs. These guys played what they wanted and it was not defined or limited by genres—they did not have a limited repertoire. Those guys were music lovers. They loved any and all good music. Howard wasn't unique in that sense.

As a testament to the hard lives, the violence and conditions of his time, Howard Armstrong told me a story about a card game, when he was with Nat Reese, when someone cheated and got caught and then shot. He didn't get killed because he cheated. He got shot because he made the mortal mistake of calling his accusers liars, which was the worst thing you can do is to question someone's honor, because when your good name is practically all you have, you are ready to die or kill for it. So, they shot and killed the guy and when he was dead they stuffed a candlestick in his mouth and lit it to give them light so they could continue playing cards. Wolf Tickets is a misnomer for the African American slang term "Woof Tickets." Selling woof/wolf tickets means "calling someone out on a lie or untruth." I wrote a song about it:

"Wolf Tickets"

Have you ever seen that old Geechee trick of pitching a defective knife
And while your foe fumbles for it you pull your good one and you take his life
Kids these days have made to cut that old caper obsolete
And so I stood there staring at that pistol lying at my feet
And selling wolf tickets when my blood comes to a boil
I'm selling wolf tickets I'm just like a rattlesnake in his coil

Brother Armstrong told me of a time when life was so cheap it was a damn shame
He said they stuck a lit candle in a dead man's mouth so that they could continue their skin game
I'm so glad that game that they call skin went out of style
If you laid those dead cheaters down end to end they'd stretch on for miles and miles
From selling wolf tickets, he had a bullet in his head, he was selling wolf tickets
His blood ran candy apple red

You've got your reputation made of trying to go for bad
But that don't make me feel afraid and it only makes me sad
'Cause I wonder what you're scared of and why you walk so hard
Why you keep on barking like a little dog in the dark
Selling wolf tickets, what makes you so scared
Selling wolf tickets, have you got those hell hounds in your head

Selling wolf tickets when my blood comes to a boil
Selling wolf tickets I'm like a rattlesnake in his coil
Selling wolf tickets he had a bullet in his head
Selling wolf tickets his blood ran candy apple red
Selling wolf tickets what makes you so scared
Selling wolf tickets have you got those hell hounds in your head

Marvin and Turner Foddrell

John and I did a tour of Virginia with Turner Foddrell and his son Lynn—a Piedmont blues tour. We went out for a few weeks and then we came back home and later on that year we went out again for a while. But I remember seeing the Foddrell Brothers, Marvin and Turner, at the Smithsonian Festival. I consider them members of the DC blues community even though they lived further out in Patrick County, in the town of Stuart, Virginia. They didn't come to DC that often, but they didn't live far from DC. They were definitely part of the scene. The Foddrell Brothers were great fingerstyle players with a huge repertoire of Appalachian and Piedmont blues and roots songs. They were so good and so well-known and so well liked that even when they weren't in DC, their presence was there. When they showed up it was a special occasion and celebration, and they were highly respected by everyone. They were regulars at the Blue Ridge Folklife Festival organized by Joe Wilson.

Henry Townsend

Henry Townsend was a good friend of Chief Ellis. Henry and his wife would stay with Chief Ellis and his wife. When Henry came to town, he would play Wolf Trap or the Smithsonian Festival, or the Kennedy Center. Whenever he came to town, he would stay with Chief Ellis. They knew each other from back before they moved up from the Deep South. Whenever they were around they would welcome me and call me to come over. It would be just like home, sharing food and drink. Once Chief found out who my father was, and that he knew my father back home in Alabama, he said, "Well, I'm not going to give you liquor anymore, because I knew your people." Being with those guys was just like being back down home, because we would hang out together and play music. More than that, I would just sit and listen to them talk. Henry Townsend's wife liked to cook, and Chief's wife liked to cook, and they'd cook the food I remember from down home in Alabama, down at my grandmother's. That's what I remember most about them, that it was just like a taste of home, a real kinship.

Fris Holloway and John Dee Holeman

Fris Holloway was a piano player that played and buck danced with John Dee. John and I even played Carnegie Hall with them once. Both of them are featured in Eleanor Ellis's film *Houseparty* at John Jackson's house. Fris has this cheesy portable keyboard almost one step below a Casio, and it was a bad little machine with a terrible tone, but he was a good player. John Dee was good friends with just about everybody in the DC community. We all knew him and everybody still holds him in high regard because he was a great player and singer. Like many of those older guys, he preferred to plug in a guitar more than play acoustic. The last time I performed with him he was proud of the fact that he hadn't lost any of his vocal range and was showing off how high he could sing and all that. John Dee Holeman—of course he's a great flat-foot buck dancer. I've come to understand that the term "buck dance" wasn't widely used in the African American community—it was simply called "dancing." That's basically what it was, dancing, flat footing, a percussive dance. John Dee was very well recognized for that ability along with Algia Mae Hinton.[8] Because of Eleanor's film *Houseparty*, there's a whole new community of young hip-hop dancers for whom John Dee is a hero, because they saw him dancing in that film and wanted to know more about him. In fact, some of them have gone down and visited him and Algia Mae Hinton in person. Of course, neither one of them is dancing anymore. The direct link to that now is Williette Hinton who is Algia Mae's son. I brought John Dee out to Centrum a few times and he just loved that. I remember late one night we were in one of the buildings where people held late-night jam sessions. I walked into this room and there was John Dee sitting at the table—leaning way back with the guitar, and he had his hat way on the back of his head, cocked to the side, and he was playing to six women sitting on the other side of the table looking at him. It had started to rain and John Dee had made arrangements with my harmonica player friend Grant Dermody to get a ride back to his sleeping quarters. Grant came up to me and said, "Phil, I'm about ready to go back over to the housing. Tell John Dee I'm ready to go." I went up and said, "John Dee, your ride is here." All six women turned around and looked at me and poked their bottom lips out and I told Grant, "Never mind—he's good. He's got a ride."

I will always treasure those guys.

In 1984 we did another album, *Dog Days of August*,[9] which was critically acclaimed and won us the W. C. Handy Blues Music Award for Best Traditional Album of the Year. Not bad for a record we taped in John's living room. This was our first album with Flying Fish, recorded in John Cephas's living room with Pete Reiniger recording it. *Dog Days of August* was the first album we did with Joe Wilson as producer and I wrote the title cut. The W. C. Handy Award is like

the Emmy or Grammy of the blues. I think it was because the album was natural, it caught us at our best, and John's voice was hard to beat and there wasn't
anyone doing what we were doing as an acoustic blues duo. This album established us and solidified to me that we were on a serious upward career track.
That award gave us the confidence to make music a full-time career and to dedi-
cate ourselves to being professional musicians. We then knew that what we did
was important and had value and was going to be successful in the long term.
John played "Hard Time Killing Floor" by Skip James. My original "Roberta" was
on this, and Joe Wilson said, "Well, you know, it sounds good when you guys
sing together." We didn't have another song that we sang together on, and that's
how I wound up making up "Roberta" on the spot, because they wanted another
song like we did "Let It Roll." People liked that, how John would put harmony on
my singing. Joe Wilson wrote the liner notes on this one. He says, "John and Phil
are bluesmen, but they ignore the rules. At a time when fusion and wall-shaking
electric sound is the norm, they perform with acoustic instruments and with an
intensity that causes noisy halls to hush."

We worked with Pete Reiniger on several projects after that. He was probably the best studio soundman at that time—probably the best studio guy in
the country for recording acoustic music. He worked for Smithsonian, and he
worked for the festivals, and he was definitely the best. After a while he and John
had a falling out, because Pete was a perfectionist used to people having a professional attitude in the studio. John was not very professional in the studio and
not very comfortable. I think we were ready for this session, but there were some
after that where we weren't that well prepared and where Pete had to figure out
a way to make things work. John would lose his patience and get on Pete's case
for things that were more like mine and John's fault. At a certain point Pete just
had enough and stood up to John, saying, "You can't disrespect me in my own
house like this," because the studio was in his house. He just lost his patience
with us, because he was trying to fix stuff that he probably shouldn't have had to
fix. Things would have been better if we had been better prepared. John never
accepted responsibility for not being prepared. Joe Wilson was trying to keep
the peace and had us listen to his bad jokes and bad song lyrics that he was making up. If he jumped in there it would always be on John's side and his attitude
was that Pete shouldn't have lost his patience.

For me, reflecting back on all those albums we did over our career, I admit
that for many of them I wasn't satisfied with the recordings at the time. I always
felt like we could have done better. Maybe it's just normal artistic self-doubt. For
many years I did not even listen to the recordings we made, but for this writing
I reacquainted myself with the albums. After a long hiatus, upon listening after
all that time, I was reminded of what I knew already, that playing with John
Cephas was such a different thing than playing with the younger folks I'm play-

ing with now. I think that it's just a matter of the times that John came up in, and those times—they don't exist anymore. The atmosphere in which he developed his playing style and his skills was the real deal. He came directly from the tradition. Today, we're trying to continue and to re-create it, but when he was starting out as a blues musician he was playing within the African American community at house parties. It was the golden age of house parties and jamming and playing for people that were dancing and partying. He had a level of energy and a rhythm on the guitar that most of the younger guys now don't have. The younger people came up playing and preparing for small clubs and concerts. They would prepare for the listening room environment by rehearsing and practicing, whereas John came from a time of just knock-down-drag-out partying and playing all night long, and people being noisy, dancing, fussing and fighting and laughing and eating and all of that. That just develops a different type of musician than someone who comes up and their main experience is concert halls and coffeehouses.

Listening again to our own body of recorded music confirmed that. The other realization is, upon reflecting on my own feelings at the time that we should be tightly rehearsed, that it could be much better if we could spend time preparing. It is different now. We made some very good music, records that were critically acclaimed, award-winning, and well-loved by our audience. The truth is that our records are a lot better than I remember. Looking back, I realize that if we had done the recordings as is the standard now, like picking these tunes out, playing them over and over again so we have them down airtight, and then going into the studio and playing what we rehearsed, we might have wound up with something that was just dead on the tracks anyway. I now realize that a lot of what I dislike about recording music today is exactly what I was pushing for at the time. Like in a lot of other instances where I butted heads with John, in the end he turned out to be right.

After we returned from the tour of South America and the Caribbean in 1984, Barry Lee arranged a tour of California, to two festivals. The first was up in San Francisco and then another date at the Long Beach Festival down in Los Angeles. There was about a week to ten days in between those two things. Those were the only breadwinners. Somebody got us a gig in Berkeley the night before or the day before the San Francisco Blues Festival, which was a two-day event. We shared that stage with everybody from Robert Cray to Albert Collins. We went on to some smaller venues. One thing I remember during that trip is staying in Barry Lee's father's house for a few nights, and how much he liked John Cephas. Barry Lee's father was said to be not the most enlightened man as far as race, but he referred to John as "salt of the earth," which was basically true. John just had this inherent dignity about him. Everybody could love him.

In California, we rented a car and we drove to San Francisco. After the Long Beach Blues Festival, we had a couple of days to kill before our flight back, and John decided he wanted to go to Mexico. We set out, packing a bag with a bottle of black rum on the dashboard and, as we were driving through Gilroy, John fell asleep while he was driving. When we got into Mexico, we didn't know that you weren't allowed to take a rental car across the border. We got stopped by a Mexican motorcycle policeman on the way back to Tijuana and this guy extorted every penny we had. We had no choice but to pay him because we were caught red-handed with an open bottle of rum in the car. He made you pay right then on the spot, just stealing. That's the way he was trained to collect "the fine" in advance of the trial. He let us go after he took just about all the money we had. He was just waiting to recognize a car that had a rental tag. It was a planned shakedown.

Nineteen eighty-seven was a big year. The most wonderful event was the birth of our second daughter, Martha Faith Wiggins. We still lived at 18th and Kalorama Road in Washington, DC, right in the heart of Adams Morgan. In 1987 Cephas & Wiggins won the most prestigious W. C. Handy Award as Entertainers of the Year.

Eliza was about three years old when Martha was born. Thank goodness I was home for Martha's birth, because I still feel bad that when Eliza was born I was out of the country. That was difficult for my wife Wendy. Martha was born in the same hospital I was born in, the Washington Hospital for Women. I was there, probably about three o'clock in the morning as the shift changed. A new, elderly nurse came in and she introduced herself, and my wife Wendy told her that I was also born in the same hospital. The nurse stopped and she walked up to me and took a good look and said, "Well, I don't remember you."

Martha was a big baby. Maybe nine pounds. When she came out her head turned blue because she wasn't getting enough oxygen at birth. There comes this big beautiful baby with a blue head, and I'm, "Oh, my God, what's going on?" But it was fine. It was great to be there for the birth.

Those were the best years, living in Adams Morgan in an apartment at 18th and Kalorama Road with our two children. Our best friends all lived in the same building and there was great fraternity and mutual support. Our best friends were Sulay and Lydia, great people who lived upstairs. As it turned out, we were having daughters at the same time. They were great. Sulay was from Ghana and Lydia was from the Midwest somewhere. Like my wife and me, they were an interracial couple. Sulay was this incredible spirit of a guy and a real music lover. Both of us had huge collections of reggae music. I was working at the law firm as a messenger, but I didn't make a lot of money. There were times when Sulay and I were broke at the same time and struggling. To get through the hard times we would celebrate by getting a half pint of Jack Daniels and a six-pack of Dos

Equis, and drink "depth charges," playing reggae music loudly on the stereo. That's when you pour a glass of beer and then you take a shot glass of liquor and set it inside, then you chuck it down in one breath. That's how you get high. Our group of friends, we were all interracial couples and we all had daughters. It was great because we all passed baby clothes on to each other and we all took care of each other in that way. We would go up to Lydia and Sulay's apartment or to Mark and Jo's and our toddlers would play and within three minutes of being in each other's house none of the girls had the same clothes on that they had on when we walked in. That's how it was back then: we had our little tribe and we all took care of each other. Jo and Mark and Wendy and I, we would take trips together. None of us had much money but we had a good life and great times. During that time, I would have big New Year's Day parties and we would eat black-eyed peas and collard greens on New Year's Day. There were always people, always music, there was always—I imagine if I lived there now it would seem tiny, but at the time it seemed like we had plenty of space and it was always full of life. Life was great, but it was hard, too. Working at the law firm really sucked. It was weird having to spend the days dealing with this office mentality and being around a bunch of rich lawyers, and basically being on the low end of the totem pole. My music career was taking off, and I had a day job and family obligations. Cephas & Wiggins had a lot of gigs at that time. I came home very late at night and had to get up early the next day. Most nights I was doing music and often I only had maybe three or four hours of sleep at most. In addition to all that, I used to play in the house band at the Childe Harold. I never got tired of playing. We would play all night and then the guy would shut the door and we would just continue, and we would be playing and he would just open the bar up for free liquor and we would play music all night. I remember going to work more than once not only hung over, but actually still drunk from the night before and I just turned around and left the job. I really hated that job, and I reached the point where I felt like I could make it in my music.

After that I tried to do music full-time, and I still needed more income and I wound up with a few side jobs. One was working with the Everyday Theatre in Anacostia. The director of Everyday Theatre got a grant from the District government for me to work with youth at risk. At that time DC was the murder capital of the U.S., and Anacostia was a tough place for kids to grow up. That job was far better and it was work that I cared about and work that required much more of my talent and resources than working in the mailroom. I had to use my brain, my creativity, and my imagination. The resources I was calling on at night making music were the same resources I was calling on for the theater job. I also worked as a teacher for the Art and Drama Therapy Institute, a day-rehab for adults with intellectual disabilities. I worked there two hours a day teaching them songs and how to play harmonica. We did a songwriting workshop together. I was putting together a network of jobs that were music related that I could do to help supplement my income, and things too that were very rewarding to me in terms of doing some good in the community. At the Art and Drama Therapy Institute I got to know some amazing people, and I got to know some people with incredible challenges in their daily life that, in spite of all that, just had incredible spirit. I was able to help support myself doing that, and at the same time I was getting a lot more than just money from doing that community work.

I will never forget when we went to Memphis for the Handy Awards in 1987—we had to rent tuxedos and I was standing on the stage with John to accept that award, and John started crying when he was trying to speak, because he was moved for how far we had come. Here we were, two guys that started out playing the blues in house parties in our own African American community, and now we were being honored with the biggest award of the blues, the W. C. Handy, the Oscar of the Blues. It was emotional and humbling. He stopped talking for a minute, trying to compose himself, and the audience just went nuts. That was a great feeling, something I would have never imagined to win, the award for Entertainers of the Year. We were up against all the greats, Buddy Guy and B.B. King—that's the whole nine yards. It's not just the category of acoustic blues or traditional blues or whatever; it's the whole thing, the big award. It is unbelievable to me to this day that we got that recognition. It was like a dream. Being there, getting that recognition, hanging out with all these people who were like icons of blues. Of course, most of them were Chicago blues guys. It was just unbelievable for two acoustic players from Virginia and DC to be recognized on the same level with B.B. King and people like that. The pageantry of it, being around all these well-dressed people, just everything about it was like a dream. There we were, seemingly on top, and I still had a day job.

For me I just felt like we had arrived, we had gained acceptance and success, and I now perceived that I might be able to quit my day job, that we were established now. Now I had the confidence to support my family, my two children, by making music, to have a life and a living doing what I love to do. In some ways, it did work out like that. Because of the new recognition, our careers ascended and we were able to get some good gigs. Still, it wasn't quite as huge an impact on our careers and income as I had hoped. We had every opportunity to capitalize on what this huge award presented. We could have started actively touring on the blues circuit, but we worked only as much as John wanted to work. Once again, the difference between us was a factor. John didn't need to work as much as I did, because he had his other income, his pension. As I said, he loved being home and there were a lot of things about traveling that were difficult for him. If he had been more interested and more in need of getting out there and traveling more, pushing harder, getting bigger gigs, we could have done that. But I don't think that was what he wanted or needed. John also loved to be in control. I think that he felt like if we had a booking agent that was too big-time, that he wouldn't be able to keep control—that the agent would have more control. We definitely kept it at a level that John could handle.

In 1987 I also appeared in the movie *Matewan*,[10] a film written and directed by John Sayles. Actually, Sayles's music director, Mason Daring, contacted Augusta Heritage Center at Elkins, West Virginia, looking for a harmonica player. I think it was Margo Blevin who recommended me. I called him up and he said, "Well, you know, make me a recording and send it to me, and we'll see if you're what we're looking for." I basically sort of forgot about it. A few months later I was sitting around the house doing nothing and I thought maybe I'll make a cassette and send it to that guy about that movie. I recorded some noodling around in the cassette recorder. I had a cassette of the Marimac recording of me and John and sent them off to him. It turned out that the Marimac cassette was blank. They hired me based on my noodling around. The next thing I know I'm getting calls from wardrobe and I went there and it was literally amazing. John Sayles is a brilliant filmmaker. He did this factual film about the coal mining wars in West Virginia. It was around 1920 the Matewan massacre happened. I went down there and appeared in two scenes. My scenes were a musical metaphor for when the different camps of African American and white coalminers started to communicate with each other and to organize. There was the Italian camp, and a camp they called the natives, which was the hillbillies, and there was the black camp. They were all segregated. The main scene that I'm in is one where these two Appalachian guys—a fiddler and a guitar player—they hear this mandolin off in the distance, and they walk toward it and they wind up in the Italian camp with the mandolin player. Then you see me—I'm off by myself sitting on a stoop somewhere, and I'm hearing them both and I'm just playing along with them from a distance. Music ends up being the first step toward unity, in the old adage that music is a great unifying force and the universal language. When I did *Matewan*, it was a real opportunity to establish myself and get into the movie scene, and I didn't pursue it like I should have. In recent years, I've reached out to Mason Daring again to try to remind him of my work and all that, and I've never heard back from him. It was a missed opportunity for me.

We had by this time traveled the world to Europe, Africa, Central and South America, China, Australia, and New Zealand. In 1988 we were also among the first American musicians to be invited to the Russian National Folk Festival in Moscow in the former Soviet Union. We went there with a contingent from America in a cultural exchange program under the auspices of the Smithsonian. They sent a group of traditional musicians from lots of the different regions in the Soviet Union to the U.S., and likewise Americans went to the Soviet Union. It was still the Cold War, but relations were getting better under Mikhail Gorbachev, statesman at the time. He was the eighth and final leader of the Soviet Union. It was an interesting and somewhat unusual tour. We Americans stuck out like a sore thumb. It was me and John as a duo, the group Sweet Honey in the Rock from Washington, DC, the Badland Singers—a group of Native Americans, I think Navajo—and the Johnson Mountain Boys, a bluegrass band. This cultural exchange got started when the leader of the Soviet Union at the time, Gorbachev, sent a contingent of Russian musicians to the Smithsonian Folklife Festival. I met quite a few of them, and actually got to be good friends with some of them, including a cool duo of Tuvan throat singers of Mongolian ancestry. The art in throat singing is in the use of overtones. They also played the Jew's harp, which has distinct similarities. There is a melody created with the throat singing that makes this low growling and the Jew's harp creates this low "boing-boing-boing" sound. The overtones are almost like magic. It was amazing. When we went to Russia I reconnected with those Tuvan singers.

We went also with scholars and folklorists, including Simon Carmel, who wound up being my roommate. His specialty in folklore was customs and traditions relating to deaf people and he was himself deaf. The funny thing about that trip was that all those jokers that worked for the Smithsonian had come to realize that I was a bad snorer. They were trying to figure out who was going to room with who, and they figured out that they should put me with Simon, because he was about the only person in our troupe that I wouldn't keep awake all night. Simon was a little guy and he had an alarm clock that instead of making sounds it made bright flashes. We got to Moscow and stayed near Gorky Park in the Olympic Village, that they had built for the 1980 Olympics that the Carter administration boycotted. As we got settled in, Simon plugged in his alarm clock to see if it would work, and because of the difference in the electrical current, which was 220V in Russia, it basically blew up. But it worked out anyway, because I never got to bed before 7:00 in the morning anyway. I was in Moscow and took every opportunity to meet and talk to people and to learn about it. I made the best of every moment and wanted to miss nothing. I would come into the room at 7:00 and wake Simon up and get in the bed and sleep for maybe an hour or two before I had to get up to start my day.

I was struck by the heavy-handed Soviet bureaucracy everywhere. We had the feeling that we were being basically pushed around all the time, that we didn't know what was going on. Once we thought that we understood what was happening it turned out to be something else was happening. The basics of life, things that we took for granted here in America, were luxuries over there. One of the women in Sweet Honey in the Rock commented, "These people are so busy taking care of their military they don't take care of their people." We would go to breakfast in the morning and have coffee, and ask for a little milk and they'd say, "Well, milk is not on the menu today." Everything seemed to be rationed and scarce. One day I took a walk and I saw a vending machine in the middle of this plaza and there was this line of people standing in front of it. It was some type of drink machine. I was watching and a man walked up to the machine, put his money in, and there was a cup sitting there, and apparently the cup gets filled up when you put the money in. He stood there and drank it—and when he was done he put the cup back down and the next person did the same thing. I was amazed that everyone standing in line was drinking out of the same cup. That was an eye-opener for me of what life was like there.

Right there in the Olympic village there was a guy who operated out of an open shack with just four posts and a shabby makeshift roof with scrap wood over top. He made a fire pit where he was grilling meat all night long and selling it. That's where all of the musicians and the Russian late-night people hung out. I later found out that it was probably horsemeat, grilled over nasty scrap wood with paint on it and all. We would just hang out there and drink vodka all night and solve the problems of the world. During the first night we were there, we were hanging out late at this strange barbeque place—and a group of Afro-Puerto Ricans from California showed up. At that time, they were called Los Pleneros de la Puerta—they changed their name over the years, but they're pretty well known. They played sacred Santería music and they were into some version of voodoo. They played drums and congas, tambourines called *pleneros*. A couple of generations of them were there. They were beautiful people—two women and four or five men. They also had interesting string instruments, like a large Mexican guitarrón. I had brought over a bottle of Jack Daniels to offer some fine American bourbon to friends I might meet in Russia. We're all sitting around there having a drink and the guy who is the oldest member of Los Pleneros, who must have been pushing eighty at the time—he walked up and reached out for the bottle, and I handed it to him. He braced himself against that little shack, threw his head back and he drained about half that bottle. I thought he was going to die, an eighty-year-old man—no way he can handle that. But he was fine. From that day on I think twice before I hand a bottle of liquor to anyone.

The audience at the Russian Folk Festival mostly consisted of other musicians, the many folklore groups from the different parts of the Soviet Union. Their idea of folklore and our idea of folklore were very different. We were a bunch of different groups of people that didn't have much in common with each other except music, and we Americans did our own thing the way we would do it in our own community. All the different groups from the Soviet Union, and also from places like Cuba, they were like organized troupes of people in traditional costumes of their home regions, almost like uniforms, and they had choreographers. They all did the same routine of organized marching and dancing. The only difference among them was like costumes of different colors and styles. It was all tightly choreographed. It was different than anything I had experienced. A couple of times we were actually in front of the general public, but mostly it was other musicians, other performers.

Cephas & Wiggins were received well. But the feeling at the festival was a real strong sense of nationalism and feeling of competition. When John and I played we could tell that people were enjoying themselves, but the other performers would not show that because they were more anxious to show their skills, to be judged as the best, and to show what they're doing is better than what we're doing. It seemed like they were under pressure and not loose and enjoying themselves, as we were.

At the opening ceremony of the festival they had a big parade, almost like a marching-in ceremony. All the troupes lined up and walked around the arena inside the Olympic village. All the other groups had their costumes and uniforms on and they were prancing along and stepping high and marching along. Here we were, a bunch of diverse American roots and blues musicians, just strolling in and talking to each other, getting to know each other, because a lot of us had never met each other. I had never met the Johnson Mountain Boys. We were walking and I was talking to this guy in the Johnson Mountain Boys, and he was chewing gum and not watching where we're going. We almost stepped off of this huge platform and as we looked up out and there was the public standing there looking at us. At the end of the festival they showed a film of it, and it was funny, because they show us walking and almost falling off of the edge of this platform and they show him chewing gum. They showed this on this huge screen with everybody watching us, the clumsy, loose Americans.

They took us on a tour to Gorki Leninskiye, the mansion on the outskirts of Moscow, where Lenin lived up until the time he died, and they actually took us to the house that he was living in when he died. We went in there looking around his house, and I noticed that all the mirrors in the house were covered up with black curtains. Back here in Washington, DC, we had just recently done a performance curated by Bernice Johnson Reagon about the customs relating to death and dying in the black community, and part of that presentation was they talked about the customs in black families. There was also a custom of people covering the mirrors because there was this belief that you could see the spirit of the deceased walking around the house and you could see their reflection in the mirrors, and they would cover the mirrors. I asked our guide if they had the same belief there, and she was surprised. The interpreter posed the question to the guide and she just looked at me and said, "Yes." She wouldn't talk anymore about that at all. But it was interesting to see that that far away we had the same custom.

A year after we went to Russia, we toured China, in 1989, sponsored by the Kennedy Center—a few months before the Tiananmen Square massacre. That trip was organized for artists and arts educators. We went to the training center for children for the Beijing Opera. They start the kids when they're two years old. It was a huge complex that included a regular grade school, and schools for dance and music. One morning we got on a streetcar to go from our hotel to meet the people who were going to take us around to these different institutions. One of the guys with us got off the streetcar and left his briefcase on the train. He told the hosts and about an hour and a half later they brought it back to him—untouched, everything intact. That would never happen in the U.S. Someone would have riffled through it, taken out anything they thought was valuable, and probably chucked it in the trash somewhere. But they were able to just go and get it and give it back to him.

Our hosts wanted us to have a great experience, and they took us to a lot of restaurants where they would bring us course after course of food. But we noticed that no one ever brought us rice. In the U.S., when you go to a Chinese restaurant you get rice. But there was never any rice. When we asked about it they said, well, you know, rice is considered low class and they don't serve you rice because you're honored guests. In Beijing, the air was very bad. You would immediately tear up when going outside. It smelled exactly like my grandmother's neighborhood in Titusville, Alabama, because everybody heated their house with a coal stove and burning coal was the predominant smell on the street in Beijing. I recognized that right off.

Our hotel was within an hour's walk to the edge of town. There was a main thoroughfare where people would come to Beijing from the rural areas, bringing in raw materials to shops in the city. There was a guy with a big horse-drawn wagon with a flatbed piled high heading into town. I looked up and noticed that there was no driver—no one holding the reins. As the wagon went by, I saw the guy asleep in the back of the wagon. The horses know where to go. I had never been around the Chinese language before that and it struck me how the Chinese language was soft-edged compared to Japanese.

We also performed at the Kennedy Center Cultural Diversity Festival, a program for schoolchildren, in the play *Chewing the Blues*. The Kennedy Center basically hired a playwright to write a play that would somehow expose the culture of Piedmont blues. This program for schoolchildren was part of the Kennedy Center Diversity Program. John and I had played at the Kennedy Center a couple of times, and I think just from knowing us from our performances they came up with that idea of including us in that diversity program and writing a play that would help students delve into our culture. We performed on the Millennium Stage a few times. There was a fair bit of crossover between the Smithsonian and the Kennedy Center.

It was a big deal when John Cephas won the National Heritage Fellowship Award in 1989,[11] which made him a "Living Treasure of American Folk Music."

This award is one of the most prestigious recognitions a traditional musician can get, bestowed by the National Endowment for the Arts. According to the NEA, "The National Heritage Fellowships recognize the recipients' artistic excellence and support their continuing contributions to our nation's traditional arts heritage." We know that Joe Wilson definitely had a huge part in that, in nominating John. Of course, the main credit for that goes to John, because it was him and his life. He was 100 percent a musician and a carpenter—in fact, it wasn't like he was an entertainer as much as that he was just a musician, just like he was a carpenter, just like he cooked food—because he was passionate about everything he did. In a way, this huge award was a culmination for John to emerge from being the person he was when I first met him, someone who played music for fun and at house parties and didn't feel like it was even worth something to be performed on a stage. It was low-life music, hanging out in the juke joint or the house party, drinking and partying. Over time he gradually learned that his music and culture had value and was worth perpetuating, spreading the word, sharing with the world. He developed into that person, a cultural treasure of traditional music, and then he was finally recognized for that. It was huge.

I think that a lot of people assumed that the award went to both of us, but it was John's award alone. I think some among the general public and the presenters would assume that Cephas & Wiggins won the Heritage Award, especially people that ran venues and booked concerts. You would often hear the phrase, "Heritage Award Winners Cephas & Wiggins." The recognition definitely blew over onto me, too, in terms of our duo's success in bookings and prestige. The folks who ran blues festivals wanted to have a certain amount of prestige and class, and they liked promoting their concerts by having a Heritage Award winner perform. It was a huge award for John, well deserved and wonderful.

In 1989 we recorded our album *Guitar Man* on Flying Fish.[12] This album also won a W. C. Handy Award, our second on the Flying Fish label. To a certain extent these awards have something to do with the efforts of the label on our behalf. Flying Fish had a lot to do with it, because you need someone pulling for you in the industry. Of course, there's no substitute for the quality of the music. Flying Fish could not have finessed those awards for albums that were no good. We won several W. C. Handy Awards over the years, Traditional Album of the Year and Instrumentalist of the Year. But the big milestone for us was Entertainers of the Year, in 1987, because we were up against everybody for that category. I mean, we beat out B.B. King, Buddy Guy, and all the big names. That was a great feeling and validation. That was a milestone that established us as full-time fixtures on the festival circuit. We felt like we had made it.

The title song "Guitar Man" is actually me, but it didn't sound right to say "harmonica man." John wrote "Black Cat on the Line." "Richmond Blues" is a song John actually didn't write, but he adapted it to be Richmond instead of whatever city it was originally. The funny thing about that song—it has some of the best lyrics of any song that we ever did. But he says, "I was standing down in Richmond on the corner of Broad and Main," and if you know anything about Richmond, Broad Street and Main Street are parallel. They never intersect. One of his friends who lived in Richmond pointed that out to us when we were doing that song.

Rehearsing wasn't John's favorite thing. I think it was during this session, I remember one time we, Joe and I, had talked to John and scheduled a rehearsal. Joe and I drove down to Bowling Green, which was a two-hour drive, to rehearse, and we got there and it was late morning and John was already drunk and there were bottles of liquor strewn around his yard. He came out and he said, "I can't rehearse today, I'm beat—I'm too hung over." We talked for a while, and then wound up turning around and going all the way back home. Later, after John passed on, I was talking to Joe one day, and he said to me, "Well, John was always pissed off because you didn't have to rehearse and he had to rehearse." That surprised me that he said that, and I mean to me my feeling was that I would have loved to have rehearsed—I would have loved to have the opportunity to put in some good rehearsals in preparation for any of those recordings. Just because if we did, we'd go in there and we'd know what the hell we were doing, each song would have its own distinct quality, instead of just being like a jam session, and I wanted the chance to practice our material. But John, he just didn't want to do that. I don't know why, but he basically sabotaged all our efforts to have rehearsals; but, nonetheless, the album sounds good. At the time, we were recording them I didn't feel that way about them. I felt they could be much better. It's funny. Now that I have a chance to listen to some of them, I'm surprised how much better they sound than how I thought they sounded. I guess you can chalk it up to artists always wanting to do their best, and somehow feeling as if it could always be better.

The hardest thing for me was the divorce from my wife, Wendy, which affected everyone dramatically. Despite that personal family turmoil, during this period John and I had great travels and we made wonderful music. John at that time was going through his own troubles, dealing with diabetes and not knowing how to take care of that and not being willing to do what was necessary to take care of that condition. In many ways, due to that illness, it was a real son of a bitch to be around him, because it definitely affected his disposition. John eventually learned to manage this disease once he realized how important it was to take better care. Then his disposition also improved quite a bit. He still drank too much and should not have. As an alcoholic, he convinced himself and rationalized, "Well, I have it under control. My doctor says I can have two drinks." No doctor ever told him that. No doctor would ever tell an alcoholic—

oh, you can have two drinks. By this time, after twenty years of playing together, John and I just naturally fit together. On good nights, it felt great. It wasn't like we planned how to play a tune out this way or to plan arrangements. It was more like this was—there's all this past, present, and future in a stream, it would just flow right through us out to the people. I mean there were nights when it wasn't like that—there were nights where it was more of a struggle. On nights when it wasn't happening, I often came to find out that wasn't any indication of how the audience was receiving it. There were nights where I felt afterwards like wanting to just go crawl in a hole somewhere and hide out. Then I'd talk to people and they'd go, "Wow, that was amazing." On good nights, it was indeed amazing to play with John because of the fact we had played together so much and for so long and that we knew each other musically well. We could anticipate each other. Like many musicians, I sometimes tired of what we were playing. Sometimes I was starting to feel like, man, if I have to play "Black Rat Swing" one more time my head is going to blow off. It was starting to get to a point where John and I weren't doing anything new, weren't learning any new songs. Sometimes it started to feel on a lot of nights like we are just going through the motions. I was writing my own songs, but I knew that most of my original songs wouldn't be Cephas & Wiggins songs—most of them would never make it into our set list. So, I started to moonlight a little bit with other musicians.

Actually, I got in trouble with John for doing a gig with Eleanor Ellis. John heard about it and he was giving me this big rap about we put in much time to develop our duo and all that—basically he was just jealous.

By now we had reached fame. The 1990s were a fruitful period for us. Our career was now essentially at a peak. We were recognized internationally, had won a major award and played the best concert halls in the world, including Carnegie Hall in New York, Royal Albert Hall in London, and the Sydney Opera House in Australia. We played the Chicago Blues Festival—actually we played more folk festivals than blues festivals, mostly because of Joe Wilson's connections. We played up and down the East Coast quite a bit—Boston, Philadelphia, and New York.

We had been all over the world, from Australia and New Zealand clear across the globe making great music. The music business and the blues end of it especially is complicated. The artistic side of it is one thing, but of course the human interaction is both positive and negative. Some issues are stressful and pervasive in dealing with business, race, dealing with my culture, and dealing with how people are treated and how people react to their treatment. Some people in the music business, in their interaction with African American musicians, consider themselves to be altruistic, but actually have a condescending attitude. In this business, I've been around a lot of people that have this paternalistic, patriarchal attitude. That particularly impacted some of the older blues guys—John

Hurt and others. We know how some of their handlers were very possessive of the musicians that they allegedly "discovered." I heard many people claim, "Well, this old guy—I took care of him, I did this, did that." You know, one memory that comes to mind specifically for me is being in a hotel with Carey Bell. The leader of his band was talking about how they get paid for each gig and he'll give Carey a little bit of cash at a time and then pocket the rest—take him to the liquor store. It was babysitting. By taking that responsibility you're essentially saying this person is not capable of handling that responsibility. In some cases that may be true, in other cases it may be exploitative. But if it is true, why do business with that person? Why exploit their talent if you don't respect them as a human being, as a grown man or a grown woman? The examples of that are ubiquitous. They're everywhere. And for me, having seen that a lot, having dealt with it to a certain extent for a long time, I have no patience and lost respect for people that require that treatment. I definitely don't respect or appreciate people that would exploit that situation, to set up a relationship where they're making money off of somebody—that's a grown person that they basically treat like a child.

There have been several people over the years that I've come in contact with that were like that. It works two ways of course, in this unequal relationship. At a certain point when a musician gives up his independence and figures out that the handler is willing to take care, they give over that responsibility—and assume that they can be irresponsible and as wild and stupid as they want to be, knowing that this person is going to look out and is going to pick up the pieces.

John Ullman was our agent at the time, but we eventually switched over to the Piedmont Agency. John and I and Joe Wilson—we had been doing some gigs somewhere, and on our way home they sprang it on me that they were going to be stopping in North Carolina to meet with this guy and they wanted me to come along, and I couldn't come. I think things would have gone better if I had come with them, but at that time I had two toddlers at home and I had made plans with my wife Wendy that I was going to be home. I had those family obligations, juggling schedules with my wife and we had to balance all that. I couldn't just call her and say, "Well, I'm not going to be home for another four or five days because I got to go do this"—I couldn't do that. I had to keep my word and go take care of my kids. They went without me to meet with the head of the Piedmont Agency—Steve Hecht—and they went and met with him and worked out the arrangements for him to become our agent. The result of that was detrimental. Basically, Steve had become John's agent and not mine. There was a lot going on that I wasn't privy to, that I wasn't part of, when the deal was made and much of what came later. There was a real communication gap where John knew what was going on and I didn't. I would find out certain details of contracts and travel arrangements—mostly after the fact. They didn't communicate directly with me. Joe Wilson was working with John Cephas and they were taking care of the business—they signed the contracts. In hindsight I regret it, but it was due to certain circumstances. I could not ditch my obligations to my wife and my kids. If I had more time, and if I had focused on it, I could have fought for myself. But I couldn't do that.

John kept limits on our activities and the agents, who didn't work that hard to generate gigs for us. They mined the contacts that we had already established over the years. They basically just called those people, and then they hit them up for more money. In the scheme of things, they did a little bit to develop new work, but not that much. That probably had a lot to do with who our agent was. John's concern was losing control of the business side of it, which is funny, because he was never good at it to begin with. But I think it all served his purposes, where he wasn't away from home more than he wanted to be or more than he could handle.

In the early 1990s we did a tour of Turkey. We started in Istanbul and went to Ankara as part of a two-city festival put on by Concerted Efforts, and it was just great. In Ankara, this guy named Timel Aris showed up at the gig and he somehow got backstage, and he was talking to John. Basically, he made a connection with John and blew smoke up his butt. Then he got in touch with him after we got back to the States to come and perform in Turkey again. By this time, I wasn't working with Everyday Theatre anymore. I was working with this Video Action Fund run by activists for various humanist causes. We were working with kids through the I Have a Dream Foundation over in Southeast Washington in the Anacostia neighborhood. John got this gig for us, and it was three weeks to a month, something like that—and I was worried about losing my job but I also didn't want to blow the duo thing with John, so we went. The Turkish guy had told John, "I'm going to guarantee you this much, you'll be playing in the club four nights a week and depending on how many people show up, and it's going to be popular, you stand to make a lot more than what this guarantee is. We'll put you up in your own apartment and there will be servants waiting on you." We got there and they picked us up at the airport and drove us to this hotel late at night. The hotel doesn't look great, but we get there and he says, "Well, right now the club is closed, but don't worry. Tomorrow we'll go to Mel's office and he'll explain to you all that's going on." The next day there's a message at the hotel—"Don't worry about it—no one is coming today, but don't worry—it's okay." So that day I got up to have breakfast and then I'm sitting in the lobby of this funky hotel, and I look around and noticed these two jokers in the lobby playing with guns. They had a bunch of thugs there. The long and short of it was that this guy Timel Aris never got the proper permits. The club was in the bottom of like a condo and the guy that lived on the next floor above the condo was some city official who didn't like Timel all that much and didn't like the noise from the club. He had put in a complaint, and that's what closed the club down. There I was in Turkey, staying in a hotel full of thugs in the dead of winter in the freezing cold with snow and ice everywhere. We haven't seen the guy who hired us in several days. At that point, I wondered if we were ever going to see him, or if we're ever going to get paid. We were stuck in Ankara, a government town with not much going on, especially in the neighborhood where our hotel was. After being cooped up for several days, and not getting paid, I decided I'd go out and take a walk with one of those young hotel waiters. We went walking, and across the plaza from where we were, I saw another tall black man walking, and I just nodded at him, and he nodded at me. He came over and struck up a conversation with me. It turns out that he was the son of a well-known kora player whose father's records I had at home, Famoro Dioubati from Guinea. We started talking, and I couldn't believe I was talking to the son of this guy whose music I loved, and we managed to become friends. He took me out of that funky neighborhood up the hillside to where there were all shops. He took me to meet his older friend who was a Muslim scholar. We sat there sipping tea and talking about religion and philosophy and politics. Later Famoro took me all over Ankara. He was there in military school. During the month that we were in Ankara, we played together a few nights. All this time John pretty much stayed in the hotel. Except for one day, when I wanted to buy a gift at an Ankara museum shop, John and I headed downtown with two young guys from the club. It was a long walk and it was getting later and later. Finally, it was starting to get dark. I asked, "Well, isn't this museum going to be closed?" "No, we're almost there." The next thing you know we were standing at this gateway and a guy said he wants my camera. I was confused. "What's going on?" "Give it to him, he'll give it back later. We're going in here where you're not allowed to take photos." I could understand that the museum doesn't allow you to take photos. But, it was not exactly a museum. Where they had taken us was to the red-light district, and it was one of the most terrible things I had ever seen in my life. It was as if you were in the Washington zoo. They had all these little buildings with big glass windows and you look inside and there's all these women laying around on couches and chairs, and they were from thirteen to seventy years old. The idea was that you look in that window and pick yourself out a woman and then you go and you know. I've been to Amsterdam. I've been all over the world. I have never seen anything like this dealing with human beings before in my life. It was just terrible and unbelievable. I asked them hey, you guys are Muslim—how does that work? I found out that they have a ceremony that they perform so that for whatever time that you spend with the prostitute you're married to her. They have a little marriage ceremony so that they're not going against the Koran.

I never will forget that. It was just a horrible scene. But also, the fact that they thought that was what I was interested in—as if that's what I wanted to see on my trip to Turkey—it was an insult. Even our host, Timel, he invited us to his house for dinner. His wife prepared this beautiful meal for us and he never even introduced us to her. She was off by herself in a corner somewhere. It was this dynamic that we were not supposed to speak to her or even acknowledge that she was there. It was the strangest thing. The Muslim scholar that we talked to, he told me a story—in the time of Mohammad during the very first Muslim call to prayer—they were trying to find someone to do it and the only person that agreed to do it or had the courage to do it was an African man and ever since then, according to the Koran, it says that black people had a very special position in the eye of God because of that, because the very first call to prayer was given by a black man. The role of women in that society bothered me. One day while sitting in the hotel lobby I saw this big car pull up, and two guys get out of the back. They were chatting and walking into the hotel together, and then another door opened and a woman came out all by herself. She had to get the bags and carry all that stuff, slipping and sliding in the ice, and she was having trouble getting the door to the hotel open. By the time she finally gets herself in the hotel, the two men were sitting at the bar sipping tea together and none of them were paying her any mind.

The 1990s were also a fruitful and prolific period for recording. We released a series of highly successful and critically acclaimed albums in rapid succession: *Flip, Flop, Fly*, Flying Fish Records. 1992.[13] This album was dedicated to Wilbert "Big Chief" Ellis. This album also won us a second W. C. Handy Award. For the first time, we were no longer called Bowling Green John Cephas or Harmonica Phil Wiggins and we were now just John Cephas and Phil Wiggins. It was my suggestion, because I never did like Harmonica Phil Wiggins. John says in the liner notes, "The only difference between gospel and blues is subject matter." There is a song of John playing with the iconic jazz guitarist Tal Farlow. The clarinetist Don Rouse is on this album. His wife Sandy Rouse worked for the State Department. She was a friend of Dr. Barry Lee Pearson who years earlier booked us on the international tours to Africa and South America. I used to have a New Year's Day party where we would have knock-down-drag-out jam sessions until sunup. Don came and jammed with us on those a few times and he sounded good. I thought yeah, we should have him on the session. Dr. Julia Olin, who is now the director of the NCTA, actually sang on the album with her lovely voice. She is a good singer who had a career as a musician and she played in Nashville. She was singing on the song "Standing at Judgment."

My song "Evil Twin Blues" is credited to J. Cephas of J.C. Inc., which is a lie, because I wrote that song. It gives me credit in the small print, but on the song list they assigned it to John. That song was about my ex-wife, Wendy, who is a Gemini. If you listen to it, it's in a way a comical song, and John sang it like it's a real serious knock-down-drag-out blues song. He didn't realize it was sort of a joke, but the way he sings it, it's real tragic sounding. John had a beautiful, beautiful voice, and he never connected with or cared much about lyrics. I always said he could take your grocery list and sing it to you and it would sound beautiful. In the liner notes, Jim Squires wrote:

> It would be hard to believe that so few people could make so much music if one of them were not Wiggins, who can turn a tiny little harmonica into an orchestra; an unaccompanied mouth harp, no matter how good the mouth, often sounds like a one-legged man tap-dancing. On this album, especially on "Blue Day Blues," Wiggins' harmonica has two legs. And his prowess as a composer—long one of the great strengths of this duo—adds another dimension to their diversity.

This was a fun recording session with all those musicians. All of them—including Daryl Davis—were people I enjoyed playing with.

We recorded *Bluesmen* on the Chesky label in 1993, recorded by Bob Katz, executive producer Norman Chesky.[14] The CD cover is one of the first and only pictures on any of the albums that shows me without a hat. We left the Flying Fish label after three successful and critically acclaimed albums after the owner Bruce Kaplan died. Now we named ourselves John Cephas and Phil Wiggins. Chesky was an audiophile label with like real cutting-edge recording techniques. We were the first acoustic blues recording they ever did—and possibly the only one because their focus was classical and jazz. To me, in terms of recording experiences it was like one of the best ones I can remember and the album is one of my personal favorites. We drove up to New York and they took us to the basement of a church, where they had a custom-built microphone and they spent about an hour getting us in the right position around this microphone. They also had a small PA system with a couple of microphones set up for ambient noise from the room. Once they set all that up, and turned it all on, they left. We just sat there and played for about two hours. When we were done playing they turned it off and that was it. That's how that recording was done. I feel like it was great, because it was the closest thing to a live recording. The only thing missing was an audience. It was my favorite record of all the ones done. It was just fun and the feeling was good, and it just felt natural and it wasn't all this separation and the normal studio retakes over and over. We just did it boom, boom, boom—one song after the other—one take for each one, and then we were done. John was more natural in this recording environment, and more easygoing. I don't know if he was conscious of it, but definitely there was nothing difficult about it at all, whereas the other sessions there was always some difficulty.

I always wanted to do a live recording with John, and we never did do that. I know we're on some anthologies where they have a couple of tracks that were live, but I felt like for our duo that it was pretty impossible to capture the energy that we had or the level that we played at on a stage—I felt like it was impossible to capture that in a studio. I regret that we never did a whole live album. This is as close as it ever came to it.

After the recording, we spent the night in a hotel and the next day we had to go to the office of the record label to pick up a rough tape. Then we took a cab back to the airport and we stopped by the studio. We drove over there, and I held the cab until John came back with the tape. Uncharacteristically, I started up a conversation with the taxi driver. It turns out he was right from my grandmother's neighborhood in Titusville, Alabama. Out of all the cab drivers in New York City I happened to be sitting in a cab with a guy who was very familiar with Mr. Fortune's grocery store and Maddie Pearl, who lived two doors down from me, and knew my Uncle Wilson—he didn't know the rest of them, but he knew Uncle Wilson, because Uncle Wilson was always in the street, always running, making trouble. He knew Mr. Fortune, he knew Maddie Pearl—he knew all these people that I grew up with. It was just a crazy, crazy coincidence.

In 1995 we released our first Alligator Records album, *Cool Down*.[15] This was our debut on a label that Joe Wilson got us signed to. We owe so much to our association with the NCTA and to Joe Wilson, our producer, mentor, and friend. The gigs that Joe Wilson organized, playing at the national festivals and touring, were some of our best and most important gigs and got us the most recognition. We got a lot of good work and a lot of good recognition from the NCTA and from Joe's efforts. He orchestrated us to get on the prestigious Alligator label. We had been recording on a shoestring and on small labels.

I recall that we were at a festival playing in Chicago and Bruce Iglauer was there and Joe Wilson, and we had finished playing and people were flocking to the sales tent to buy our recording. I think we sold our Marimac reissues on cassette, a tiny label that had little or no distribution. People were flocking in to buy them up. Joe Wilson jockeyed Bruce to be in close proximity so he could see all that commerce going on. Bruce did in fact notice it, and he said, "Who owns this recording?" Joe said, "Well, right now they own it." That's what piqued Bruce Iglauer's interest in recording us, and that's how we got on that label. But we did them for Alligator, but we never did them in Chicago. Basically, John and I were one of the only groups or artists that produced our own recording and then sold it to Alligator. They are still one of the top blues labels in the world, and it was a big deal. We had met Bruce Iglauer on the road here and there at festivals, but didn't spend much time with him. A couple of times when we played for the Chicago Blues Fest we ran into him, but at that time we never went to their offices. All of our Alligator work was recorded locally and Bruce was not around. I was glad to meet him. I met him when I played with Ann Rabson on her record for Alligator, *Two-Fisted Mama*, when Bruce was actually in the room for those recording sessions. Honestly, at the time when we did those Cephas & Wiggins Alligator albums I felt like they were overproduced, dripping with reverb and all this stuff, and they all had a similar feel to them—almost homogenized. When I recorded with Ann Rabson, I felt like Bruce's input at the time of the recording was helpful and I appreciated it. He had good taste and good artistic input.

Alligator is as close as it gets to "major label" in the blues. They have international distribution and are a highly respected blues label out of Chicago. Getting on that label was a major career step for us. I know when we first dealt with Alligator, Bruce Iglauer, the president of Alligator Records, wanted to participate in order to make it a good record, and to do it under his umbrella, but John Cephas wanted to do it himself and then just send the finished tape to Bruce. I didn't have that much to do with it, wasn't in on it, but I know that's what John insisted on, and Alligator went along with it. I wrote the title cut "Cool Down," which continued the thing of my original songs being title cuts.

"Cool Down"

Well this morning's headlines read, four more precious children dead
Before one drop is shed, cool down

Chorus: Cool down—cool down. You better let your blood cool down

Your hair-trigger temper wakes and your trigger finger aches
That's such a bad mistake just cool down

Chorus
You've got your turf staked out and you want no shadow of doubt
So you're trying to take all the doubters out, well cool down

Chorus
Well the law is on the run, it seems like all god's children got guns
Kingdom come, thy will be done, cool down

I wrote this song in the early '80s when Washington, DC, was the homicide capital of the U.S. I was working with kids in the Anacostia neighborhood, which at the time was one of the most dangerous neighborhoods in Washington. At that time, they were debating the waiting period for gun purchases. Police were upgrading their weaponry in order to compete with the kids' arsenal. I got in a cab one morning with a Jamaican cab driver and we were talking about the debate over the waiting period to buy guns. He said, in his thick Jamaican brogue, "At least give a man time to let his blood cool down," and I stole that line. Grand larceny is my most often deployed writing device.

"Action Man" was written by Joe Wilson, whose idea of being producer was to sit around and write bad songs while we were working. On the CD sleeve, it's credited to Cephas & Wiggins but Joe Wilson wrote that song. I didn't want anything to do with it and didn't want my name on it. I wrote "No Ice in My Bourbon," and "The Blues Will Do Your Heart Good," so I had a few on this album. Mike Joyce of the *Washington Post* said, "Cephas's commanding voice and expert guitar work, coupled with Wiggins's soul-stirring harmonica, make for a familiar but compelling combination."

There was an album *Going Down the Road Feeling Bad* on Evidence in 1998.[16] This album was an "unauthorized" compilation issued by Evidence. Of course, it was legally licensed, but not authorized or known by us. They took our songs off previously published albums, used our names and likeness on the cover, and generally used our material without our knowledge or permission. One day we just came across this album and John was livid, whether there was a legal basis or not. Somehow, he settled with the label for a whole set of just about every album they had ever issued. It was better than having a lawsuit, but I never saw a dime from it and they are still selling the album to this day.

Things just kept getting better. In 1999 we performed at the White House for President Clinton, Hillary Clinton, and many invited guests. The president hosted an annual party inviting various musicians to perform, and he liked and supported the blues. B.B. King was always the star. I think that Joe Wilson, then director of the NCTA, had a hand in getting us invited as local DC musicians. It was me and John Cephas, B.B. King, Johnny Lang; and Della Reese was the host. We spent two full days at the White House on this major production. Day one was a complete dress rehearsal of the whole show twice in one day and then once the next day. Then we came back and did the evening of the second day. For me it was great. I was young and just happy and amazed and honored to be there and able to spend two whole days of my life hanging around with B.B. King. It was just unbelievable.

John Cephas and I had known B.B. for quite a while, John more so than me. B.B. and John were closer to each other's generation than myself and they just had this connection as two comrades or two kindred spirits. They both had a gravitas. John respected B.B., even though he was not awestruck, but in a way, he definitely acknowledged that he was in the presence of one of the blues icons, and he definitely didn't consider himself on that same level. They connected well as people and musicians. We had performed with B.B. King before, including at Towson State University back in 1986. I was a bit anxious to play this White House gig, but B.B. just put me at ease without saying or doing anything, through his vibes. He was very calm and he calmed me down. I liked talking to

him and hanging with him, glad to meet him—just to chill with B.B., who ema-
nated a powerful and calming balance. The funny thing was that my daughters
were excited to meet him and all, but they were much calmer than I was. B.B.
was easygoing and a true gentleman throughout the whole process. It was a
long, hard couple of days of playing—doing everything full out—no shortcuts.
There was no like, "Okay, we're going to do a sound check and then first we'll do
this song and then we'll move to what happens next." We had to play everything
all the way through, beginning to end, multiple times because they had to work
out all the camera angles, to get everything nailed down exactly. B.B. wasn't a
young guy at the time, but he was just a Buddha who took the whole thing in
stride. That was great and he was very sweet and kind with my daughters. To be
honest, my kids were more excited about B.B. King than they were about meeting Bill and Hillary. John and I played with B.B. in the finale. John and I were
his rhythm section. I don't think Johnny Lang was there. I think Della Reese
actually sang with us.

We traveled with B.B. King's band from the hotel to the White House and
through the security. It was fun just spending time with those guys—old road
warriors. They were laughing and joking the whole time. The first day we pulled
up to the White House, and the guards opened the gates to let us in to this one
area. The Secret Service had this German shepherd dog sniffing all around the
van for bombs or explosives. The German shepherd was gray around the snout.
One of those guys in B.B.'s band looked at him and said, "Hmm, that's a government dog." And the other guy said, "Yeah, he's going to draw a pension." As we
got through the dog sniffing and past all these heavy-duty Secret Service guys,
each one of them like a walking fortress, big old 6-foot-4 guys with broad shoul-
ders and black Kevlar on strapping automatic weapons.

We got to meet Bill and Hillary and had a chance to speak to them. I was
surprised to learn that Martha had already met Hillary because she had been to
Martha's school. The Clintons were down to earth, friendly and very nice. You
could tell they were music lovers, especially from watching Bill's reaction while
we were playing. There was one time in particular after one of my harmonica
solos that he gave me a thumbs-up gesture. That was exciting.

Right around that time we had a crazy incident at John Jackson's house.
This guy from New York was making a documentary film about Larry Johnson, the fingerpicker who sometimes came down to DC. Once he crashed our
gig at Carnegie Hall. He was there at John Jackson's house at a picnic and a
fight broke out between two of the other guests. I come to find out later that
it was all about this guy and he had a friend his own age, and he thought that
the friend was hitting on his way young daughter. They had some fierce argument about that and the one guy told his friend to leave her alone, and then he
found out that he hadn't left her alone. He pulled out a knife and cut the other

guy. He got him across the neck or across the face and the guy was bleeding profusely and panic ensued. All the women were screaming and getting towels to mop up the blood. The filmmakers didn't expect anything like that. Larry Johnson said, "Let's get the hell out of here," and his crew packed up out of there so quickly and they left in a huff. I guess hanging around these country people in real life was not what they expected. They came in to let Larry look good, like an authentic country bluesman, and instead they were cutting each other. Larry just took off out of there. I don't know whatever happened to the film they were making.

We recorded the album *Homemade* on Alligator Records in 1999.[17] This time we went into the studio with material that we were not familiar with, we learned and rehearsed in the studio. This album is probably the epitome of that. John Vengrouskie was a guy who Joe Wilson knew, who lived in a house that was owned by the Park Service. He was a real eccentric guy, and we went out to his place, a nice old house, real funky with stuff thrown all over the place. It wasn't very clean. He was an eccentric guy. We also recorded at Pete Reiniger's house.

In this session, we didn't know the songs that well. There were a couple of songs on there that were written by other people that weren't very good songs. The one John wrote, "I Was Determined"—I honestly never thought that was a very good song. I remember those sessions just basically being miserable and looking forward to when they were over.

Another album was *From Richmond to Atlanta* on Bullseye Blues in 2000. This was a compilation album comprised of reissue cuts from our Flying Fish years, a collection of older material pieced together. Frank John Headley wrote in the liner notes: "All through the album Wiggins's trusty Marine Band furnishes splendid responses to his cohort's guitar and vocals. To these ears he proves his mettle on the old Piedmont dance tune 'Richmond Blues' and on a deliciously fey version of Skip James's 'Cherryball' . . ." and "'The blues is uplifting music,' says Wiggins with characteristic cheeriness. 'It's what the blues is all about. It is music to rejuvenate you and to nourish the spirit.'" Anyway, since there is no law broken by a reissue—that's what this is.

We started off the new millennium with a bang and in 2001 we played a major blues festival in Tokyo, the Park Tower Blues Festival, on the bill with New Orleans musicians George Porter, the bass player for the Meters, and Earl King. It was a hugely successful concert. The Japanese audience loved our playing. I remember people going nuts. Chicago bluesman John Primer was there and gospel singers the Five Blind Boys of Mississippi. The funny thing was, while we were there Bernard Purdie showed up, the drummer with King Curtis.

He was this iconic rhythm and blues drummer who called himself Bernard "Pretty" Purdie. He was a very dapper and well-coifed guy, very much the ladies' man. John at that time was like a reformed smoker and you know how reformed smokers are. Somebody had a cigarette, and Bernard Purdie pulled the lighter out of his pocket. John said snidely, "You smoke?" Purdie goes, "No, I don't smoke. I just like to have a lighter to light the ladies' cigarettes." There was also this young guy, a twenty-one-year-old prodigy drummer playing with the Running Partners. He was phenomenal. I was sitting backstage with Bernard Purdie, and we're both watching this guy with our jaws on the ground, and Bernard says, "Well, I used to give him lessons when he was nine years old, but he done left home."

For me, in Japan I felt like I was way too physically big and took up way too much space the whole time I was there. Tokyo is a very crowded place and the people are in general much smaller than me. We were in this pretty fancy modern hotel and the hallways had this ambient lighting—dimly lit and atmospheric. I came out of my room, and there was a maid backing out of the room across the hall, pulling a cart, and she almost backed into me. She accidentally bumped into me and she turned around and she screamed and jumped about two feet off the ground. There was this big black man! There are two funny things that surprised me. When a Japanese person is reading English, they switch the l's and r's, and they do it like pretty consistently. When they wrote in English, like the English menu instead of "blocks" of tofu, they would write "brocks" of tofu. They would not only pronounce it, but they would actually switch it in writing—they would switch the l's and the r's. This was a big fancy hotel, it seems like they could have hired a consultant to tell them it's blocks with an l, not brocks. The reason I brought that up is because John Primer was singing, "Hey, hey, the blues is all right" and getting the audience to sing along. I was thinking to myself, I bet they're switching that—and sure enough they're all singing, "Hey, the brues is all light." I'm like yeah!

Another album on Alligator was *Somebody Told the Truth*, 2002.[18] "The Pimp in the Pink Suit" is about a guy, a DC character. I never saw him, but apparently when John was growing up there was a pimp in his neighborhood that drove a pink Cadillac and had a matching pink suit and all. And it captured both John's and Joe's imagination, and then Joe wrote this silly song, "Tell It to the Pimp in the Pink Suit."

My original song "Burn Your Bridges" is on this, an instrumental, it's a harmonica showoff song. That's also the first time my song "Forgiveness" appears on record. I wrote that song and John and I were working on it and John played it, but John just couldn't hit it. We recorded it twice. We recorded it at that session, and the first time we played it live was at Augusta and I liked that recording of it, and I wanted that recording to be on the album. But Joe went ahead and put that other one on there. The funny thing was that I was pissed that he did that, but then it turned out to be a lot better than I thought, and I was glad that he did that.

"Forgiveness"

I took a long trip south on the whiskey train.
I took Jesus' name in vain
I blew a fortune on cocaine
and I caused my own family heartbreak and shame
When I was just near about to go insane
I found forgiveness.

Chorus
Forgiveness poured down like rain on the sun scorched land
Forgiveness rushed in like air to a drowning man,
forgiveness like home from a journey of a thousand miles,
forgiveness like milk and honey to a starving child.

I let bad blood force my hand.
Revenge caused me to harm my fellow man
When the time came to pay the consequences I ran
and I ran and I ran and I ran and I ran
When my luck ran out and they had me in hand,
I found forgiveness.

Chorus
I've heard it said that an honest man is worth his weight in gold.
I'm just thinking about the many lies I've told
My reputation has been bought and sold.
I made a midnight deal at the lonesome crossroads
When they came knocking for my soul, I found forgiveness.

John did a piece with the jazz guitarist Tal Farlow, "Darkness on the Delta" with John Stewart on rhythm guitar. It was fun to do the Piedmont classic "Railroad Bill" and Skip James's "Sick Bed Blues," which John liked playing, as well as Robert Johnson's "Last Fair Deal Gone Down."

In 2002 we issued *Shoulder to Shoulder*, again on Alligator Records.[19] That was a shitty session. I remember being miserable the whole time. We weren't ready to make a good recording. I was happy to have Ann on there, but for some reason John and Joe didn't like her performance on the recording. Andrew Volpe, John's girlfriend's son, wasn't a very experienced blues bass player. He was a rock and fusion style player. I don't know why John wanted him on the session but he didn't fit in. He would walk out in the middle of a take to take a cigarette break. He had all kinds of issues. He's doing good now, but at that time he was a mess.

"Ain't Seen My Baby" is credited as a John Cephas song—"Ain't Seen My Baby, the evening sun's going down"—I don't know who wrote that one but it wasn't John. He wrote "I Did Do Right" but I never thought it was a very good song. "All I've Got Is Them Blues" was credited as a Cephas and Diamond song. I don't want to dish dirt on John, but he wasn't always accurate when he gave songwriting credit to people. There was a woman named Diamond and she wrote that song. John put his name on it and actually she got angry about that, because I mean she wrote that song straight up. It's not a great song anyway.

The album was also well received in the blues world. *Living Blues* said Cephas & Wiggins "remain today's premier blues guitar and harmonica duo." The *Washington Post* said, "Remarkable guitar and harmonica duets. Their infectious rhythms and supple melodies combine tasteful fingerpicking with impassioned harmonica solos."

That was our last hurrah with Alligator. Our last album together was on Smithsonian Folkways, *Richmond Blues*, Smithsonian Folkways, 2008.[20] This was our last album together. I remember being pretty miserable and not that into it and feeling like it wasn't that good. And, honestly, at the time I said to myself—and I never said this out loud to anyone—I thought that would be my last recording, because I felt this was not going anywhere musically. I felt like we were just going through the motions. I didn't feel at all connected to the songs, or excited about them, or that we were putting that much feeling into it. It's funny, but when listening to it today it sounds so good.

By 2003 I was living with Judy LaPrade, who I had met at the Augusta Blues Week. We had a house on Kennebec Avenue in Takoma Park, Maryland, about a block and a half from where we live now. It was this cute little one-floor, one-bedroom house sitting way back from the road, so that as you pass by it on the street or on the sidewalk you didn't know it was back there. The house had been built by landscapers and they planted all kinds of rhododendrons and mountain laurel in the yard. From the front, all you could see was a jungle of rhododendrons with giant blossoms that you don't often see in people's yards. It was beautiful back there. We had a real nice wooden gazebo with a hot tub in it like a nestle deck. When we were buying the house, we had a friend who was a contractor who was supposed to help us inspect the house. He walked around with his little pencil and pad and didn't say much of anything—and he gave us the go-ahead to buy it. It turned out that what we didn't know was that the house was basically built on a cement slab with like no rebar or anything, and it was a foundation that it was built on, and directly in the pathway of a creek. For the first couple of years that we lived there we didn't notice anything, except that when it rained we would notice that there was water standing in our yard.

A neighbor had cut down all the trees and put up a parking lot, and the water just ran off his place into ours, and after a while we noticed that when it rained there would be several feet of water in our backyard. Eventually, we figured out that the water was running underneath of our house, causing a shift so that it wasn't sitting on a flat surface. Then pipes would burst, and the foundation was giving out and starting to sink. The framing of the house would rest on the pipes and break the joints, and that's what was causing that. And after a while there was a big crack and it got to the point where we had to turn the water off. We could only turn it on for a little while each day to fill pots and buckets because the pipes were always bursting. It was just a big mess. Because it was our home we dealt with it, and much of our belongings were damaged. I lost a collection of precious photos and albums. My photographs were all gone, the documentation of my whole career, just ruined due to mold and mildew from all the moisture from the leaking.

One day our friends Paul Watson, a harmonica player, and his wife Judy Watson, a good piano player, came over for dinner because we hadn't seen them in a while. They confronted us with what we tried not to face up to, stating, "You know, you need to move from here. This is ridiculous." We knew they were right. At that point Judy was working in Willow Street Yoga as a massage therapist, and one of the women that worked in the office had a nice little wood house, and she let us stay there for the summer. At first, we didn't know what we were going to do about our house because we still had a mortgage and all. We ended up putting it on the market and we sold it for the property value as a tear-down so we could pay down the mortgage and get out from under that debt. Of course, we didn't have a house at that point. We moved into this, a one-bedroom apartment that we're living in now. The people who bought it tore the house down and rebuilt. And those folks who tore down the trees and caused the drainage problem said, "Oh, good, when they tear it down and build a new house, that's going to make our property values go up." Once we moved out and the house was full of our stuff and we were having to pack it all up and put it in storage, the guy across the street came and stole a bunch of shit out of our garage—bicycles and tools and things like that. So that was the neighbors in that neighborhood.

Of course, the insurance company, their job is to deny any responsibility. They count on people suing to make them do what they're supposed to do. Unfortunately, we didn't have the money to hire a lawyer. We had flood insurance, but not "the right flood insurance." "We don't cover that" was their answer. We didn't get a penny. Because property values were so high we were able to pay off the mortgage, but we walked away with nothing. We did a benefit concert to raise some money to just cover the expenses of moving. I remember talking to a friend that day, and I said, "You know, it's a pretty bad situation, but nobody died. We lost our house, but I didn't lose my home, because that woman over there, that's my home." It was great that many people showed up to support us and help us to make this transition and we appreciated it, but in the scheme of things all we lost was a house.

In 2004 I played on an album *The Prodigal Son*, by the great DC blues man Memphis Gold. His real name is name Chester Chandler. On this album, he was joined by local musicians, bassists Willie Hicks and Larry Self, and the harmonica player Charlie Sayles, a local acquaintance with whom I shared the stage several times. The Nighthawks' drummer Pete Raguso was also on the record.

This was also the time when Lynn Volpe came into John's life. The first time I met her was when she came over to our house with John. She came into the kitchen, the epicenter of where the crack that extended from the kitchen through the living room. And Lynn walked through and said, "Whoa, this is like a funhouse." And I'm like, "It's not that much fun, Lynn."

John had diabetes and he was not taking care of himself. During that time, he was an angry, paranoid person and it was hard for people to get close to him. I don't know what put the fear of God in him, but at a certain point he quit drinking for a while. About this time, because we were at Augusta and the day before the last day of the teaching week we would go to this real nice restaurant on the outskirts of Elkins, and I remember getting everybody to raise their water glass to John because he had gone through that whole week without having a drink. I realized how difficult that was for him and I wanted everybody to acknowledge that. We drank a water wagon toast. He got in better shape and was a nicer person so people could stand to be around him, and he got himself a new girlfriend. He called me up and he said, "Phil, I got a girlfriend. She's two-thirds Japanese." "John, how does that work? How can she be two-thirds Japanese?" He didn't explain it—but that was just one of John's expressions. We had been on one of those Masters of the Steel String Guitar tours and he cracked his toe. Because of the diabetes it wouldn't heal. He eventually had to have that toe amputated. Lynn worked at the doctor's office and that's how they met. John had already split from his wife. At the same time, she was very attracted to him and she told me that because he was such a neat person and sharp dresser and all, that when he first started coming there she thought he was gay. He asked her out because she had been flirting with him hard. It was great for me, because by that time making music with John and doing business with him was difficult.

Lynn was a reasonable person and she kept John organized and she kept me apprised of what was going on. She basically was the line of communication between me and John, and that was great for me. I was glad to see John happy and doing better and taking better care of himself. But the main thing was I was appreciative of having Lynn because she helped me to deal with the business of working with John. John at a certain point also just pushed his first family and grown children out of his life. He just didn't want to be bothered with them anymore. When he died, he left them nothing and he left everything to Lynn. Whatever happened in his personal life, he set his children up to be angry and bitter and to be in a position where they were not able to get any closure from him. John's wishes were very clearly stated. It seemed like he reached a certain point in his life where he just didn't want to be bothered by them anymore and he pushed them away. That's a terrible thing to say, but it's what I saw. He didn't want them to come visit him.

My own daughters had graduated from high school and Martha moved with their mom to New Bedford, Massachusetts. Eliza had just left home and moved to California. It was hard for me when they moved away. I went to visit Martha in New Bedford a couple of times. At this time in my life I wanted to explore playing with some other musicians and to explore some different music. In all of my travels with John to festivals and gigs all over the country and all over the world that I thought it would be fun to play with others. I reached out to a whole bunch of them but I have not made that happen in that time. One guy I had thought about playing with was Don Vappie, the New Orleans banjo, guitar, and mandolin player.

I was with him and a bunch of other Louisiana people in Bangor, Maine, when Hurricane Katrina hit and I got to know him from being at different festivals. His wife was there with him. After that Katrina disaster, Don and I would go to play at the festival and she stayed in the hotel and just watched CNN. It was a terrible event and it took those people a very long time to get back home, and some of them never did get back home because their homes were destroyed. That's how I got to know Don Vappie, and he said yes. I also wanted to play with the Holmes Brothers. I was thinking it would be great to have them sing backup and harmony on some of my songs. Over the years after that, they'd say, "When are we going to do that, Phil?" Sherman Holmes still talks about it, but I never managed to pull enough money together to fund such a project, to pay for the studio time and all that. I never had enough to spend on that, rather than paying rent and child support and health insurance. Don Vappie came out to Centrum a couple of times, and we spent time playing together.

We were at this place called Garth Newel, in the western side of Virginia in the Blue Ridge Mountains at a high elevation, and John started complaining. Well, for one thing, we got there and John was doing his typical freak-out, because no one was there to meet us and we were trying to find our rooms. John was going up and down these stairs and getting agitated. We had an early day gig and when we were done we planned to spend the night in that beautiful place. But John wasn't feeling well and said, "I'm short of breath. I can't breathe. We need to get out of here. I need to go home." We went home and then the next week he went to the doctor and they told him that he had pulmonary fibrosis and that there was no treatment or cure for that. They also told him that he needed to stop performing and traveling.

I think we did one or two gigs after that, and that was that, he stopped performing in 2007. I remember the last gig we had after he was diagnosed and they said that he shouldn't be performing. He did it anyway. I felt like it was a good gig. A friend of mine videotaped it, and when I watched it I realized how out of breath John was. It was in Ashland, Virginia, at the Ashland Coffee and Tea concert venue. Tim Kaine was there, the governor of Virginia, who was later the vice-presidential running mate with Hillary Clinton. I remember standing next to him, talking to him. None of us knew that this was going to be our last gig. He only lived for two years after that—maybe not even that long. He was diagnosed and then he was quickly gone. I remember him saying that he didn't want anyone to come see him. In 2009 John won the Library of Virginia African American Trailblazer Award. He couldn't go to accept it, so I went to accept it with Rick Franklin in Richmond. At that time, I hadn't seen John in a while, because he didn't want visitors. They had made an acceptance video for this event of him sitting in his living room talking. It was a real shock to me to see him in that condition, to see how much worse he had gotten. It was heartbreaking to realize how quickly his health had declined over the past couple years. I was with him all the time and I didn't notice it.

Shortly after that Lynn called me up, said, "If you want to see John, you better start heading this way." Barry Lee and I hopped in the car, and we got to his house fifteen minutes after he had passed on. We arrived too late. When we got there a bunch of his family, his daughters and their husbands, were hanging out in the front yard and we got there and we went in and a couple of his daughters came in behind us, came in with us, and they immediately started getting into an argument with Lynn, claiming she won't let them see John. The hospice nurse was with Lynn, and she explained that there were certain things that needed to do be done in preparation before anyone could see him. That was proper and also what his wishes were. But they were getting in Lynn's face. I stepped in between them and I said, "You know, I don't know, I'm not picking sides with anyone, but right at this moment is not the time for you to be confronting her about anything." They heard me and backed off. Then Lynn came to me and said, "Well, you know, he doesn't have a shirt on and we're not strong enough to lift him up. You've got to come and lift him up so we can get his shirt on." I went in and he was laying there dead, and I lifted him from the waist up and we laid him back down. It was a natural thing in a way—felt good to be useful one last time for my friend and partner. The mourning was hard, because John and I had spent a lifetime together. I was in the deep shock and sadness of mourning.

I think that his illness was caused by his work at the Armory. When I first met John, he was a pretty heavy smoker, but they say that smoking does not cause pulmonary fibrosis Particulate pollution causes it, like breathing in sawdust and fumes, the stuff he was working with as a carpenter all the way into the 1990s. They had OSHA and all that, but John never paid much attention to that stuff. I'd go in and see him working at his shop at the Armory and he wasn't wearing a mask.

John did not want a funeral. His last wishes were to be cremated and Lynn arranged that, but his family went to the funeral home and collected his remains and they took them and had a funeral anyway. They buried him somewhere down near Occoquan, Virginia. I didn't go to that because that's not what John wanted and I've never gone to where they buried his remains. I mean, my whole thing about death is that it doesn't make sense at all to make a big fuss about once the life is gone what is left behind. I remember for example when Flora Molton passed. I'm not a person that will go to a funeral and go up to the open casket and gawk over the remains, whatever they are left behind when a life leaves. It's not important to me and that's not how I want to remember someone. I don't want that image. When I went to Flora's funeral, there was some woman, Kate, and she was like, "Phil, go look at her." I was like, "Kate, I'm not going to do that." She wouldn't let it go. She just kept bugging me—"Go look at her." I know that John did not want a funeral so I did not go. Jon Lohman went to that funeral and he told me that they did have an open casket, which was absolutely against what John wanted.

We held a memorial celebration for John at the Smithsonian on March 29, 2009. The memorial was at the Baird Auditorium of the Smithsonian Museum of Natural History at 10th and Constitution Avenue, N.W. There was a house party jam/reception after the memorial at Westminster Presbyterian Church at 400 I Street, S.W. I was in the house band with Mark Puryear on guitar, Harold Anderson on bass, and Daryl Davis on keyboards. Rick Franklin, Eleanor Ellis, Diamond Jim Greene came from Chicago, David Lay, and Dudley Connell performed. I did a set with Corey Harris and one with Rick Franklin. Bill Wax of XM Radio was MC and Barry Lee Pearson gave the eulogy. Speakers included Barry Bergey from the National Endowment for the Arts; Daniel Sheehy, Director and Curator of the Smithsonian Folkways; and Bruce Iglauer—founder, owner, and operator of Alligator Records.

Rick Franklin and I we were playing music as the people were coming in. Corey Harris and I had been scheduled to play. The reason why I asked him that because in my mind I thought it would be best that after I finished speaking that the very next thing that people hear is music. During the ceremony, I talked about how much he loved gardening, and about how John, for a person that traveled all over the world, was uncomfortable a few miles down I-95 away from home. And that the very best John was John in his garden and that nothing in life excited or made him happier than putting a seed in the ground and watching it grow—and that he had also planted seeds all over the world with his music and that I've seen those seeds take root and sprout and bear fruit, and that fruit falls and those seeds take root and produce more sprouts and on and on. The way I set it up was as a continuing cycle so that it would be natural just to have music.

Sometime after his death I wrote a song for John, and these feelings emerged:

"Goodbye, goodbye, goodbye"

The full moon smiles so bright and high
The next night the moon is about to cry
Me and the moon hate long goodbyes
Goodbye, goodbye, goodbye
Goodbye, goodbye, goodbye

The sunset is such a fancy show
I guess the sun just hates to go
If only she knew like I know
So long, dry long so
So long, dry long so

I bid fare ye well to my good friend
I know someday we'll meet again
And he will greet me with a grin
Come in, come in, come in
Come in, come in, come in

After John's death Lynn shared some sweet things with me. John had told her that he felt that the best years of his life were touring, recording, and making music with me. That warmed my heart. She also exposed me to some of the bitter blues, some of the stuff that was going on where I wasn't included in some of the royalty payments and business dealings. Right after John passed Lynn was very generous with me. She shared a certain amount of money with me from John's estate, but there were things that I discovered—especially in terms of who was credited with writing certain songs that hurt me. John was not a songwriter. John maybe wrote two songs during the time that we were playing together: "Back Biter Blues" and "I Was Determined." Other than that, he never wrote any songs. I was writing songs the whole time we were playing together, most of which never made it onto our set list, but I did have maybe about a dozen songs that we played, like "Roberta" and "Guitar Man." When we first started playing together, I was writing these songs and I would go to the

Library of Congress and register them. I felt like I'm writing these songs, we're doing them together—I registered them under Phil Wiggins and John Cephas, and I put his name on them too. That was a mistake on my part. John and I, we were happy making music together and I never considered that there would be any problem. Unbeknownst to me, John was communicating with Alligator and would credit himself as songwriter. Now, in terms of what Alligator knows or believes, John Cephas wrote "Roberta." They have that down wrong. I think some of the other songs, too. Financially, I don't know that anyone is making any money off it, but it's just a big disappointment for me to discover that he would do that.

Right around the time of John's death, we were working with the Mid-Atlantic booking agency through the Maryland state government. They had booked a bunch of Cephas & Wiggins concerts for which they had gotten grants. When John couldn't do the gigs anymore, some of the concert venues backed out, but some of them honored those contracts with me, and whoever I brought with me. I did most of them with Corey Harris and a couple with Rick Franklin. That lasted a long while. After those gigs ended, I was still with Piedmont Talent at the time and they weren't getting any other offers. After a while when those gigs from the grants ended, things got slow. I realized that I had to start over. I was doing some stuff with Nat Reese and Reverend John Wilkins. Reverend Wilkins and I went to Portugal together. I was able to piece together some stuff, but it got scarce. Locally, I played with Rick Franklin and Eleanor Ellis. Rick and I played the Bristol Rhythm and Roots Festival. I was still working off and on with the Art Drama Therapy Institute with adults with intellectual disabilities, and I was doing some harmonica seminars.

After losing my lifelong musical partner it was naturally difficult to deal with mourning a friend, someone so close in my life. Basically, I was just trying to move forward and I came to the realization that mourning is not a linear process. It's not a process of going through these stages and then you're done. It seemed more like it was in cycles of mourning. I was, moving forward, going around, and now circled back again. I still feel like that. I'm still going through cycles of dealing with that loss. It has to do with John, with missing him as a person and a friend, and also missing him as a musician. I still haven't met anyone that is as strong a musician as he was. I don't know if I ever will. After his death, I also had to figure out what to do from there, where to take my career and how to survive and thrive.

I had to start all over—alone.

Cephas & Wiggins during their first European tour with the American Folk Blues Festival in 1981.
Photo by Axel Küstner.

Cephas & Wiggins, 1982. Photo by Axel Küstner.

Cephas & Wiggins at B.B. King's Blues Club on 42nd St. in New York City, 1999. This photo is on display at the Smithsonian National Museum of African American History and Culture. Photo by Bibiana Huang Matheis.

John Cephas at B.B. King's Blues Club on 42nd St. in New York City, 1999. Photo by Bibiana Huang Matheis.

Cephas & Wiggins on tour in Germany, 1999. Photo by Axel Küstner.

With President Bill Clinton at the White House Oval Office, 1999. Public domain. White House Press Office.

Phil Wiggins and John Cephas with B.B. King, 1999. Public domain. White House Press Office.

John Cephas and Valerie Turner backstage at Madison Park in New York City, 2007. Photo by Lynn Volpe.

John Cephas teaching a seminar in Dr. Barry Lee Pearson's course at the University of Maryland, c. 1982. Photo by Myron Samuels. Courtesy of Josh Samuels.

Phil Wiggins, Nat Reese, Etta Baker, and John Cephas at Augusta Blues Week, 1985. From the archives of the Augusta Heritage Center of Davi & Elkins College. Photo by Doug Yarrow. Courtesy of Phil Wiggins.

Chapter Three

CARRYING ON THE LEGACY ON MY OWN

The period after John's death was a time of turmoil, change, and, naturally, of self-reflection. To a certain point down the line, before John passed, after more than thirty years, I had admittedly been feeling tired of playing the same songs, the same old repertoire. Many musicians experience this sense of boredom and desire for something new and different. John was not expanding, not learning anything new. Every new song that I brought to him he shaved off the edges, and so we wound up playing different versions of "Black Rat Swing" over and over and over again. Admittedly, before he passed, I had lost interest. The passion sometimes wasn't there anymore. On most nights, I would have a hard time getting the energy up to play well because I felt bored by playing the same stuff over and over again. I've never told anybody that until now.

After John passed, I was just saying 'yes' to whoever rang my phone and that got me into all kinds of crazy things. The first thing I faced after John died was filling the obligation to perform at already contracted gigs, in a series of concerts for John and me, where the venue itself was raising part of the funds through grants. In some of those situations the grant was still being applied; other times they lost the grant because John had died, but they were still willing to fund the concert on their own.

As I suddenly found myself alone, I was reaching out to a lot of different people to explore musical opportunities and to try out new and interesting arrangements, and, I needed a partner to play these gigs with. During this period of playing on, I connected with various musical partners. At the same time, my life was complicated as I learned that I had a serious heart condition. Just before John died in 2009, I noticed symptoms of being short of breath, especially when I laid down, and chest congestion. I thought I had a cold or something and I was self-medicating. Someone gave me some antibiotics but then I hit a stretch right before John and I took a trip to South Carolina to play a blues festival in Salisbury. By the time we got there I hadn't slept in probably three nights. I called my sister who is a nurse. I told her my symptoms and she ordered me to go to the emergency room right away. She said that once I told them my symptoms they would not keep me waiting. I checked in and there was a room full of people waiting—and sure enough, five minutes later, "Mr. Wiggins?" They took my pulse and listened to my heart, and the next thing I knew I was lying in a gurney flying down the hall, watching the lights going over my head, like in a movie. The next thing I knew I'm in cardio intensive care. They told me I had congestive heart failure, atrial fibrillation, and cardiomyopathy. I figured that I would tell them my symptoms, they would just give me some pills, and I would go on and play my gig. While in the ICU it hadn't even sunk in enough for me to even be scared about it. It was all just comical to me. They gave me shots to drain the fluid out of my lungs and they kept me for four days. Then they said, "Go home and go to a cardiologist right away." I did that. The cardiologist said, "Well, you need a valve replacement. But your heart right now is too beat up to go through that. I'm going to put you on a regimen of blood thinner because it's dangerous what was going on with the heart." They put me on blood thinner and some other pills to regulate my heartbeat and blood pressure. They planned to do that for six months, and hopefully at the end of six months I'd be able to withstand the heart valve surgery. After six months, I went back in and they looked at my heart again and surprisingly said, "Well, you know, you're still an afib, but other than that your heart functions are normal. You don't need the surgery." I was very relieved about that. I still have afib and still take pills to regulate my heartbeat and take blood thinner and blood pressure medicine. I take Warfarin, which is basically rat poison, so to drink alcohol is toxic and foolish. But, I do drink a little and feel like I do it in moderation most of the time. I probably should eat a heart-healthy diet, less red meat. The funny thing is that I love greens, which you would think is healthy and a good habit; but it impacts my blood thinner, so I'm not supposed to eat them. Touring and playing for me in terms of that stuff is difficult anyway, because I never eat dinner. I try to make arrangements to have some food after the performance. Then of course you want to just relax, ventilate, have a drink, sit around with your friends and talk, and I'm usually not hungry by then. I skip a lot of meals.

Nonetheless, that didn't stop me and I had to carry on my work, to play on. Some of these gigs that John and I had booked, I played with Corey Harris, and that was interesting. It was great working with Corey as a musician. He is a very talented player. Most of the younger guys that I wound up working with after John didn't have the experience of coming up in house parties and gigs within the community where it was your job to lay down a rhythm that was big and fat enough so that people could dance to it over people laughing and talking and carrying on. So not having had that experience, a lot of them missed that strong sense of rhythm that John had. Corey was an exception to that, because he has a powerful rhythm. My own theory about that is it has to do with his strong connection with African music and particularly the West African guitar players. For him it was definitely about the rhythm.

Right after John passed and I was starting to play with all these other people, I realized several things. For one thing, I realized what a narrow comfort zone I had. Like playing with John, it was always one particular rhythm that I got good at. But when I was playing with Rick Franklin or with Corey Harris and other people, I was struggling to hit my stride. It was a great feeling, but it was also a rude awakening. I was used to this one thing, one way of playing, and so it was interesting to get all of a sudden thrown into the necessity of learning other people's rhythms. But it was great because it was new and fresh. I was expanding. For example, playing with Corey was refreshing. He has such a strong, loud voice in comparison to John's beautiful, soft warm voice. As a rule, when John was singing, my best job was to be as out of the way as possible and to help support the rhythm as much as possible. John had a little bit of a challenge with the rhythm, but also his voice was so pretty and soft, I didn't want to get in the way of it at all. I used harmonica as percussion whenever he was singing. Now playing with Corey, I could play in unison as long as I played softly, or I could play a countermelody or a counterpoint. It worked because it wouldn't overpower his voice as much as for the other people I had played with.

For me, working with other partners was naturally a learning experience. As Corey and I were working out songs together that was evident. John and I had a pattern of singing a couple of verses and then to take a verse as a solo, and then sing a couple more verses, and then maybe another couple of verses solo. I noticed that in playing with Corey that wasn't happening. My first impulse was to say, "Well, okay, now you sing a couple of verses in the beginning, and then you take a guitar break and then I take a harp break, and blah, blah, blah." But then I thought to myself, well, maybe I should be a little more open-minded about that instead of dictating what should happen, rather than make a statement to ask questions and see what develops naturally. So, basically, I said to Corey, you know, sometimes John and I, he would just give me a solo break. We went with doing that on some songs, but on a lot of it we did not. Corey said, "Yeah, that is not what I do." I could dig that, and it made more sense for a person coming from a much stronger connection with African and Delta blues styles. I just let it go like that and it developed into a cool thing where it wasn't so much about harmonica solos, but it was more about the overall groove, and to my liking it was more about the dance. It was more of an African approach to our music than a Western approach. I enjoyed that about working with Corey.

I first knew Nat Reese from Blues Week at Augusta. He was playing in a duo with Howard Armstrong for a little while. When he came to Augusta there was a young participant, Wim Stynen from Belgium, who just loved the music, especially John Jackson, Howard Armstrong, and Nat Reese. So, he put together a tour for us in Europe, in some of the former Eastern Bloc countries and part of the U.K. We toured Europe in 1995, it was John Cephas and me, Nat Reese and Howard Armstrong, Doug MacLeod, and John Mooney from New Orleans—a white slide guitarist with a real gravelly voice. On that tour, I got to know Nat Reese. Later, after John died, we did some recording together with Jon Lohman, the Virginia state folklorist and director of the Virginia Folklife Program at the Virginia Foundation for Humanities. I went down to Nat's house with him, and we did a few gigs. People who heard the recording praised it profusely, even though it was never released up until now, and hopefully it will see the light of day. What I remember most about that session was that we got to a hotel out there in Virginia, and Nat and his grandson Danny were staying in a room together and they both smoked like chimneys. I went in there in the afternoon one day and hung with them and rehearsed tunes with the plan of getting up the next morning to do more. The next morning, I could not physically make myself go to their room, because I couldn't stand the idea of breathing that smoke in there. I called them up, "No, I'm not coming. If you guys want to rehearse, we'll have to do it somewhere else—not in your room and not in my room." We also played at the West Virginia Music Hall of Fame in 2009 and at the Richmond Folk Festival in 2010.

Nat was a sweetheart of a person—just great, happy and generous—a pleasure to spend time with, and a great musician. At the point when I met him and got to play with him, he had forgotten more about music than I ever knew. He played all these great swing tunes, but he didn't play a good, clean, clear chord progression. You would hear the tune just boiled down to the essence of it. He played odd chords—a fistful of notes more than an actual chord. It was a learning process for me to play with him; but, like anything, if you keep your ears open you can work it out. You just have to listen and figure out what your best contribution could be—what's the best thing that you can add at a particular time, whether it's just rhythm chops or melody. I love all those old swing tunes and torch songs and stuff that he did, but I wasn't good at it—but I got pretty good at faking my way through them. It wasn't until after he passed on that I actually learned a lot of those songs note for note, until I could play the melodies. I was just a little bit behind that time. I remember wishing that I had known them that well when he and I were playing together. I loved playing with Nat Reese and I had high hopes that something could work out for us.

The period right after John died was lean times. After John passed away things were slow. Nat and I played together at least once a month, but that wasn't enough. Initially, I did pretty well because of all those gigs that John and I had preset, the ones that had the grants and all those I played with Corey. Then all of a sudden, by 2011, those ran out and I looked at the income and gigging situation and realized, wow, I've got nothing. It was coming into focus for me at that point that realistically I was almost starting over, which was something that caught me by surprise. I didn't realize that that was going to happen. At that point, it was a real struggle just to barely make it. For a period of time I did some work at the Art and Drama Therapy Institute—I did whatever I could do.

In 2011 and '12, I had a few gigs with Chuck Brown, a player I really admired, the legendary DC bluesman and the father of Washington's famous go-go music, which he practically invented. It's an amalgam of blues, soul, and funk, very original and a big deal on the DC scene, a style that later influenced hip-hop and rap. He could play some deep blues and gigging with him was enjoyable. Great memories. When I first met him, we were doing a show for the Washington Area Musical Awards, sometime in the late '80s. I was at the venue warming up on the harmonica when he and his entourage came in. He came over and leaned an ear in to hear what I was doing. After a minute, he made a gesture with his hand like trying to shoo away a fly and said "freelancing!" In 2011, when we were to play together for a showcase of National Heritage Award recipients, we rehearsed at Archie's barbershop. After we had played just a couple songs halfway through he figured we were ready. He wanted me to hear what he had been working on in the studio. It turns out that he writes horn arrangements. Hearing them was when I understood his aesthetic. They were airtight and immaculate and not a wasted breath. He was not at all a fan of flights of fancy.

Then Nat died in 2012. It was a hard blow because I had high hopes that we could do more together. The mourning process for John Cephas was still fresh on my mind, and I felt a painful feeling of, "They're all dying on me." Nat Reese was just a delightful, generous, joyful person to spend time with, and in terms of repertoire, I couldn't imagine a better person. He played everything from blues to jazz. He and Howard Armstrong both came through that period of time, the Great Depression in the 1930s, when itinerant musicians traveled all around, including to the different coal camps. By necessity they had a varied repertoire, because from night to night they would be playing for a couple of different crowds—one night they'd be playing for hillbillies; the next night they'd be playing like the Italian camp or the Polish camp or the black camp. They had to cover all those different types of music in order to keep those people entertained. That was Nat and that's what made it so much fun to play with him. We covered such a great variety of music, and it was all challenging for me to be able to hang with him. His voice had distilled all these life experiences. He smoked like a chimney and his voice had all that gravel, and you could hear a faint hint of a melody. It was just beautiful to me to hear that tiny bit of melody coming through all that gravel, and at the same time, just the style and presence with it.

I loved the way Nat Reese sang. Singing is probably the most important thing in what we do, and so many of the younger players who did not come up in the period when the blues was a natural part of the community, they sing in a voice that is not theirs—even Corey sings in an affected voice that it's not his natural voice. With Nat Reese, John Cephas, and all those folks from that generation it was their pure natural voice with no pretense, no affectation. You think of Louis Armstrong singing and you think, at what point did people decide that this is good singing? Satchmo's voice was so gravelly and he was distinct with the phrasing, timing, and style, and the choice of melodies. With Nat, even though the melody doesn't leap out at you, there's a melody there and it's beautiful and it's deliberate. He made these aesthetic choices. That's what I remember about Nat. In terms of my ability to play well, I'm affected strongly by who I'm playing with. Nat Reese just gave me so much great energy and inspiration that took me in directions I wasn't used of going. What I remember most about playing with him is just being able to have my ears wide open and my mind wide open and being able to accept what he gave me and respond to it.

When Nat died, for me it was mostly the sadness about losing him as a friend rather than losing yet a second partner. Of course, I liked making the music together, but mostly I enjoyed just listening to him and being around him and now that door was shut. I missed hearing the sound of his voice.

After Nat died, I played with the Reverend John Wilkins a bit. He's the son of Robert Wilkins, who wrote the famous song "The Prodigal Son" that was covered by the Rolling Stones. I met him at the National Folk Festival in Richmond. The National Council for the Traditional Arts (NCTA) had brought him and his daughters up for the gig. Reverend Wilkins lives in Memphis, but his church is in Mississippi and he's got his daughters to sing gospel music with him. I met him there and then he came out to the Centrum Port Townsend Acoustic Blues Workshop. We spent a week out there, and I got to know him better and we hooked up. The NCTA hired me to accompany him at a festival in Nashville—I remember that it was hotter than hell that weekend. I came home and I had a bad case of dehydration—which I didn't know at the time. I knew I was feeling faint. We figured that out because my sister is a nurse. We got a couple of gigs together.

In March 2010, I played on a Blues Cruise with Corey Harris. Right at the end of that blues cruise I flew from Florida to Portugal where I met up with Reverend Wilkins to perform in Lisbon. It was great. Guy Davis was playing the night before us so we went to hear him play, and we hung out with him for a day. The next night was our performance and he stayed to hear our performance. After Portugal, we played the Telluride Festival in Colorado in September 2012.

The Reverend Wilkins also has a motorcycle club and he is an avid Harley-Davidson rider. His singing sparked things in me, and inspired me the most when I was playing with him. I loved playing with him. His voice was so powerful and steeped in gospel and he inspired me to play all sorts of deep roots sounds. I had new sounds coming out of my harmonica that I didn't know were in there, based on what I was getting from both his playing and his singing. His guitar playing is very raw and basic, but also very powerful and rhythmic. He's not that much older than me but very interesting. For a preacher, he's very open-minded, a think-on-your-feet person, rather than being dogmatic and set in his ways. Even though he had recently had back surgery, it wasn't hard to convince him to go exploring around Lisbon. We went up into the hills where they were making port wine and they had all these great little cafés up in there and wine cellars. They served inexpensive small plates of food and you could sample the port wine. We must have hit a half a dozen of those. There we ran into this crazy old Portuguese street guitar player who was playing blues and gospel music, sitting by himself wearing raggedy clothes. We sat and listened to him for quite a while and talked to him. It was just a crazy coincidence.

I liked playing with John Wilkins and still had plans and hopes to work with him in the future, but at the time I wasn't looking for a permanent partner. With him, it was a dynamic of me as his sideman. He's not the person that would have been open to an equal partnership. Also, he didn't have the versatility to do a lot of the varied music that I now wanted to do—and actually have been doing since John's passing. I realized that I wasn't looking for another person to enter into another permanent duo partnership where I would be the accompanying backup person. I wanted to explore lots of different types of music, and especially to play my own compositions, and that's what I have been doing ever since.

In 2013 I reconnected with Frank Matheis, a music journalist and radio DJ who had been following my career for a long time. He approached me about writing an article for *Living Blues*, one of the most important blues magazines in the world. That cover story "Phil Wiggins—On His Own but Not Alone," appeared in 2014 and was the first article that gave me real prominence as a solo artist after Cephas & Wiggins. In the course of writing that article we decided to collaborate on this book. After the publication of the *Living Blues* article, I discovered and experienced that people here at home didn't think of me "on my own" until that article came out, detailing my new efforts. The Cephas & Wiggins brand prevailed. When I traveled overseas it was different, especially in Australia where I did a lot of PR including radio, television, and print articles. In Australia, I was becoming known on my own merit after Cephas & Wiggins, much more than here. Of course, there were a few music industry people that John and I had developed relationships with who understood where I was at, but a whole lot of them didn't.

In many ways, it was like having to start all over. In part, I accept that it has always evaded me how to take advantage and maximize the effect of publicity, how to sell myself. Since John's passing, I've played the Kennedy Center, the Library of Congress, and blues festivals on my own—and I tried to build my career back up to the level where John and I were at when John passed. But, I didn't know how to do it. The *Living Blues* article helped me increase recognition and awareness, and it was just a great piece of publicity material to give to people, with the prestige that *Living Blues* carries, to be on that cover of that respected publication. That definitely got the attention of people. The whole blues scene basically had ignored me. What used to be the W. C. Handy Awards, that John and I had previously won, and now is now called "the Blues Award," the International Blues Challenge, that whole circuit—those blues music industry people. For one thing, the scene has changed and it seems that most popular now is blues rock. That's what people are calling blues now. Basically it's twelve-bar blues, loud bass and drums, and it's just a conduit for extended guitar solos. That's not what I'm about. Now, when they see acoustic blues musicians they think, "Oh, this is music for sitting on the back porch." I have to be careful when I say that, because I feel like John and I were able to overcome that stigma. I think that at the time that John passed, he and I had achieved status. We were on the main stage, and people knew that and didn't have any doubt of that. I think that I'm getting back to that point now, but it's been a long and slower process than I would have thought it would be. When you go to festivals there are mostly electric bands. In many festivals now you find old guys that used to play rock in the '60s and '70s, a lot of them British former superstars, or whatever. Now that they're old and washed out in rock 'n' roll and they're headlining blues festivals, pushing the real blues players out of the way. That's what they put on main stage and often there is hardly any representation of African American musicians at these festivals, which is more than absurd. If there are any acoustic acts they are usually sidelined on a smaller stage called the "back porch stage" or the "shack stage" or in the ditch, or whatever. That's where that music, the true blues, is now relegated. They rarely think of acoustic music as main stage.

I played the Telluride Festival several times since John passed—with Corey Harris and with Reverend Wilkins on the main stage. But it's hard to overcome that reality. Many people came to me and said, "Phil, you know how you can make a lot more money? Just go electric." I have no interest in that at all. I play the traditional country blues.

In 2015 I was at a rehearsal. It was late afternoon, pouring down rain, and I had just left the house in my raggedy jeans—the same clothes that I was gardening in. While I was at the rehearsal, I got a call from Josh Kahn, who works for the Creative Alliance, which is headquartered at the Patterson in Baltimore. The Holmes Brothers had been scheduled to perform there. Popsy Dixon had just passed away, and on the day of that performance Wendell Holmes went into the hospital. Sherman was there by himself. Josh had connected him with this young guy, Brooks Long, a very talented singer and guitar player who had been Wendell's apprentice in the Maryland Apprenticeship program. Brooks Long and the great drummer Eric Kennedy were in the gig. So, Josh called me up, and he said, "Phil, you know, we have a room full of people down here ready to do this thing, and Sherman is basically on his own because Popsy passed and Wendell is in the hospital. Could you come sit in?" Judy brought me a shirt and I got the train down there and got an Uber to the Patterson Theater. I showed up and those guys were all dressed nice, and I was wearing a half-decent shirt and dirty blue jeans from gardening. Sherman was basically in shock that day, so having recently lost my partner, I could relate to where he was at, and it was good that I was there. They started the show with the gospel song "Amazing Grace." Eric Kennedy and Brooks Long sang some beautiful harmonies with Sherman. After the first song, I got up on stage and I played the whole night with them. It was probably one of the most amazing nights of music that I have ever played, and felt more useful probably than I had ever felt. I know it did Sherman's heart good for me to be there. I was able to inject some energy into the whole thing.

After that, he called on me to do some other gigs with him, including at the Library of Congress. In the meantime, after a while of us playing together, he had me thinking about how to help him continue—and again I realized that I wasn't looking for another partner. Sherman has a huge, beautiful voice and fantastic energy—he's like a force of nature, to use that cliché. I love playing with him, and some of my most memorable moments were with him. In 2016 we played at the Richmond Fest, and I got to play with him and this combo, the amazing women gospel singers the Legendary Ingramettes, who sang on his recording as backup singers. In the meantime, Sherman was at a funeral down in New Orleans and ran into my buddy, guitarist and singer George Kilby Jr. Sherman had told George about how he was having a hard time getting work and staying busy and paying his bills, so George took it on himself to help Sherman get booked. From that point on we also played in a trio of me and George and Sherman, three songwriters. In each set, we were able to each do several of our original songs. It was just an embarrassment of riches because we had so much original material among the three of us. I still look forward to doing more of that.

Right now, I play in various ensembles, with combos depending on the gig opportunity. It feels great. No matter what the group, no matter what happens, it's going to be a good time. I've been drawn to people who are a joy to be with and to play with as people, friends, and travel companions. They're people that are considerate, that life isn't just about them; it's about all of us all together and having a good time and taking care of each other. I feel pretty good and optimistic that, if I live, I have a lot more to contribute and I am having a great time right now doing a lot of different things. In a sense, I'm actually slowly moving back toward where I started, playing string band–inspired blues and swing music, great melodies of old songs. I feel like at this point I have moved on from Cephas & Wiggins. Of course, John will always be part of my life, but I feel like at this point I'm standing on my own and I have my own projects and they're pretty far removed from Cephas & Wiggins. I will never outlive the influence John had on my life, but at the same time I just get a twinge of a feeling, like I'm not swinging on John's coattails anymore. I feel like I can stand on my own two feet.

All that is true, but I don't know if I ever will find an equivalent to John Cephas, or if I need to. Even though at times I think that I miss having what we had, I'm reluctant to say that I could ever replace John. I haven't found a partner like John, but lately I haven't thought about it that much, and maybe that's not what I need. Now, I am searching for music that is as fully satisfying in terms of content, feel, and expression. I am enjoying playing with the young musicians, excited by the youth and the energy of the bands I am now leading. When I was playing with John I was letting the music, the harmonica playing, stand on its own. Now young people encourage me to tell more stories, to talk more and to put everything not only in a historical context, but put myself out there, which I discovered people enjoy and appreciate. I've also discovered I do have stories to tell.

Just about every note of music that I ever played in my life has been dance music, but rarely has it ever been presented as that. Most places that I go to perform, people are sitting on their butts and listening. It's not what the music was made for. This music was the soundtrack for parties. It was dance. So right about the same time as I had wanted to bring dance back where it belonged, I had the good fortune of two dancers coming into my life—Baakari Wilder and Junious Brickhouse. In several of my current ensembles I bring on either of these fine dancers and artists to celebrate and demonstrate that heritage. When we perform, we'll inspire people to get up off their butts and show them how it's done. They both have amazing rhythm that just jumps out at you, and you can't sit still when this is going on. That's a major part of my new ensembles. I had known about Baakari Wilder, who is a brilliant tap dancer from Maryland and came back into my life through the Dovetail Ensemble. Now he often performs with my group the Chesapeake Sheiks. He is a brilliant dancer and as much a musician as he is a dancer because his dance is percussive in style. Baakari plays the song's rhythm and adds a layer of percussive basis. When we were forming the Chesapeake Sheiks, I tried to figure out if we should have a drummer. The phrase came out, "It takes a good drummer to be better than no drummer at all." At the same time, I thought to myself, well, having Baakari instead of a drummer is even better. When he dances for the Sheiks, it takes that band to a whole higher level. Comparatively, Junious doesn't make a sound when he dances. It's more show and fun and movement. I invited Junious to the Augusta Blues Week in 2016 and 2017. He brought the entire dance troupe and they had so much fun and sparked up the entire event. For all the years I have been teaching at Augusta, they never had proper representation of the dance traditions that went along with the Piedmont music that they were representing. They would always have someone who they'd call the blues dancer, but it was someone that the

Augusta office hired. They never consulted with the staff of the Blues Week, and that person never fit in with what we were doing. They fit in a little more with the swing dance stuff, but to me it wasn't compatible or in any way connected to the Piedmont buck dancing. When I first started going to Augusta, John Jackson and Cora Jackson were there. But no one ever thought to call on Cora, because she used to teach young girls in her community dancing, to invite her or to ask her to join in and show people the dances that came from that community. It was a huge missed opportunity.

I love leading the Chesapeake Sheiks and am inspired by their respect for the music and for me, which is gratifying. They're so talented that I just feel happy and fortunate that they want to make music with me. These young guys seem to channel the old spirits and they seem to have the strongest connection with the roots of the music we call Piedmont blues—and the great thing about that is that because they're younger with that real strong connection to the past and with their vast energy, they push me forward. The Chesapeake Sheiks are Marcus Moore on violin, Matt Kelley on guitar, Ian Walters on piano, Steve Wolf on bass, and Baakari Wilder on feet—on tap dancing, a brilliant performer who can dance the melody of a song with his taps. Marcus is a great violin player. He's from Alabama, so we have that in common as my family roots are also in Alabama. He is actually a classically trained violinist, but his father also turned him on to the black string band players, which he also internalized. I met Marcus at Archie Edwards's Barbershop. I happened to wander in there one day—on one of my rare visits—and Marcus was there with his father. They both were familiar with Cephas & Wiggins, and they knew some of my music. I enjoyed jamming with Marcus that day. The wonderful thing about these young guys is that even in the time we've been playing together I've witnessed incredible growth in them as musicians. Ian is just a fabulous pianist, a guy who plays with soul and passion. One of the untapped resources in the Sheiks is that we have some good singers, and Marcus has a pretty high voice. I'm looking forward in the future to getting him to put that out there a lot more.

The bassist, Steve Wolf, is in my age group. I've known about him for a long time, even though I've just gotten to know him personally since he joined the Sheiks. Before, he played a long time with Danny Gatton and the Fat Boys, and he brings strong experience and virtuosity. The Sheiks is my main squeeze right now, my band. I love that band, I love those guys, each one of them is a wonderful musician.

It all got started after I met Ian at Augusta, when I had a gig at the Bluebird Festival in DC, with a trio of me, Harold Anderson on bass, who is a very cerebral jazz player, and guitarist Mark Puryear, who is also a musicologist. At the last minute, Mark Puryear reneged on the gig and said, "Oh, I'm going on vacation." He hadn't let me know and it was less than a week before the gig. I panicked and called Marcus, Ian, and Matt. Harold let me know that even though Mark reneged, he definitely was planning to do it and he was counting on it. That's how the ensemble was founded. After that gig, I realized that these were some great players and that I wanted to do more with them. Later Steve Wolf joined us on bass. After our first gig together, I realized that he was a great player, a powerful soloist with rhythm, but also a very lyrical diverse player with broad abilities. That's the Sheiks. We started getting together at the barbershop, learning swing standards and string band songs. It was exciting for me every day to get up and learn how to play and practice these melodies with this new ensemble of young guys, full of energy and hunger, and respect for the music. Our repertoire is equally inspired by the legacy of Martin, Bogan & Armstrong, Nat Reese, and the Mississippi Sheiks. We play a variety of styles, including Delta blues, finger-style blues, and acoustic country blues. It's all string band music, which intersects with jug band music, torch songs, pop songs—you name it—but all filtered through that country blues aesthetic with acoustic instruments. Very little of it is twelve-bar and eight-bar blues. We revive songs by Louis Armstrong, Slim and Slam, Lewis "Rabbit" Muse, and other obscure songs.

In 2014 we released a live CD, *No Fools, No Fun*.[1] This recording was made in the memory of my friend Nat Reese, who reminded me how much I love the music of the black string and swing bands of the golden era: the Mississippi Sheiks (from whom I stole the name) and many others. We had the Chesapeake Sheiks CD-release performance at Publick Playhouse in Cheverly, Maryland. It was one of the few occasions where I got to play for a predominantly black audience, and from the second I stepped out on stage and opened my mouth, there were people talking back to me from the audience. It's a real African and African American thing that there's no separation between you and the audience. If you say something and it sparks a reaction from somebody, you are going to hear it. It was wonderful, because it made it very much fun for me and fulfilling and easy because it gave me energy that whatever I put out was coming back at me, giving me the response. That's part of our contribution to this culture: no separation between the audience and the performers. The audience does not sit quietly on its hands and applaud in between songs. People were talking back to me. It was wonderful.

I love playing with the House Party: Rick Franklin—guitar, Marcus Moore—violin, and Junious Brickhouse—dancer. The violinist Marcus Moore is also in the Chesapeake Sheiks. Marcus Moore is originally from Alabama and he has a background in classical music and also in jazz and African American string band music and blues. Rick is a very steady and calm player, joyful and fun, but I felt like we needed a violin, an instrument that was once very popular in the blues and is now coming back strongly. Junious is mainly an urban hip-hop dancer who has now connected with the blues. Junious is from the North Carolina Piedmont region and he also spent a lot of time with John Dee Holeman, Algia Mae Hinton, and Williette Hinton. The House Party ensemble pushes the energy and we try hard to work together to inject fire and energy into the music. Junious is the director of Urban Artistry, a dance troupe out of Silver Spring, Maryland. We were introduced through Clifford Murphy, who was the Maryland folklorist at the time. Clifford connected us together and told me that Junious wanted to learn harmonica, and he encouraged me to reach out to him under the Maryland Apprenticeship program to be my harmonica student. Junious had a musical wakening while serving in the military. He was deployed in the Middle East on several tours and found himself being that far away from home and in those hostile environments needing to connect with home, trying to find a way to keep himself grounded.

I also love to play with Eleanor Ellis and Rick Franklin in the Phil Wiggins Tidewater Trio. That ensemble is the perfect combination. Rick is easygoing and mellow, a fine guitarist who plays steady and pretty. He has been a long-time friend and musical partner who plays challenging songs that have something special to them. He comes from Virginia and grew up listening to this music, learning blues from records, and later at Archie Edwards's barbershop, from listening to and learning from John Cephas and all the pickers there. He is a fine Piedmont-style guitar player. Rick and I go way back. We were having kids at the same time together. Rick is my good friend, one of my favorite people to spend time with, because he is such a loving person and a huge, gentle spirit. One of the main reasons why I make music with him is just because I enjoy spending time with him. On my website, I have a little write-up that I think reflects this ensemble nicely: "Rick brings the joy. Eleanor brings the fire." I feel like that's true.

Rick likes double-entendre and hokum songs. He's not that drawn to the down and dirty or the mournful blues; he's more into beautiful and uplifting songs that are a little funny with double entendre, tongue in cheek, and a bit risqué. We play "Stagger Lee" in the Skip James style, even though he never played the song. It's so pretty the way Rick plays it, that I just take the opportunity to completely indulge myself. We play a verse and then he sings a verse and then I play a verse. I must play at least half a dozen verses of instrumental solo on that song, just because I love the way he plays it so much. It's for the audience in the sense that if they see me enjoying it, maybe they'll enjoy it too. But mainly it's just for me to enjoy it myself. The way Rick plays and sings, he definitely could have much more recognition than he has. I don't know if that's because people underrate him or if it's to do with the choices he makes for himself. Rick made an album with Michael Baytop covering the songs of bluesman Frank Stokes called *Searching for Frank*. That and Eleanor's album *Comin' a Time*: those are two of my favorite records ever made by anyone.

I've known Eleanor Ellis for a long time and we've been through a lot together. We're both alumni of the Flora Molton University of Life. We have a lot in common. Especially in these most recent years, I just enjoy whenever we spend time together, whenever we're sharing a stage together. For me it's just pure joy and for some reason I'm just able to relax when I play with Eleanor. I'm able to play to my full potential and hopefully to help her do the same. I love playing with Eleanor. She's a very unique person originally from Louisiana. I don't know much about Louisiana, but it seems to me like definitely growing up there has a lot to do with who she is and how she navigates. In a way, she's very conscious of what's proper, and of etiquette, which sounds funny, because she's not square at all. She's a very determined, strong woman who has a style of properness and respectfulness of people. She's a great player. Making music with her, it's obvious she's been playing for a long time and works hard at it. She acquired great skills as a result of putting in the time. Eleanor has a beautiful natural voice. When you hear her speak it's almost like she's singing with a very musical accent and her melodic inflection. That's what comes out when she's singing, and she's just a beautiful, beautiful singer. I love playing with her. She knows a lot of great songs, so it's a lot of fun. I recognize Flora's influence on Eleanor, who doesn't even realize it, but very often she's channeling Flora, and I recognize it. I'm aware, "Oh, there's Flora again." She doesn't shy away from anything, and she works at it until she gets something powerful. That's what I love about her. Eleanor figures out a way to provide the rhythm and at the same time make a strong statement in an instrumental verse so it says something; it comes across as a good, powerful solo. The only problem is that when she and I travel to gigs together the two of us get lost, because I have the worst sense of direction on the North American continent and she has the second worst. I feel lucky anytime I get to share a stage with her.

Another current collaboration that I am very happy with is my duo work with the Australian singer and guitarist Dom Turner in Australia. Dom and I just connect well. People all over the world loved Cephas & Wiggins music and responded positively to it. In the 1980s we toured in Australia, where Dom Turner and the Backsliders would open for us—or what they call in Australia, the "support act." I got to know Dom and to be good friends with him. We spent a lot of time traveling together and kept in touch. When John passed away, Dom reached out to me and said he was planning to come to the U.S., and we did a little tour of Western Virginia playing four or five gigs together. Then he invited me to come to Australia. I've been going to Australia quite a few times ever since then, and I love playing with Dom. He's a great player with wonderful aesthetic. He fell in love with the blues from about as far away from it as you can get geographically. We have similar tastes, instincts, and inclinations, which results in us sounding and feeling as if we've been playing together a lot longer than we actually have.

There are many blues lovers worldwide, including many good musicians, who feel the music deep down. Sometimes these folks have a very romanticized perception of the blues, and I don't see how they could understand it the way we African Americans do, because they haven't lived the history of the black struggle in America. The people who have lived through or have direct connection to the experiences of oppression, during the era when this music was created, will know how the music and the whole African American culture are integrally linked. Dom Turner somehow gets it, and it's fun to play with him. I think he feels the music on a deep level and approaches it with a lot of respect. We understand each other musically very well and have a strong musical and personal connection. We regularly tour Australia, and playing with him has been one of the most musically and personally satisfying gigs of my career. I feel that a lot of Australians and Europeans are far enough away from it so they can have a different vision of the blues. In a lot of art forms, you see that happening. Some of the most beautiful writing about New York City was by people who were not from New York. Many blues musicians, and audiences, are from faraway places.

It's interesting, when thinking about the universalism of the blues, that some people are looking at the blues from an innocent position of ignorance of the actual blues history and culture and also how much it has changed. I spoke to a woman standing outside of a bar—I forget where we were, maybe Perth, Australia—and she said, "Man, I would just love to go down to Mississippi and see the real bluesmen just standing on the corner playing." Those days are over, but this woman had a frozen-in-time, romanticized, and stereotypical vision of what's going on in America.

The fortunate thing for me was that I got to meet a lot of my heroes and the true icons of the Delta and Piedmont blues, to know them as people, as family. I had much respect and admiration for those people. It's a necessary part of life when people work closely together to make this music, to travel, record, and work together in a lifelong partnership. You don't put each other on a pedestal. To us, music is like bread and water, a necessary part of life. It helps to sustain us. It helps to keep us going. It's not some act to get dressed up for and sit on a stage. It's part of our life, like eating and working and sleeping, and making music or hearing music and celebrating with music. That to me is the unromanticized reality of it.

Dom and I see eye to eye on a lot of things. Like one of his pet peeves is Australian guys that try to sing and talk when they're performing like they're Americans. That's also something that bugs me, but more so about Americans that try to sing and talk and act like they're eighty-year-old black men from the Mississippi Delta when they're nothing of the sort. Dom has a beautiful voice and he sings in his natural voice and accent. There is no posing and putting on. He does the music because he loves it and he does it like he does it; he doesn't try to do it like the person that he learned it from. That makes our playing together much more natural—just real. It's two people doing what they do and meeting in the middle—coming at it from different sides of it in a real, sincere, and honest place. It's just a joy. When I step on the stage with Dom, I'm full of confidence, because I know that what we're about to do is going to be heartfelt and energetic and in one way or the other it's going to touch people.

We played at Byron Bay, the biggest blues festival in Australia. It was great— in a huge tent playing for a couple thousand people going crazy with just us two acoustic players on stage putting out enough energy to rock an audience. The people in Australia are down to earth. They connect with you and don't sit on their hands. They're not polite. They respond. They have a lot of curiosity about where I come from and my culture and the culture that created the blues. When I tell stories, they love it. We played in the city of Darwin on the northernmost coast of Australia, and up there I came into contact with more indigenous peo- ple than I ever had before. I got to be friends with a guy—Goharu—a beautiful singer and guitar player. The region around Darwin is a beautiful part of the country, almost like being on a tropical island. I know a little bit about Austra- lian history and of course the history of how the invaders and the people that came from Europe and settled in Australia, the history of how they dealt with the indigenous population—it's horrendous. Traveling with Dom it was great to have an opportunity to meet some indigenous people and to talk to them and to get a little bit of the history and culture from them firsthand. In Australia, I also found my stride as a storyteller, because I felt that it was important for me to share about the heritage and culture of the blues they were hearing, being that it is so far outside of their own culture. Ever since then, I have incorporated stories and background information into my repertoire, and people respond well and appreciate it. Some people even said that they like the stories as much as the music. The difference in Australia is that the audience responds to it in a virtual conversation.

We recorded an album *Owing the Devil a Day's Work*.[2] The title comes from something my mother always said about left-handed people, derived from the ancient belief that left-handed people "owe the devil a day's work." The title fit because both Dom Turner and I are left-handed. Dom has a nice voice and sings like himself and he hangs his Australian accent out there for the world to see. He's got these friends that were in the pop band, Midnight Oil, from Australia. One of them owns the studio. He came there, set up a couple mics, turned them on, and left. Again, we just sat there and played for a couple of hours, essentially a live recording. The only thing missing was the audience. It was real natural and it felt good.

I'm out on the road with George Kilby Jr. quite often. George is a great guitar- ist and singer and we tour quite a bit. George feels like we were both in the same boat when we met, because he had also lost his playing partner, Pinetop Perkins. Actually, at the time that Pinetop had passed on, he and George had not been playing together for a while anyway. The difference that sets us apart is that with John Cephas and me, we had equal billing as partners—Cephas & Wiggins—both our names were out there. There would not have been Cephas & Wiggins without Wiggins. I feel like it was different, because with George it was just Pinetop Perkins and his band, where George was the arranger, the bandleader. He helped produce a couple records with Pinetop. I was encouraged to work with George after I got to know his songwriting style, which seemed to be very compatible with me. I realized that he would be a good songwriting collaborator, including on songs that I was working on and had trouble finishing, or coming up with the right groove. My skills were in playing with words, and I felt like I could be helpful to him with his lyrics, to cut out the fat in some songs, to point out some good plays on words. I felt like we could be a good combination, which turned out to be true, because we do collaborate well. In the beginning, it was never my idea that we would do a lot of playing and traveling together, but now we do several tours a year, going out for a couple of weeks at a time. I've been going and meeting up with him in Colorado often and just staying out for maybe a week. We also go overseas for a couple of weeks once a year.

I met the Seattle-based roots and blues duo, Ben Hunter and Joe Seamons, out in the Northwest at the Centrum Port Townsend Blues Week. Ben Hunter took my harmonica class. He only had one harmonica and it wasn't the right key. Ben Hunter plays fiddle, as well as guitar and mandolin. His partner Joe plays banjo and guitar. They're both just great singers. The great thing about Centrum was being able to spend nights jamming with those two. They have a huge repertoire of music from the nineteenth century to the present—obscure old-time music ranging from blues to Appalachian ballads, much of it pre-blues. They are young guys, brilliant musicians, and serious students of music—almost perfectionists. It's wonderful for me to play with them. They won the International Blues Challenge in Memphis in 2016. I enjoyed the chance to tour in Europe with them and to play on their excellent album *A Black & Tan Ball*. I will be doing more with them, I hope.

As I am making my own way, playing with different people, I sometimes reflect on the acoustic blues, the so-called Piedmont blues. Many people that are playing acoustic fingerstyle blues today, playing well and helping to get the word about this music out there, are people that were inspired by John. I think he deserves a lot of credit for that. Because of John, and people like John Jackson and Archie Edwards, that music is in good shape today. You have young people now that are into it—there's that direct connection. It also seems like there is renewed interest in the old roots and blues music, and that young people have recently discovered the recordings done by Alan Lomax and Worth Long.[3] A new generation is now mining those songs. You have on the one hand people who have sat and played with and learned from and with John Cephas or John Jackson or Archie Edwards—and then you have those people who have come to the music from the field recordings. It's a strange thing in a way, because sometimes the young players are trying to recreate the old recordings note for note. Some of the people even dress up like it, wearing the garb worn during the 1930s. The funny thing about some of those people is that they don't know that much about the history or the culture that produced the music that's on the Lomax and other recordings that they've heard, like the Harry Smith *Anthology of American Folk Music.* Too often they don't actually care. All they care is that they can sit down and play and re-create that recording like a photograph. That's an interesting phenomenon because in a way it's good that they're going back and hearing this old music. But in a way, it's not like it's treated as a living music. People are interested in re-creating a recording that they heard, to lock it in a museum.

Good songs should be about something. If you don't have an idea to communicate, why even open your mouth? I don't like it when songwriters trivialize the blues experience. A good song will have something important to communicate or a story to tell, or even something to put out there in the world that will make people happy and uplift people. All those things are meaningful. People will never cease to struggle and never cease to suffer and never cease to work hard. They will never cease to want to survive and succeed and to celebrate. All these topics existed when this music was first being created and all still exist. All the needs and necessities that caused music to emerge, and especially the original blues, still exist today. Of course, black culture, the American and African American cultures, have changed quite a bit. Now people have access to much more information. Cultures come into much more contact with each other than they used to—with a much broader sharing experience taking place; but the same basic needs are still there. We've become inundated with technology, and in some ways so separated personally because of it; if you allow it, technology can isolate people. Today, people need more real contact. That's what the blues is all about. What's going to happen? Are people going to forget how to talk to each other and how to treat each other? How to allow each other their dignity? I think so. I think it's happening. I think that in some ways it's become even more important that this music is here, because people need it. People need the blues.

Yet, to me, the modern blues scene has a big negative side, like the annoying blues-rock and a lot of stuff that's being called blues now that isn't actually blues. At the same time, there's a lot of modern music that's a direct continuation of the true blues because it's connected to the root and it's the natural growth and future of the blues.

There are a few players worth mentioning, people who I care for and admire. Some are outside of the DC area that are vital to the broader community. After years of all of us teaching, our students are nationwide and even worldwide, carrying on the legacy. The students we taught have dispersed. There are two musicians in Queens, New York, Valerie and Ben Turner, known as the Piedmont Blūz duo, who directly carry on the music taught to Valerie by John Cephas. I consider Valerie and Ben to be family and feel a strong connection with them. I love them both, and feel totally at home with them. Valerie is probably John Cephas's most accomplished student. Her husband Ben plays just the right thing on washboard percussion. Erin Harpe, from Annapolis, is making a big name for herself fronting a band in Boston. She learned from her father Neil Harpe and she was influenced by Eleanor Ellis. Her career is on the ascent and she is terrific. There's Diamond Jim Greene in Chicago, the wonderful Lauren Sheehan in Seattle, all playing the music they learned from their respective teachers, John Cephas, John Jackson, and me.

Other great players fit into the tradition. There is Samuel James up in Portland, Maine. A lot of what he does is individualistic, acoustic blues, but some purists would listen to it and think, "Is that blues?" To me what he plays is exciting, because it's modern and new, but it's got a very strong and natural continuation of what started at the roots. It's great, because he has a very young "what's going on now" perspective and aesthetic and a way of coming across that's very contemporary, but he is also very deep with the great past. I love playing with Jerron Paxton. He's a musical genius and a wonderful person, an encyclopedia of American music from the eighteenth century to the 1940s. It's as if the spirits of those musicians of the bygone era are just flowing through him. He plays piano, guitar, banjo, violin, harmonica. But it's not like he just plays one of them well and then fools with the rest of them; he's brilliant on every single one of them. He's not satisfied unless he's being challenged. When we get together to play the same tunes that we're both familiar with he is always pushing the limits, expanding boundaries. I know it's a cliché, but he's an old soul in a young person. Another great player is Mike Lightnin' Wells, a true Southern guy from West Virginia who now lives in North Carolina. He has been longtime friends with John Dee Holeman and Alga Mae Hinton, and he's an encyclopedia of old music, country blues and all types of old popular music—dance music, torch songs, pop songs. He's one of the few people I know who can keep up with Jerron Paxton in terms of repertoire, and he has very good taste. Lightnin' is one of the best ukulele players I've ever heard, and a great guitar player and singer. He has inspired many people in the DC scene. Also, Andrew Alli, a harmonica player from Richmond, is not typically a country blues player in the Piedmont style. The first time I met Andrew was at this harmonica gathering in Mississippi, the Hill Country Harmonica, and I loved his energy and playing.

As artistic director at the blues camps, I am trying to figure out who to bring to Augusta or who would be good to come to Centrum to represent these old masters. Since that generation is gone, I'm reaching out to these young people, terrific new players who will make big names in the future, like Jontavious Willis from Georgia and Marcus Cartwright from Louisiana, both rising stars in the acoustic blues. That's where the spirit of the blues is now. We have to be careful that the blues-teaching retreats don't become old geezer camps, where it's just a bunch of fat, old white guys sitting on their asses learning blues licks and playing shuffles. We need young people to vitalize the music, bring energy and a wide variety of styles. There is lots of good music made today that I feel connected with.

DC is my home and it is important to me that the local blues continue as vibrantly as ever. Locally, the Archie Edwards Blues Heritage Foundation carries on in Riverdale Park, Maryland, where they sponsor concerts and jam sessions, as well as music workshops. It's a good thing and it creates a central meeting place for local players of all skill levels. My hope would be that people come to the new barbershop jam sessions and seminars to carry on the actual legacy, to learn it, to grow and stretch. Michael Baytop is the heart and soul of the Archie Edwards Foundation. To this day he continues to be a strong influence on the direction that it has taken. He fosters the spirit of openness and generosity that's pervasive there. There are a few other people, like Miles Spicer, who was Archie Edwards's and Michael Baytop's student. Miles has shown amazing growth over the years—and he definitely carries on the legacy and has come into his own. Jackie Merritt has grown in her guitar and harmonica playing, singing, and songwriting. Jackie and Miles both are great songwriters and that's one of the things that I like about their group, M.S.G. Acoustic Blues Trio: they are not just preserving Archie's legacy, they're carrying it forward into the future by creating new songs, which is important in terms of perpetuating this music that we love. There are also a couple of very good harmonica players in the DC area. Recently I brought Geoff "Stingybrim" Seals to Blues Week in Augusta to teach beginner's level harmonica.

That same joyous spirit is carried by another harmonica player in the Washington, DC, scene—Jay Summerour. People often say, "Whatever he's on, I want some of it." Whenever you see him he's overflowing with joyous energy. Players like Donna Fletcher as well. Resa Gibbs is an amazing singer. Another student of John Cephas's is Marc Pessar, who was John's apprentice. I've made some nice recordings with him. He absolutely loved John and spent a lot of time with him just because he admired him so much. Harold Anderson is a wonderful and very cerebral bass player. For a brief while we had a trio, he and I and Mark Puryear. We simply went by our names: Wiggins, Puryear, and Anderson. We only did a few gigs, sometimes billed as "Phil Wiggins and Friends," and on one gig we were billed as Three Deep. Mark Puryear and I seem to speak the same language, and I love the music he plays. For a long time I felt that I would love to have done a combo with Mark, but I could never get him to commit and actually the same thing was true with Harold.

It's music, dance, and food that makes community. Family, food, and music always belonged together in my life. It was all about the house party, and it goes all the way back to the African aesthetic of music being part of life; music is not entertainment. Music is part of life—just like eating and sleeping and drinking water. Before Piedmont blues was played on the international stage it was music that people played in their own home while they were eating, while they were celebrating. I remember being at John's house and we'd be playing music in the kitchen while people were cooking and we'd eat a bite or two between songs. It was just part of life. It wasn't like it was a performance. Music was part of the party. Food and the music is part of celebration that includes music, dancing, eating, laughing, talking, arguing, getting things straight, telling the truth, telling lies, having fun, having conflict—all that is part of the celebration of blues. And food is a big part of it. It's just like you play some, you eat some, and then you play some more. Everybody had a garden. Everybody grew fresh vegetables. John Cephas had field cress and also fresh corn and then we baked cornbread. Potatoes—cooked potatoes, plus potato salads—all those kinds of things. People lived in the rural areas. The so-called soul food was developed by people living in bondage and having to make the best of what was left over, what was given to them after the white people were done and took all the good parts of the meat. For instance, black folks did not get the best cuts of the ham and what was left was the ham hock and the chitterlings, and the things that were basically thrown away. African American people had to figure out how to make the best of those things, and they did. A lot of what you will find on menus in real fancy restaurants is something that Africans and African Americans figured out . . . okay, it's tough meat, let's just cook it very slow on low heat for a long time, and you'll wind up with something that's tender and flavorful.

That's how we developed soul food specialties. We typically had beans and rice and greens for New Year's, called Hoppin' John, but we always had black-eyed peas and greens for New Year's. Hogshead was a thing for Christmas. I like to cook what they call "peasant food"—dishes where you wind up putting a lot of different things in the pot and it takes a while for the flavors to bloom. You put in your celery and your onions and your garlic and all, and then it starts to slowly develop. A lot of the dishes actually taste better the next day as leftovers. I like to cook poultry. I've been fortunate to have traveled a lot in my life—starting as a kid and growing up in a military family. I like the traditional African American dishes, like black-eyed peas and ham hocks and cornbread, stuff like that, and I cook a couple of African dishes like ground nut stew with poultry. In Africa, the meat was not the main thing. The meat was more like seasoning, because it wasn't that easy to come by. Ground nut stew is made of chicken and greens and onions and ground peanuts. For African food, you use different spices that would be considered here as baking spices, like cinnamon, nutmeg, and cloves and allspice. And you make a chicken broth. It's like a stew and it's wonderful.

I also cook *arroz con pollo*, a South American dish, with roast chicken and you make broth and it's got olives, pimentos, and saffron in it and garlic, with lots of onion and chorizo sausage. You put all that in with the rice, and as it cooks down the flavors start to bloom. In all these dishes, you take simple ingredients and you take your time. You may not have a lot of money to buy a lot of ingredients, but you have the time. I've always felt like for me that it's not so much that you spend a lot of money on food but that you spend time preparing it well. That's what makes the difference and that's what makes good food to me. I make my own hot sauce. The main ingredient I like to use is habanero peppers—which I grow behind my building. I usually plant about eight plants a year, and it gives me enough to make a couple dozen jars of jerk sauce, which I got from my first trip to Jamaica. We were traveling along going from Kingston on our way to Montego Bay and we stopped by the side of the road at this little shack where this woman was selling jerk chicken and jerk sauce. I wanted extra jerk sauce, and I took my spoon and stuck it in the jar and the lady said, "That's hot." I said I'm used to hot, and I put it on my food and it lit my mouth on fire and she just looked at me and laughed and said, "Hah, I warned you." I was like—I have got to find what those ingredients are. The first thing I had to figure out was habanero peppers. They're what we call scotch bonnet peppers, which they use a lot in the Caribbean but also a lot in Africa. They have a very distinctive taste that I had never had before. That's the main ingredient to jerk sauce. Then allspice, brown sugar—or sometimes I'll use molasses—a combination of spring onions and Vidalia onions. I use lime juice, a little bit of pineapple juice, and the baking spices—a little nutmeg, cinnamon, cloves in there. It makes a thick sauce. If I'm cooking with it I'll either use it direct, or I'll thin it down some with more lime juice and more pineapple juice to make a marinade. That's my jerk sauce, and then I'll make a straight hot sauce with habaneros and vinegar and water and a little salt and garlic and ginger. And that's how I make a hot sauce.

I am sixty-four years old this year, in 2018, and I plan to keep making music for as long as I can. Right now, I've had a few big successes, but I could always use more gigs, better income and steady work for myself—and my bandmates. I don't have a record label or a manager. I embody the word "independent"; yet, it's a struggle to make ends meet. I think if people knew how close to the edge I live they would be surprised, but I'm getting better at taking care of that. The world has changed and we can do more for ourselves than we used to in the old days, but I acknowledge that I am not the most self-promoting person. My partner Judy always says that I'm pathologically against self-promotion—too humble, whatever that means. But, the two basic areas in which I have an absolute huge ego is that, number one, I never wanted to play like any other harmonica player. I always thought that maybe someday, the same way that people are trying to learn to play like Little Walter, or Big Walter or George Harmonica Smith or Sonny Terry—maybe they'll listen to me and say, "Oh, Phil Wiggins had his own sound. I want to try to learn that sound." The other place where my ego comes out is in my songs—I'll just make up my own. I've been doing that ever since I started trying to play music on the harmonica and I've always loved words.

I don't consider myself famous. Of course, I know that I've been doing it a long time and that my name is out there, and I feel good about that. I guess I want to get better at self-promotion, to get smarter at that part of the music business. There are musicians that are good businessmen, and to their credit hard workers at that aspect of it. I feel like I'm not one of those people. In a way, I'm lazy because I focus a lot on the art and the craft of it, but on the business part of it I need to get off my ass more. I know that. But I also know people who are putting musical crap out there, and because they are good at the business end somehow people fall for it. I don't know what to say about that. I know that it's not me. I work hard every day at making good music and writing good songs.

I'd be lying if I didn't say it feels good when I realize that someone recognizes me or acknowledges me for my life as a musician. It's very satisfying. If I have to reflect on my music, I can say that it is my desire to take this little instrument, the harmonica, which took me around the world, to be the absolute best that I can be—to be open to learning, hearing, and listening. For me it's not about fame. It's almost like a form of paranoia, but I feel like once you start reading your own promotional shit, and believing it, that throws an obstacle in the way of growth. I never want to stop moving forward, to stop listening to everybody and anybody and learning. It's the same thing with the songwriting: I'm a person that, for some reason, all my life people have told me their secrets. I value that, because I feel like somewhere in those stories, in those secrets, are keys to survival and to thriving and living well. I don't want to miss those. It's a blessing, in a way. A lot of times it's like, "Whoa, I wish you hadn't told me that." But in the long run I feel like it's a blessing that for some reason people trust me with their secrets, with their stories. I feel like I've learned a lot in life and how to navigate through life from the stories that people have shared with me.

In 2017 I had the amazing honor of being selected for a National Endowment for the Arts National Heritage Fellowship. It is commonly referred to as the "Living Cultural Treasure" award, because that's how it started when the U.S. copied Japan to give out this cultural award. Before me the great Sonny Terry won it for harmonica, as well as Elder Roma Wilson, the gospel harmonica player. Other great people won it—Bill Monroe, John Lee Hooker, B.B. King, Earl Scruggs and Lester Flatt, and people like that, and my peers like John Jackson, John Cephas, John Dee Holeman, and Warner Williams. Now, I won it after more than forty years of playing.

We had the award ceremony at the Library of Congress on September 14, 2017. It was an incredible honor, which is gradually coming into focus for me personally. It is going to be a long process of understanding what it means. At the same time, being recognized and accepted in the company of these great players is a profound honor. It is humbling and in some ways overwhelming to be among these great artists and musicians who are driven to be the absolute best at what they do. The fellowship is slowly coming into focus for me.

I am deeply grateful for all the decades I spent playing with John Cephas, but this award was won for my music, my contribution to the instrument and the blues, to teaching and overall for my own life achievements. I am on my own and this profound honor completely pulls me out from under the shadow of John. This award recognizes me for my work, not for having been John's partner. The people saw enough value in what I do to want to recognize me. That goes a long way towards giving me confidence and self-respect.

The fact that it's given out by the United States government is an interesting situation for me in a period of time where we have made some huge leaps backwards as a nation. As an African American musician, this was of course going to be on my mind through this whole process and it's interesting to be receiving this particular award at this time in history. Rather than to write a long political statement, let my song "Igbo Landing" express my sentiments. Igbo Landing is a historic site at Dunbar Creek on St. Simons Island in Georgia. At this location, there was a mass suicide in 1803 by captive African Igbo people who took control of their slave ship and refused to submit to slavery. They all decided to die together rather than to live a life of subjugation.

"Igbo Landing"

There wasn't no beacon of hope and freedom,
no promise of the American dream
There wasn't even any Ellis Island.
What greeted those people made them moan and weep.
As they rowed up into Igbo Landing and
saw so many Africans chained and bound
That sight inspired some of my forefathers
to jump into the Dunbar Creek and drown

Chorus
And now you say you want your country back,
to make the "greatest nation" great again.
Well I've heard that there have been some good old days
but I don't know where nor remember when.

There wasn't no sheriff like the one in Mayberry,
shut down the jail on Thanksgiving Day.
If they caught you on the road without money and papers,
I'm here to tell you partner there was hell to pay.
They would detain you and they'd fine you
and they'd throw you in jail
And when you couldn't pay the money fee,
they'd ship you down to Lee County Alabama
and make you go to work in the lime quarry.

And now you say you want your country back,
to make the "greatest nation" great again.
Well I've heard that there have been some good old days
but I don't know where nor remember when.

My uncles got themselves a brand-new bicycle
from working at Mr. Fortunes store
It was meant to be used to deliver groceries
all around Titusville from door to door.
Well they took that bicycle out on a spree,
just having fun as children will.
The sheriff caught them and he pistol whipped them
and then left them lying bloodied on Dynamite Hill.

And now you say you want your country back,
to make the "greatest nation" great again.
Well I've heard that there have been some good old days
but I don't know where nor remember when.

When thinking about that fact that I'm recognized as a "national cultural treasure" of the United States of America, what does that mean? Finally, I came to the realization that the wonderful thing about this recognition is that it is about the best about our country, where different people came from every corner of the globe to add their perspective, their aesthetic, work ethic, and skills to make this country what it is. That is almost the opposite of what a lot of people think of when they talk about patriotism or being patriotic. That to me is true patriotism, what there is to love about this country, the amazing and wonderful variety of cultures and ethnicities and ways of thinking and ways of doing things, and that all became woven together to make this country what it is.

Here is the transcript of my acceptance speech:

Remarks by Jane Chu, Chairman of the National Endowment for the Arts and Acceptance Speech by Phil Wiggins during the National Endowment for the Arts Heritage Fellow Award Ceremony, September 14, 2017, Library of Congress, Washington, DC.

JANE CHU: Our next NEA Heritage Fellow is Phil Wiggins. (Applause.) Phil is from Takoma Park, Maryland, and he is a virtuoso on the acoustic harmonica. He was born in Washington, DC, and he is a long-time fixture in the Piedmont blues community. He learned and he performed alongside blues and gospel artists like Flora Molton, Archie Edwards, Wilbert Big Chief Ellis, as well as National Heritage Fellows John Jackson, Warner Williams, John Cephas. Phil has a passionate dedication to teaching and mentoring and advocating. He has taught blues in schools, served on nonprofit arts boards. He has been a cultural diplomat who has performed on multiple continents on behalf of the U.S. State Department.

And for his extraordinary mastery of the blues harmonica and contributions to American music, the National Endowment for the Arts honors Phil Wiggins. (Raving Applause.)

PHIL WIGGINS: That's an advantage to being local. (Laughter. Responding to loud applause) I have to say I'm pretty amazed to be standing here this evening. Woo, I never imagined when I was a kid and with my toy harmonicas trying to figure out how to make music on them, huffing and puffing on those toy harmonicas, that those three inches of metal and wood would take me to every continent except Antarctica. So that's pretty amazing. When you've been as far away from home as I have been in my playing life, you think a lot about home. And, when I think about home, my first association with that word I guess is from hearing my mother talk about home. Whenever she talked about home she was talking about Titusville, Alabama. And I could tell she was thinking about home or that she was talking to my grandmother, because her Alabama brogue would come back really strong.

And I remember when I left home to go to college—I went to live with my aunt and uncle in New Jersey—and my mother gave me this patch quilt to take with me. My aunt and uncle, they didn't have an extra bedroom for me to sleep in, so I slept on the floor for two years under this patch quilt that my mother gave me that my grandmother had made. And I remember my mother looking at that patch quilt and saying, "Well, that's Aunt Precious—that's the dress she wore to prom. And that's the suit that Brother Wilson wore at graduation." And I thought that patch quilt is an amazing symbol of this country that we call home.

It's a strange time to be thinking about that, and to be feeling about that, and I am so happy to be a part of this celebration, because it celebrates what that patch quilt symbolizes. It symbolizes this patch quilt of beautiful deep cultures from all over the world that came to make up this country that we call home. And it's not that home that these folks that are going around waving confederate flags that they want back; it's the home that's represented by all these wonderful artists and crafts people that make the country that I am glad to call home. Thank you. (Applause.)

Just as I concluded that acceptance speech, the first to jump to his feet to enthusiastically extend his hand to me was Thomas Maupin, the old-time white buck dancer from Murfreesboro, Tennessee. We had already formed a friendship backstage. Later, Maupin's grandson, who had joined the buck dancer on banjo during the concert, gave me one of the greatest compliments ever, by saying "You could play a dance all by yourself."

It makes it that much more meaningful to me personally that I was nominated and recognized by people from the general public. I thank Matt Watson for going through the whole nomination process and for all the people who supported it. This fellowship honor, the highest award the United States bestows on its traditional artists, is not based on any commercial concern or sales. To be recognized and appreciated by other musicians, musicologists, and music journalists, and to be in the company of other traditional artists, makes it very special. It feels great to be recognized by people that know about the music, the history, and the culture that created it. That's what makes it as powerful as it is and what makes it worth continuing. They found me doing what I love to do; and, to be recognized for doing that, just means a lot to me.

I still have lots of good things ahead. I hope that I will keep growing and learning, getting better at what I do, in particular writing more good songs. I feel like I've made a lot of progress with my singing and I'm continuing to just get better at that. Mainly, I just want to put songs out in the world that are useful, that help people or make people feel good—to inspire people and help to sustain people's spirit. That's what I hope for. I also hope to work more and for better pay so that I can live better. But the main thing is to just keep good, useful, helpful songs in the world.

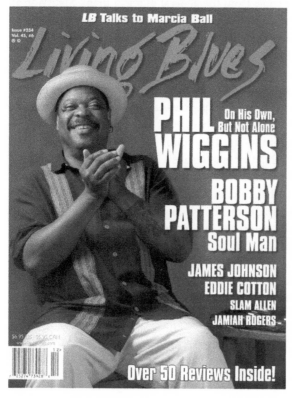

The 2014 cover story in *Living Blues* magazine by Frank Matheis validated Phil as a solo artist and set the stage for the writing partnership of this book. Photo by Bibiana Huang Matheis.

The Chesapeake Sheiks during the 2017 NEA National Heritage Awards ceremony at the Library of Congress, when Phil Wiggins was awarded the National Heritage Fellowship. Photo by Bibiana Huang Matheis.

Phil's acceptance speech at the NEA National Heritage Fellowship Award ceremony at the Library of Congress, 2017. Photo by Bibiana Huang Matheis.

Phil letting loose, 2014. Photo by Bibiana Huang Matheis.

Phil Wiggins and Houseparty, 2014: Phil, Marcus Moore, Rick Franklin, and Junious Brickhouse. Photo by Michael G. Stewart.

Phil Wiggins and Dom Turner in 2016 at the Narooma Kinema, Narooma, New South Wales, Australia. Photo by Julie Fox.

Rick Franklin and Phil at the "new" barbershop in Riverdale, Maryland, 2013. Photo by Bibiana Huang Matheis.

Phil and Corey Harris at Jazz at Lincoln Center in New York City, 2013. Photo by Bibiana Huang Matheis.

At the 2016 John Cephas Tribute festival in Bowling Green, Virginia, the "new generation" who carries on the traditions. Back row from L to R: Warner Williams, Jay Summerour, Jackie Merritt, Rick Franklin, Resa Gibbs, Marc Pessar, Phil Wiggins. Front row L to R: Miles Spicer, Eleanor Ellis, Valerie Turner, Benedict Turner. Photo by Frank Matheis.

Jerron Paxton, Phil Wiggins, Marcus Moore, Valerie Turner, Benedict Turner, and Frank Matheis at Bo's in New York City, 2014. Photo by Bibiana Huang Matheis.

Blues women carrying on the legacy. Eleanor Ellis, Jackie Merritt, Resa Gibbs, and Valerie Turner, 2015. Photo by Frank Matheis.

Eleanor Ellis at Augusta Blues Week in Elkins, West Virginia, 2016. Photo by Frank Matheis.

Chapter 4

PHILHARMONICA—ADVICE FOR HARMONICA PLAYERS

As a harmonica player, I am often encouraged to give advice to younger harp players. Playing the harmonica is a very individual thing, but let me try. Some people consider the harmonica as a toy, so when people see it coming they often have low expectations—anything that comes out of it, if played reasonably well, the audience will eat up. If you spent a lifetime mastering it and playing it the best way it can be played, people are astonished. "Wow, he did that with that little thing." Like any instrument, to play it well, to master it, is a whole different thing. For me, after more than four decades of playing, on a good night, my music is not something that I think about. When I'm in the right zone, my ears and my heart and my mind are wide open and all this stuff is just like passing through me. That comes after years of playing and experience. Newcomers or intermediate players need to think about it as they play. When I am at my best, I am able to communicate what I'm trying to say to an audience—to connect strongly and to have them feel exactly what I'm trying to get them to feel, and to have them know what I'm trying to tell them. That is the main thing. For me that's what making music is about—communicating. That's why I do it.

Here is the best advice I can give:

FIND YOUR OWN VOICE

I've met many people whose approach is, "Oh, well, I heard Little Walter or I heard Sonny Boy and I want to learn how to play like them," or "I want to be able to play these licks"—and they never even think about the main purpose of music, that is to express yourself. It's a way of putting your ideas out there, of

173

connecting and reaching out to people and letting people reach you. That's what it's all about. Once you know that, then the rest comes naturally.

I was lucky that when I first started playing harmonica, I was unaware of many different harmonica players. The only harmonica player I was familiar with was Sonny Terry. But I never tried to emulate him or anyone else. I just liked and enjoyed the music of Brownie McGhee and Sonny Terry. I didn't listen to copy. At the time, when I was first trying to figure out the instrument and what I wanted to do with it, the piano was probably my favorite instrument. My father collected a lot of great piano records. Even now when you listen to my playing, when I solo, it's the right hand of the piano, the triples and such. I stole a lot from that and also from horn players. For a time, I was listening to a lot of Louis Armstrong and to different clarinet players and trumpet players from New Orleans, and I stole a lot of the phrasing, trying to emulate the sound of a trumpet, of a muted trumpet, or the clarinet. Of course, the harmonica for me is like my second voice, probably even my first voice. The harmonica has a very vocal quality, and so I literally try to make it sing, to use my hands to shape the sound, to give it a certain tone quality—like a vowel sound shape.

When I'm teaching harmonica, I tell people the idea is not that you play what I'm showing you, the melody or the riffs, note for note. Basically, what I'm trying to do is give people an alphabet and then hopefully they can take that and write their own words and their own sentences. I'm saying, "These are the building blocks. Build something with them that expresses what you need to communicate." That's my main hope for anybody that I teach.

I like "honesty." There are certain musicians where there's a level of theater involved and a level of acting. To me, what touches and moves me is when musicians express themselves completely honestly and down to the bone. Some players are a character and the whole time that they're on the stage they never drop character and you don't get to see the real person. Theatrics is a skill and an art; it's just not what gets me. I like honest musical expression.

FIND THE HARMONICA THAT FITS YOU

I use Hohner Marine Band harmonicas because I feel that they have the best possible tone. The soft wood comb gives it a nice, rich tone. Tone is very important and so is good taste. Good tone starts with your body, the way you shape your mouth cavity as you're drawing in on a note. To get the optimal tone I like to have a big open cavity as I'm playing. It almost feels as if I'm yawning with my mouth shut. I know what I like to hear and try to make those sounds.

TONE

Too many harmonica players are playing but not hearing or listening to what they're playing, because if they were hearing it, they would choose to do something different, a better sound or a better tone. In terms of tone you have a wide spectrum, from big beautiful tones to thin nasty little ones. The whole range is useful, because the main thing is to express a feeling and an idea. Human feelings run the gamut from euphoria to downright depression. The tonal range of the harmonica has a similar spectrum. It's all done with your body—with your mouth, your face, and for me also with my hands. I use my hands as just about every note of music that I play is shaped to some degree by my hands, whether it be tight—like drawing the sound—putting the sound out through a tiny little pinhole of my hands that are cupped so tight that I can feel the suction in my hands. Or a big open hand, but still shaped around the back of the harmonica so that the sound is wide open. Taste, of course, is something you either have or you don't. It can be developed over time, but musical sensitivity, taste, the ability to know when to leave space: those are things that are harder to learn than tone. The trick is not to overplay and play the right thing.

PLAYING WITH OTHERS

Harmonica players in particular need to be conscious of the fact that their most important tool is their ear. Too many players play and don't appear to be listening to anything except themselves. Some just have bad taste, because if you're going to play well in an ensemble, you want to play the right thing. Before you make a sound, what's the thinking behind that? Particularly when you're playing with a combo or ensemble, the goal should be that the whole ensemble sounds as good as possible. If you're thinking, "Well, I've got these great licks and I'm going to get them in, I'm going to fit them in"—then you're not playing in the ensemble. You need to be thinking, "What needs to be happening right now? Someone is telling a story—how can I strengthen the story? How can I support the story they're trying to tell? Right now, while they're telling the story they need to be free with the time, so maybe I'll be the one that's holding down the meter. I'll be the one that's hitting in the backbeat so that they can stay in rhythm—they can be as free as they want to be and still have rhythm."

You can take any blues song and you can put harmonica to it as long as you have the right key harmonica, and just wiggle it around and it's pretty hard to hit a wrong note. But ask yourself: Are you playing the song? Are you supporting the song? Are you emphasizing the melody? Are you supporting the story? You can repeat phrases that you get from the vocals—in call and response. Usually there is a strong vocal phrase or guitar phrase that you can pick on. Be wary of overdoing any one thing. Sometimes, if someone does a strong phrase, a three-note phrase, for example—it's best just to leave that alone. Sometimes you can weaken a strong phrase by jumping in right behind it and filling in all the space around it. Sometimes a phrase just needs to be by itself in order to have its full strength to breathe. If you listen to what's given you, either by the vocal line or by another instrument, or just the basic melody of the song—if you steal from that, if your ears are open and you're taking input from what you are hearing around you, then you're supporting the song. Those are hints to help you play in an ensemble. You need to be mindful of the total sound. You have an arsenal of sounds and licks, of call-and-response, of rhythm choice, of playing hooks, repeating phrases from the instruments as well as from the vocals. Sometimes the very best choice is to do nothing, to leave the space, to let the vocals stand out.

IT'S NOT ABOUT THE GEAR—IT'S ABOUT YOU

The other thing many harmonica players focus on is the gear they use, the microphone, the amplifier, and even various sound effect pedals and accessories. The sound that you play on the harmonica starts with you, starts with your body and your own physicality. That's what creates the tone. To me, the only purpose for amplification is to make it loud enough so people can hear it in the back of the room. I don't subscribe to trying to get a sound produced by something other than myself—by a tube amp or mic. I don't feel like that's part of making the harmonica as my voice. I feel that having a Green Bullet mic shoved in your hands and the harmonica right up against it only gets one monotone sound. I play right through the PA and use any decent PA mic. I use a combination of my hands and the distance from the microphone to shape the sound and the volume. Sometimes it needs to be played at full volume and with the hands open, in which case I'll back way off the microphone so it doesn't come across too loud. Other times I'll play with my hands airtight, with only sound coming out of maybe a hole the size of a pinhole. In that case I'll get right up on the mic so that you can hear that sound muffled, but it's a distinct sound. I like to work the mic, on the stand for tone and dynamics, meaning the loudness or softness of the harmonica.

TECHNIQUE—CHOOSE WHAT'S RIGHT FOR THE MOMENT

Because the harmonica is my own voice, I don't subscribe to some of the rules that are sometimes thrown out by other harmonica teachers. One technique that is much touted is tongue blocking, that every note that you play should be tongue blocked. For me, a rule of thumb is that I will tongue block when I'm using anything from the number 4-hole and higher because it fattens up the sound. Once you get to the 4-hole and higher, to me the harmonica starts to sound a little shrill and thin. Use tongue blocking, and other techniques, like tongue slapping where for a split second you hear more than one hole and then bam down to the single hole.

TASTE

What is good playing? Is it the riffs, or the speed, or whatever? I make choices based on my own aesthetic, which other people may not share. I think there is such a thing as good taste and bad taste. What's bad taste? Of course, beauty is in the eye of the beholder, and ear, but perhaps playing random licks that have nothing to do with the tune, or noodling, or playing super-fast for its own sake: that to me is bad taste.

I hope this helps you. Play well.

The real Blues Brothers. Jerron Paxton and Phil Wiggins at Augusta Blues Week in Elkins, West Virginia, 2016. Photo by Frank Matheis.

Top L to R: Marcus "Mookie" Cartwright, Benedict Turner, Valerie Turner, and Jerron Paxton. Front L to R: Resa Gibbs, Geoffrey "Stingy Brim" Seals, Andrew Alli, Eleanor Ellis, Phil Wiggins, and Frank Matheis at Augusta Blues Week in Elkins, West Virginia, 2016. Courtesy of Frank Matheis.

PART II

The DC Acoustic Blues Scene

Esther Mae "Mother" Scott, circa 1978–'80. From archives of the Travellin' Blues Workshop. Courtesy of Paddy Bowman.

Flora Molton and Eleanor Ellis, circa 1978–'80. From archives of the Travellin' Blues Workshop. Courtesy of Paddy Bowman.

John Jackson at the 1999 Clearwater Hudson Festival. Photo by Bibiana Huang Matheis.

Bill Harris, the proprietor of the famous Pigfoot club in NE Washington, DC. Photo by Dexter Hodges.

Willie Gaines and Phil Wiggins, circa 1978–'80. From archives of the Travellin' Blues Workshop. Courtesy of Paddy Bowman.

Archie Edwards, circa 1978–'80. From archives of the Travellin' Blues Workshop. Courtesy of Paddy Bowman.

N.J. Warren, Michael Baytop, and Richard "Mr. Bones" Thomas at Archie's original barbershop, 1999. Photo by Paul Kennedy.

Archie's Barbershop, 2007 Bunker Hill Rd. NE, Washington DC, was the place to be on Saturday afternoons when musicians gathered for acoustic blues jams. Photo by Paul Kennedy, 1999.

A typical Saturday afternoon jam session at Archie's Barbershop, 1999. Photo by Paul Kennedy.

The M.S.G. Acoustic Blues Trio: Jackie Merritt, Miles Spicer, and Resa Gibbs, 2013. Photo by Frank Matheis.

FLORA MOLTON

—Frank Matheis and Eleanor Ellis

Flora Molton was a beloved and legendary street busker in Washington, DC, a truehearted and kind lady who was a fixture of Washington street life for over forty years, rain, shine, or the cold of winter, sitting on the corner of 11th and F Street in front of the Woodward & Lothrop department store. She played a beat-up old guitar with a tin collection cup tied to it, tambourine by the foot. Legally blind because of cataracts she had since birth, she worked the corner, always wearing her thick glasses that allowed her minimum sight, just enough to see figures and shapes. She had a life marked by rejection, difficulty, and hardship with three strikes against her as a blind, black, and poor woman. She overcame whatever obstacles she faced and made it through life because of her strong faith in the Lord, her love of music, and her kindness and inner strength. Her early musical influence was the gospel music of her community, as her father was a preacher in New Hall, West Virginia. As was commonplace, he did not approve of the blues, but Flora still developed a taste for the music of Ida Cox, Ma Rainey, Sippie Wallace, Sara Martin, and Bessie Smith.[1]

Flora was born on March 12, 1908, in rural Louisa County, Virginia. In 1937 she came to Washington, where her brother was a pastor. Singer and lecturer Bernice Johnson Reagon said:

She was forced "to take to the street" to support a daughter and son—classified by the government as blind, she was considered "unfit" for employment. Throughout the Depression and World War II, she drew on her religious convictions for song material and, despite hostile police, managed to survive off the meager offerings placed in her tin cup: (Molton said) "Well, I'm going to tell you, in the early part long time ago, when I first started, they gave me fits. I would come back home and I would pray and cry and go back the next day and I'd say 'I ain't done no harm.' The gentlemen policemen, some of them were so nasty, they talk so nasty . . ." Molton was unable to get any long-term work, even after trying several training and social programs. "You see, I got so many promises. I just got disgusted. I just took to the street for mine . . . but work, no. If it hadn't been for the street, I would have been dead . . . I tried hard. I sat down and said, 'I wish some Good Samaritan would come by and would hear me or something.'" That day did not occur until sometime in 1963 when Ed Morris, a white guitarist, listened to her and began to understand her form of expression. He arranged for her to give a performance for the first time at a coffee shop.[2]

Together with Morris, Molton went on to play clubs, festivals, concert halls, and on radio.

She told her musical partner Eleanor Ellis what her typical day of busking was like:

> I caught the bus down there or a cab back or my niece came down there. And I usually take pretty much the same things with me, such as my work tools. My guitar, and my cup, and the cigar box I put in the guitar. And when I have tapes, I take them. I take my guitar, my harmonica, and my horn, the one I sing through . . . when I first got out there, people would look on me just as maybe a beggar or something like that. I didn't ask nobody but they would look at me. I'd get a lot of scorn. And different people would come along and say I didn't have to do that. But see, they didn't know my situation, because I always wanted to be independent.[3]

She sang only sacred songs, which she called "Spiritual and Truth Music." In every way, hers was deep roots music, in some ways simple sounding, but actually harmonically complex, emotive, and captivating. Bernice Reagon explained:

> Undaunted, Flora Molton continues to compose and sing, expressing through her music a special loneliness and dignity. During the 1940s she concentrated on developing guitar techniques which would create a sound representing the sum total of her feelings. . . . Her own style requires the use of a piece of steel or a metal ring to fret the strings. A wailing, whining and screaming tone results when she slides the metal on the neck of the guitar. Mrs. Molton fingers with the steel in such a way that a warbled tone is manifested. Dissonance is accomplished by her grouping of sevenths and thirds together. She also fingers three strings at a time; but if the sound of a train is desired, she fingers four strings at the time. The combination of techniques produces a chordal wail with a buzz effect, a quality present in traditional African music. Flora Molton refers to her music as "a lonesome, mournful sound," but she calls it a "country" sound rather than the blues.[4]

Eleanor Ellis reminisced:

> I met Flora formally—I'd seen her around—but I met her formally in about '82 when Myron Samuels had a festival out in Oxon Hill. He asked me to give her and Larry Wise, her harmonica player, a ride. I did. I rode them out there, and then we did our

sets. They did their set, I did mine. On the way back, that was when Flora asked me to play with her, because Ed Morris had died. I thought I'd give it a try—it might be interesting. I went over to her house and she gave me some tapes that she had made of her and Ed playing. I had an idea of the repertoire and Ed's arrangements and stuff. I worked with the tapes and I thought I had some stuff down, and I went over to have my practice with her and this was a big lesson to me, because we were going along singing and she was singing and I was playing, and some of the songs she played. I just put it in drop D, because she was always in open D, and I just played a little bass thing going, because she didn't change chords. She hammered at it with her slide, but she didn't change chords. There were some songs she wanted to sing which were in different keys or they had different accompaniment, so I had to learn some of those. We were doing one of them, I don't remember which one, and all of a sudden, I realized I was not in the same place Flora was. She was back there and I was way ahead, or whatever, and that taught me a good lesson which is that the singer calls the shots, that people don't always do stuff in a metronomic way; they do it as they feel it. She was doing it as she felt it. She might hold it for a long time and then change the phrase of the quarter or anything. So that was a valuable lesson and one that a lot of people probably could learn. Because if you listen to the people who are playing this music, some people are right on, you know, right on the structure, but a lot of people are not. And so that was a good lesson that I learned. . . . First of all, she never gave it up. We went on a tour of Europe for three months, and she played in clubs and festivals. But that was her day job, was playing on the street when she was home and she was equipped for it. She had it together. She would get a cab down there and get a cab home. She had a little amplifier. In the summer, she would have an umbrella keep the sun off, and in the winter, it would be freezing cold, she'd have gloves with the fingers out to play. She had her Pignose amp when I knew her and a tambourine on her foot and she had a harmonica too. She loved harmonica. She blew on it literally—she didn't play it particularly, but she used it for the train song "Blow That Train." When she made the recording for L+R, she would sell those records on the street. On Memorial Day when people have crosses that they put up—or they decorate the graves of war people—on Decoration Day when you might decorate a grave, she used to make Styrofoam crosses and stick flowers on them and sell them. She was prepared—she had it down. When I knew her, she was singing in front of Woodies—a big display window, ritzy rather upscale department store with models and—not models, but mannequins all dressed. And then Flora was right in front of that. It was a contrast. A lot of people who grew up here or were here from when they were young remember her. People still remember her.[5]

When people dropped money into her tin cup, Flora Molton always put on a big smile and always said "God Bless You." Many people needed that blessing and warmly remember those kind words to this day.

JOHN JACKSON

Just about everyone who ever had the pleasure of knowing John Jackson will attest that he was one of the kindest, sweetest, and most wonderful people they had ever met in their lifetimes. He was almost universally beloved.

When John Jackson went over to England he was billed as Mississippi John Jackson.[1] The mild-mannered, good-natured Virginia native, an important and much beloved member of the DC blues scene, gently protested, "But I've never even been to Mississippi,"[2] but apparently over in England the blues comes from Mississippi, and that is that. That shows a shallow level of respect for the dignity and artistry of musicians. Some folks presumptuously act as if they own the blues, and even take dominion over it according to their own imagination. John Jackson didn't need to be marketed as something other than himself, as he was one of the finest songsters of the late twentieth century. Jackson was an exquisite instrumentalist and versatile musician who mastered complex fingerpicking and a wide repertoire of music on guitar, banjo, and harmonica. He was a true cultural treasure of American roots music. Like his friend John Cephas, Jackson was awarded the National Heritage "Living Treasure" fellowship from the National Endowment for the Arts in 1986, a huge honor for a brilliant musician whose life was filled with hardship and sorrow, but who internalized it through personal kindness and musical expression.

John Jackson always appeared neat and debonair, in his trademark fedora hat and a bolo tie, like a country gentleman. He often took the stage with a sports coat, even during hot summer shows, looking good as the best-dressed man at the concert. Perhaps because for most of his life he wore work clothes, first as a poor kid raised on the Virginia mountain farm as the seventh of fourteen children, then as chauffeur, butler, and gravedigger.

He was born in Woodville, Virginia, in Rappahannock County on the foothills of the Blue Ridge Mountains, on February 25, 1924, and grew up in Fort Valley. His parents, Suttie and Hattie Jackson, were tenant farmers. As a child, living conditions for his large family of fourteen children were hard in the Great Depression as black folks in an already poor rural mountain region. Yet, Jackson's family fared well as they ran a successful subsistence farm, in nineteenth-century conditions, still without electricity and indoor plumbing. It was commonplace for children during those days to work to help support the family. Starting at a young age, John Jackson learned the meaning of hard labor, and he was deprived of an education. For his family, it was a matter of survival, of assuring that there was food on the table. Jackson always said that they never had a food shortage with the family raising their own livestock and produce, with enough to sell and to pay the rent. He never openly stated that they were "poor," but it is evident that his childhood was one of hard work and toil. The family had little money, but they had enough to eat, and cultural riches in music. From early on, the conditions for his musical development were in place, as both of his parents exposed him to music.

He talked and looked "country" and he was an uneducated man, and some folks drew wrong conclusions from that throughout his life. Surely he encountered his share of discrimination, from whites for well-known reasons, and from some blacks for being "country." Jackson alluded to some of the suffering he encountered in life, and his attitude in overcoming his hardships, in an interview with Dr. Barry Lee Pearson and Cheryl A. Brauner in 1985:

> I'll tell you, there was no one was raised up that had no rougher time than I've had. But I really don't like to talk about it, 'cause whole lots of times if you talk, I always have a feeling I'm talking to make people feel sorry for you, or sad, or trying to say somebody mistreated you. I really appreciate the way I was raised 'cause if I wasn't I wouldn't have the chance I have today, or the understanding I have. I really appreciate the way I was raised by my family and by my self-experience. There is no way in the world I would have ever learned what I know if I hadn't had this real hard drag-out time.[3]

Jackson hardly ever spoke of the details of what these "hard drag-out times" were, but his former manager and friend, Patricia Byerly, shared an anecdote that he had shared with her:

> John was called to the selective service for his draft physical and evaluation. The white Army evaluator asked him, "Have you ever had the crabs?" John responded, "No, I never ate nothing like that." Because of that statement and because he was illiterate, he was promptly declared as "retarded" and dismissed from military service. The problem was that he believed this assessment, and that he went through a large portion of his life silently perceiving himself as retarded, or at least as a lesser man, until I spent hours to convince him that this assessment was nonsense and just stupid and ridiculous, racist and ignorant.[4]

He was branded and stigmatized because he was illiterate and because he didn't know about the sexually transmitted crab louse, which he mistook for the

Maryland Chesapeake Bay blue crabs, a delicacy that everyone in Maryland and Virginia knows. How was a poor black man from East Virginia who had never been to the ocean and never had a chance to try crabs, to make the cultural shift to the undesirable insect that nobody in his community had heard of? The silver lining of this incident was that he was not drafted into a war. Assuming that he would have been eligible for service at age eighteen, that would have been 1942 at the height of World War II. Most people who knew John Jackson could not well imagine him as a soldier, as he was meant to be a musician. Of course, the utterly unwarranted classification that caused personal humiliation and degradation was cold racism in its most primitive form.

Imagine if those fools who would unfairly brand Jackson in this way would find out that he was a National Endowment for the Arts National Heritage Fellow, the recipient of the highest honor the United States bestows on its traditional artists.

Actually, the people who knew John Jackson will attest that, quite to the contrary, he was anything but retarded. Indeed, he was most intelligent, even brilliant, as well as musically talented. He knew countless songs, and even short conversations with him revealed knowledge of a vast musical repertoire, possibly hundreds of songs. As he was unable to write the lyrics or melody down, and generally had to remember all things in life without the benefit of taking notes or documenting anything, he developed a powerful memory. His was an oral history, a large body of knowledge that he retained for a lifetime. Perhaps because his mind was not filled with useless information for its own sake, he had the memory of an elephant. He was a remarkable storyteller, a witty man with a wry country humor, who recollected details and names with fascinating sharpness. His brain was able to compensate for his inability to read and write by developing ways to use his mind in other ways, as a walking songbook of American roots music—all from memory. In order to imprint hundreds of song lyrics, the music and melody to memory, the brain must be trained to quickly absorb and retain information, which requires almost superhuman concentration. This manifested itself in anything he did, including when he toiled as a gravedigger. The people who knew him attested that when he dug a grave, it was a spiritual process. He saw the act of digging the grave as God's work that he had to perform with absolute perfection, with an almost Zen-like focus. His manager Patricia Byerly recalled:

> He had the ability to focus on things that was extraordinary. He talked about digging graves, and how people would laugh at him because he was a gravedigger. He'd say, but not in front of them, he would say, "That's okay, it doesn't matter what they say. Laying people to their final resting place is God's work and not everyone can do it. You have to be called for it." When he was digging a grave, he was always very respectful. He concentrated with total focus and made the grave perfectly

symmetrical, with clean lines and corners. He concentrated with such intensity until it was immaculate. That's why they asked him to dig Robert Kennedy's grave. So that was one of the things that made him extraordinary.

Phil said:

John Jackson went through some hard times in his life, some serious stuff. Yet, he didn't let it get to him. He always had a sunny disposition and he was just the sweetest, nicest man there ever was. Other people who complain so loudly didn't go through half of what he went through and they are bitter and angry at everyone and the world. Not John Jackson. He was just a sweetheart of a man who never let anything affect his good nature.

In the greatest paradox, Jackson, a virtual saint of a man, used to sing a Jim Jackson song "I'm a Bad, Bad Man," by the Mississippi singer of no relation. Almost farcically, he sang the refrain:

I'm a bad, bad man
Nobody knows how bad I am
I don't care for police, judge and a jury
I'm a man from the bad, bad land

Then, he made up his own stanzas with story lines about cutting people, beating them over the head with a rock in all sorts of ominous, violent escapades. Nobody who knew him believed a word of it and everyone chuckled.

Jackson spoke plainly and simply with a thick regional dialect. His beautifully melodic native speech would be worth a philologist's study, as Jackson had a tendency to insert extra vowels into words, creating a lilting downward glide of the letter, followed by a sudden raising, not unlike the blue note. He pronounced "bad" as "ba-ye-ad" and "am" as "a-ye-m," "door" as "doo-ah." Apparently, the black community in Rappahannock County had developed unique linguistic elements, virtually a pocket of a distinct dialect, because of the segregation and isolation of that community since slavery days. When John Jackson moved to Fairfax, Virginia, in 1949, even the other black folks were unfamiliar with his rare East Virginia dialect that was a "singing way of talking." His actual singing had a warm tone, ethereal and gritty with a real twang. Combined with his unique dialect, his singing was both idiosyncratic and compelling.

John Jackson told Frank Matheis in 1987:

We played blues and mostly we just liked songs. If we heard a song, on the radio or on the record, and if we liked it, we played that song. We didn't call it anything except a song and the name of the song. My favorite was Jimmie Rodgers. I liked just about everything he sang and so did we all. I learned a lot of his songs and I love to play them still. I also played blues from the records and learned all those songs. We played everything if we liked it.

The ragtime and blues virtuoso Arthur "Blind" Blake was a primary influence, and some of Blake's advanced guitar technique shone through in Jackson's playing. There were few who mastered the complicated guitar styles of Blind Blake and Blind Boy Fuller as exquisitely as John Jackson. John Jackson also cited Blind Lemon Jefferson, Jim Jackson, Barbecue Bob, the Mississippi Sheiks, Bessie Smith, and many more as influences. He played numerous country and western and blues styles, including Merle Travis–style picking, Delta-inspired slide guitar, and just about anything from the Appalachian and Piedmont folk and pop repertoire of the 1930s to '50s, of both the black and white communities.

John Jackson's banjo playing was very similar to the typical Appalachian clawhammer style and picking patterns of Doc Watson, Dock Boggs, and Roscoe Holcomb. Indeed, Jackson would be equally at home with Appalachian banjo players from Kentucky clear over to the Carolinas as he was to the regional blues guitar players like John Cephas and Archie Edwards.

His father died in 1940 while working in the field when Jackson was just fifteen, a dramatic experience for any family, especially with fourteen children and a farm to tend. At age twenty, he married his wife Cora Lee Carter, his lifelong partner with whom he had seven children. He was still performing at dances as a recently married man, but he stopped playing music at age twenty-two in 1946. After a violent and threatening incident while playing a party gig, he felt lucky to get out alive and gave up gigging, in an often-told story that is also recorded on "Why I Quit Playing Guitar," on his second Arhoolie album *Country Blues & Ditties*. In 1949, he moved his family to Fairfax Station in northern Virginia, twenty miles outside of Washington, DC, in pursuit of better opportunities. He worked in various jobs as butler, chauffeur, and later as gravedigger, playing music only at home. He didn't pick it back up as a performer until 1964, other than playing for his family around the house here and there.

Folklorist Chuck Perdue, professor of folklore and English at the University of Virginia, brought John Jackson out of his self-imposed hiatus. Perdue was a folklorist who was active in the region as one of the founders of the Folklore Society of Greater Washington and the National Council for the Traditional Arts (NCTA). In a story that could be right out of a Hollywood movie, he was filling his tank at an Esso station where John Jackson was sitting with the local mailman, who was taking guitar lessons. The mailman had been bugging the reluctant Jackson to teach him guitar after he was impressed by his instrumental skills after hearing him play at home for a group of children. Jackson met him at the gas station and they were playing just as Perdue showed up. The amazed folklorist established a connection to Jackson, and the rest is history. Perdue introduced Jackson to the regional folk and blues scene and helped him launch his professional career. Unlike some others who "discovered" old bluesmen and then took advantage of them by pulling them into exploitative contracts, Perdue helped Jackson without expecting or receiving payment. He was in it for the love of music and he changed the course of Jackson's life.

Perdue brought Jackson into the local coffeehouses and introduced him to virtually everybody on the regional blues scene and exposed him to a wider audience, including a concert for the Folklore Society. He and his wife Nan accompanied John Jackson to venues along the East Coast and effectively helped launch his performing career.

That eighteen-year hiatus and self-imposed musical isolation apparently didn't cause him to forget the songs, the lyrics, or lose his chops as a player. Maybe he practiced more at home than he alluded to in subsequent interviews. Considering that he played completely from memory, he could not even read up on the lyrics. If he still had the records he learned from they could have been an auditory reminder, but as documented, he lost all of them when moving to Fairfax in 1944, so he needed to rely in large part on his remarkable memory. He told Dr. Pearson: "That's the way I mostly learned to play was playing behind the 78 records. And what happened to those records? I had about five hundred 78 records; and the man that moved them broke up every one of them. And so, when I got into the music, I still remembered all these blues tunes that I still had in my head when I quit playing in 1946."[5]

John Jackson only played music as a sideline until well into his seventies. In the DC area, he was revered by his fellow musicians and by his audience. Late in life he started to learn reading and writing basics, an act of emancipation he described to his teacher, his manager of fourteen years, Trish Byerly, as "I'm free." The gravedigger who many looked down upon because of his perceived lowly station in life ended up playing for President Jimmy Carter and getting honored as a National Heritage Fellow by the National Endowment for the Arts for his role as a teacher and traditional artist. He played major music festivals in Newport and the Philadelphia Folk Festival, and the Smithsonian Folklife Festival, the Festival of American Folklife, and the American Folk Blues Festival and many more worldwide. He traveled all over the world and met his peers Lightnin' Hopkins, Brownie McGhee, Sonny Terry, Furry Lewis, Sam Chatmon, Jesse Fuller, Fred McDowell, Bukka White, Son House, Johnny Shines, B.B. King, Albert King, Bob Dylan, Jack Elliott, Joan Baez, Bonnie Raitt, Leon Redbone, Roosevelt Sykes, and many more over the years. He toured Europe in 1969 with Chris Strachwitz, and recorded for Arhoolie in Stuttgart, Germany. He also toured in Asia for the State Department in 1984 with Ricky Skaggs, Buck White and the Down-Home Folk, and Jerry Douglas.

John Jackson told Dr. Pearson of how he wanted to be remembered:

> I think I've been discovered as a bluesman, [but] I'm more of a songster than a bluesman, because I play music other than blues. But I would like to be remembered the same as Josh White, or Blind Boy Fuller, or Blind Blake. I really would like to be. Of course, I don't say I'm as great a blues player as Blind Blake or Blind Boy Fuller and those people, but I would like to be remembered that way.[6]

Shortly before John Jackson's death in 2002, when he knew that he had terminal cancer, he often told his manager, when reflecting back on his life and career with grateful satisfaction, saying "Didn't we have fun? Didn't we make many friends."[7]

There are few men who were as successful, satisfied, and personally kind and decent as John Jackson. Everyone who knew him remembers him as one of the best and the finest. Once, Frank Matheis heard an audience member say after a John Jackson concert, "He's the best blues guitar picker since Blind Blake." John Jackson would have loved it. It may well be true.

ESTHER MAE "MOTHER" SCOTT

Musicians treasure the connection to the past, and for Phil Wiggins it was an early opportunity to play with a remarkable woman whose career goes back to her teenage years singing and dancing with the traveling Rabbit's Foot Minstrels: Mother Scott. Mother Scott left home at fourteen to tour and she had performed with Bessie Smith.

Esther Mae was born on March 25, 1893, in Bovina, Mississippi, the seventh of thirteen children of plantation sharecroppers Henry S. Erves and Mary Liza Erves. She worked in the fields starting at age five picking cotton, and had occasional schooling at Clover Valley Baptist School but never learned to read music. She left Mississippi in 1941 and moved north to Baltimore and New York before settling in Washington, DC, in 1960. During those years she worked as a housekeeper and baby nurse.

She sang with Louis Armstrong and was a friend to Elizabeth Cotten. The *Washington Post* called her "One of the last survivors of the great era of Mississippi blues singers."[1] She said that she left the minstrel show after two years because she was tired of "bathing out of a pickle barrel." She left to go to New Orleans. It was there that she taught herself the guitar, although she did not have the two dollars to buy one. "I was sweet," she recalled, "so some of the boys would let me learn music on their guitars." One of her early tutors was Charley Patton.[2] She told *Sing Out!*: "Sometimes I would sing spirituals and sometimes I would sing blues. It didn't take much to get the blues because you always stayed blue anyway. I tell you what the blues mean. The blues is when you feel sorry for yourself. That's what started it. It's from slavery."[3]

Esther Mae Scott, affectionately known as "Mother Scott," moved to Washington, DC, in 1960. It was not until the Travellin' Blues Workshop pointed to her as a local cultural treasure in the 1970s that her name started to resonate more widely in the local region, and she cut her first album at age seventy-nine: *Mama Ain't Nobody's Fool* was recorded at Track Records in Silver Spring in 1971.

While in DC, she met the Rev. William A. Wendt of the St. Stephen and the Incarnation Episcopal Church, who saw the powerful musical history that lived through Mother Scott. He bought her a guitar and encouraged her to start performing again, which she did, mostly centered around church activities. She was also active on the local scene, which led to light touring to other churches and schools, and to some local radio and TV appearances. As a deeply spiritual woman, she was committed to her church group, "Mother Scott and Her Children Celebrate Life Together." She loved to sing spirituals and gospel, particularly "This Little Light of Mine" and "God Called Adam." She was also a strong-willed advocate for civil rights and justice. In a frequently reported episode, she once gathered "a Cox's Army of Blacks" to confront the pastor of a local church which once refused to admit blacks. "We walked in and them walked out," she said.[4]

Mother Scott, the beloved matriarch of the DC blues, died of a stroke on October 16, 1979, at the Washington Hospital Center. While she is largely overlooked in today's blues annals, directories, and histories, the musicians of the DC blues scene who had a chance to play with her, including Phil Wiggins, fondly remember her not just as a poetic, musical soul, but as a spiritual leader in her community. Her recorded interviews and radio appearances reflect a hilariously funny and witty persona, and the people who knew her remember most her open heart and gentle voice, filled with kindness, warmth, and comfort to all. The loving name "Mother" fit her most excellently.

WILBERT "BIG CHIEF" ELLIS

The Alabama native Wilbert Thirkield Ellis, referred to as "Big Chief" since childhood, was a self-taught barrelhouse pianist in the tradition of his cited influences—Price Lanier, a local pianist in his region who later settled in Detroit; and, the more famous Birmingham boogie-woogie and blues pianists "Pine Top" Smith, Walter Roland, and Jabbo Williams.

The larger-than-life persona Big Chief Ellis was born in 1915 to a religious family and raised in a suburb of Birmingham, Alabama. He told interviewers Ira Selkowitz and Susan Day:

> ...I had no piano, not even a radio. My parents were very religious and they didn't allow blues to be played around the house. My father was a minister. I really learned on my own 'cause I always loved the blues...One of my favorite players Price Lanier and another one was Smokey....The weirdest thing that ever happened to me was when I was a kid. This was when my parents found out I could play. This white guy from Siluria, Alabama came to Birmingham looking for Price Lanier (who) was out of town playing, and the kids on the corner told him that I could play the piano. Then he came down to my house and my parents didn't even know I could play piano. So, when he asked my mother could he take me to Siluria to play for this party and my mother said, "Well, my son doesn't play a piano." And so, I said, "Yes, I do, ma." So, they carried me up the street to where a piano was, and my mother heard me play and this guy heard me play. Well. She was astonished. "Where did you learn to play like this?" She still couldn't give me permission to go until my father came home. So, this guy waited until my father got home and then my father said, "Well, he can't play no piano." So, my mother said, "Yes, he can and you should hear him." So, my father heard me play and my father gave me permission...[1]

After high school, in 1936 at the height of the Great Depression, Ellis briefly hoboed around and eventually went to New York. In 1936 he married his life-long wife Mattie Lee Pennington. He joined the Army in 1939 and returned to bartending in New York City from 1942 to 1955.

Besides playing piano, he made his main living as a gambler, a vice that he was so good at that he got banned from many establishments for "reading factory stamps," meaning he could decipher the backs of the cards. "Only about three people that I know living can read them. I learnt it from a guy up in New York that made cards so you know what's on top or in the hands."[2] To reach the level of technical prowess as a self-taught pianist in such difficult skills as complex boogie-woogie piano, which is fast, intricate, and rhythmic, requiring focused timing, requires intense mental acuity and the capacity for computing and quantification, as well as creativity. These are the same skills needed for reading cards. Big Chief Ellis was a powerhouse of a player and a man of considerable intellect, or he could not have accomplished what he did.

Ellis was mostly inactive in music from 1955 to 1972:

> I gave up music in '55 for twenty years. I wasn't making no money at it, the record companies took all the money I could make. I didn't get no royalties so I worked bar and gambled. I decided that if I go to work for a living, I ain't playing for nobody. I got rid of my piano and organ and I didn't even listen to blues no more, that's how disgusted I was. People misuse you, take your money. When I tied myself up with "Sittin' In Records," they recorded six sides one time, three months later they recorded six more. I'm out of work for the next year, couldn't record for nobody (because he was tied down by a contract which prevented recording for other labels) and I wasn't getting no money from them. They did you, they took advantage of you.[3]

> He was quoted as saying, "Never got no royalties. In fact, my 'Dices' hit the Billboard. And I never got . . . not a penny royalties from that. Practically every record company I recorded for owes me money right now."[4]

He moved to Washington, DC, in 1972 to open a liquor store. Soon after he was contacted by local radio personality Dick Spottswood, who encouraged a comeback. In 1974–75 he played the National Folk Festivals, in DC and at Wolf Trap, and the Philadelphia Folk Festival. He recorded an album for the Trix label in Hyattsville, Maryland,[5] in 1976 titled *Big Chief Ellis featuring Tarheel Slim and Brownie McGhee and John Cephas*. Tarheel Slim aka Alden "Allen" Bunn was a versatile guitarist and baritone singer and a friend of the Big Chief. The album was recorded by Wilson, of the NCTA, and produced by Dick Spottswood and Peter B. Lowry. On the album cover, Ellis is shown with a full Native American chief's headdress, a call to his ancestry as his mother was a Black Creek Indian. His father had Irish blood in him, as Ellis explained: "My grandfather was Irish. I knew my grandfather, he owned the whole plantation in Eutaw, Alabama."

He formed the Barrelhouse Rockers in 1975, a band that included John Cephas on guitar and James Bellamy on bass. Phil Wiggins was asked to join the band in 1976. Big Chief Ellis told the story:

I played with Johnny Shines out at the Smithsonian Festival. I was out there three weeks. I was over in the Afro-American ... what they call it market-place. I had my group with me. I got a band now, four piece ... they local D.C. musicians. Well, the fact about it, I picked one up at the Smithsonian Festival. Then I picked another one up at a party. My guitar player he's originally from Bowling Green, Virginia. John Cephas, he's a good blues player, but he's not a lead guitar player, like say Bobby Radcliffe. Phil Wiggins, he plays harmonica with me now. James Bellamy, he's playin' bass with me. I had Phil come over when he finished playing with Flora Molton, to play with me. So, Johnny Shines told him he could play the blues, too, if he could play the spirituals he could play the blues. So, he came over and played the blues and then ... from then on, I've been having him with me. He plays some good blues. Did you see me in the Inaugural Parade (for Jimmy Carter). I was in the Alabama float. I had the whole group. Then I played for one of the Inaugural Balls at Union Station. I was on the stage with the square dancing.[6]

In 1977, Big Chief Ellis retired to his native Alabama, where he died of a heart attack at age sixty-three. His imprint on the local blues scene looms large to this day.

BILL HARRIS

There was never a bluesman like "Guitar Bill" Harris and there will never be another.

When he took the small stage of his Pigfoot blues and jazz club on Hamlin Street in Northeast Washington, DC, where the specialty was soul food like pickled pig feet or chitterlings, the first sign that things were different here was his nylon-string guitar. He used to get on stage wearing a straw fedora and declare that he had a Spanish classical guitar made in Puerto Rico that plays old-time black blues, saying in nearly every show that he was "classically trained and blues bred." Indeed, he studied classical guitar at the long-defunct Washington Junior College for Music. Listeners were treated to a genre-bending concoction of music that was at once fascinating, utterly unique, and totally captivating. Among his many witty stage wisdoms was "I live in Chocolate City, with Vanilla suburbs, and I play the blues."[1]

The bard from rural Nashville, North Carolina, who wrote and arranged rhythm and blues tunes for the Clovers in the 1950s, slipped in classical guitar riffs á la Andres Segovia, advanced jazz progressions á la Wes Montgomery and Kenny Burrell, with Spanish flamenco á la Paco De Lucia, mixed with a bit of Lonnie Johnson—all that in mournful and wailing country blues songs he learned as a kid in North Carolina. In the middle of the song he would throw in "North Carolina pig hollers"—a two-note, loud "woooooooeeeeee"—that could blow the wallpaper right off the club wall. Then he tore into some old country ditty sounding like a Spaniard from Andalusia as much as a bluesman from North Carolina. Despite his jazz sophistication, he always kept true to his love for the country blues, a staple at the Pigfoot. He told the *Washington Post* in 1983, "[At home in North Carolina] the uppity people, they looked down upon it because it was plain low-down dirty blues."[2]

Harris was a major celebrity in DC. In November 8, 1978, he was honored with "Bill Harris Day" in Ward 5. Former mayor Walter E. Washington said, "Bill Harris brought honor to himself and the District of Columbia through his world-renowned artistry as a jazz guitarist, composer and musician . . . and has freely shared his rich talents as a scholar, teacher and mentor of countless young people." Harris accepted the honor by saying, "It's not what the city has done for me. Washington has given me the self-confidence and opportunity to get some of my ideas over musically and business-wise."[3] Unfortunately, he may not have been as a good a businessman as he was a bluesman. The club only lasted from 1975 to 1981 when the IRS took it. They eventually took his home in 1987 for not paying taxes. It's hard to see what the government could have gained by taking away his livelihood, the only way he could have earned the money required to repay the back taxes.

On December 6, 1988, "Guitar Bill" died at the Howard University Hospital of pancreatic cancer at age 63. His legacy remains as one of Washington, DC's most accomplished musicians. He was a brilliant composer, teacher, club owner, and friend to many. Famed jazz guitarist Kenny Burrell said after his death, "To sit and jam—that's something Bill . . . always encouraged at the picnics and at Pigfoot. He's always wanted young people to play . . . he's made a great contribution to the music as a teacher, especially around the Washington area."[4]

THE FESTIVAL OF AMERICAN FOLKLIFE (SMITHSONIAN FOLKLIFE FESTIVALS)

Performing at the Festival of American Folklife, often simply called the Folklife Festival, was one of the most important early career experiences for Phil, backing up Flora Molton and meeting some of the greats of the country blues in the period of 1974–78. During those years the festival actively showcased acoustic, rural blues and exposed this roots music to many thousands of visitors.

The festival defines itself as "An international exposition of living cultural heritage annually produced outdoors on the National Mall of the United States in Washington, DC, by the Smithsonian Institution's Center for Folklife and Cultural Heritage. For two weeks, every summer over the Fourth of July holiday, the Festival is a free-to-the-public community based educational event." Ralph Rinzler (1934–1994) was founding director of the Festival of American Folklife, one of the largest annual cultural events in the U.S. capital that usually includes daytime and evening programs of music, song, dance, crafts, and cooking demonstrations, storytelling, and other cultural education programs. The festival encourages audience participation to converse with people presented in the program.

In the 1970s there was a recognized need to establish greater diversity and to give exposure to African American culture, which had been largely shut out of mainstream cultural events. The Smithsonian created an African Diaspora Advisory Group under the leadership of Folklife Festival assistant director Gerald Davis. There was a two-week pilot program at the 1974 Folklife Festival, followed by an even more ambitious two-week program at the 1975 Festival, and culminating in a twelve-week program for the Festival in 1976 to mark the U.S. bicentennial.[1] Phil performed with Flora Molton at each of these events.

James Early, now the director of Cultural Heritage Policy at the Center for Folklife Programs and Cultural Heritage at the Smithsonian Institution, recalled meeting Phil for the first time:

> Phil Wiggins was playing with Big Chief Ellis. He was a teenager, a young adult 16 or 17 years old maybe—sitting on the side of the stage on the ground, and he was

blowing his harmonica along with the group. I recall that Chief Ellis stopped and said, "You got to get on this stage." Because we were young black Americans negotiating our way in a public space where race was the dominant screen for negotiation—not knowing our way around the Smithsonian Institution—and someone like me, who had not come out of research of the music, it was a black-white paradigm. I certainly didn't know how to think about the impact of what was going on, other than that this was a powerful ideological-slash-intellectual educational construct to talk about the connectivity of people of African descent. But what it meant to the participants—the musicians, the cooks, the dancers, the weavers—I did not have a broad, deep thinking beyond probably the sense that, yes, each individual feels proud to be able to display his or her voice, or whatever their artistic expression. . . . You had this older black woman who could hardly see, and the indelible image of this older black woman with this youngster, this young man Phil Wiggins playing with her. . . . They didn't come from the organized professional musician tradition. The music [of Flora Molton with Phil Wiggins] went deep inside all of us, and certainly inside of me, because for whatever intellectual understanding that I lacked at that time about "Folklife," they touched me deeply. . . . Ralph Rinzler had been at the apex of this new notion called "public folklore." This is not just an academic exercise . . . this is not just about the brilliance and the beauty of the compositions and the lyrics and the way that they objectify their personal lives or the social space in which they live. This is about the fight against racism, the fight against poverty. It's about building a new humanity of black and white together. I did not have those narratives at that time. So that's my memory. I have watched Phil Wiggins over the years with that as a backdrop, and I can now speculate about how that event had an impact on him and other musicians, about the apprenticeship relationship [between Flora and Phil] and how a validating institution like the Smithsonian was for that. . . . When I see Phil now, we may run into each other here or there, he's the same Phil Wiggins. Now, he's world-renowned and famous. But if you don't know who he is you won't know because he's another fellow walking down the street, but he is carrying this tremendous imagination, this extraordinary talent. . . . It was verified by all those old guys who say, "Hey, young boy, you've got something. I know you think I've got something—otherwise you wouldn't be hanging around here. But you've got something." To see him and John Cephas become famous worldwide, after seeing him around Johnny Shines and all of these people, is so good to see.[2]

THE GAINES BROTHERS

The acoustic blues in the nation's capital has a long history. Nobody can go back in time and name all the fine players who might have lived and played there without ever achieving fame and recognition. Even during the 1970s, when Phil Wiggins was already active on the music scene, there were mysterious and unsung players of fine reputations who never recorded. Among them are the brothers Leroy and Willie Gaines, friends and musical compatriots of Archie Edwards, who often joined the jam sessions at Archie's barbershop. Their peers on the local scene exalted these players, but they are now missing from the blues archives. Both John Cephas and Archie respected them, but unfortunately, as far as we know, the Gaines Brothers never made a record and played only within their own community. There is hardly any historical record of them, and they remain an enigma. Judging by the accolades and respect the others had for them, they must have been amazing players. When Archie Edwards mentioned the guitar players of the region in an interview with Dr. Barry Lee Pearson, he listed the Gaines Brothers right up there with the best of the region, most of whom went on to achieve a level of fame that the Gaines Brothers would not get to experience: "You know, the guitar is pretty famous here on the East Coast. So, I think you can find lots of blues players around here, like John Tinsley, the Gaines Brothers Willie and Leroy, John Cephas, Flora Molton, John Jackson and his son James. They're all from Virginia."[1]

Archie Edwards told Dr. Barry Lee Pearson:

We'd have Saturday night gatherings at the barbershop. The Gaines brothers, Leroy and Willie Gaines, different people sit around, play the guitar, drink a few beers, a little whiskey. He could holler so loud that your windowsill would rattle. Good Lord say, "Willie Gaines, get out there on the mountain and holler!" He'd wake them up. Yes, sir, Willie Gaines get up on some mountain and yell, he'd wake everybody down in the valley. That boy had a voice on him, and he was so stout he could take his guitar strings off it, come back on it, and pull the strings off it. He ruined so many guitar strings on me that I said, "Wait a minute. My guitar strings don't wear out like this." I said "Willie, you're so strong that when you pull back, you tear the dad-blamed strings up." Yes, sir, he was something. And Willie could dance, too. He was an all-around guy.[2]

The German photographer Axel Küstner, who first recorded Cephas & Wiggins on his Living Country Blues album series, remembered that Archie Edwards took him to see Leroy Gaines in his home in Washington in 1978, and he took one of the few remaining photos of him. Axel Küstner recalled:

After we interviewed and met Archie at the barbershop, Archie had met the Gaines Brothers, and then Archie took him and me over to meet Leroy Gaines, one of his buddies. We went over to Leroy's home that evening and I did some tape record-ings. It was some instrumental piece or some pieces I did not at that time know the title. He jammed with Archie and some with Tim Lewis, but one song that I could remember was "Rattlesnake'n Daddy," and "Lovin' Spoonful" . . . Probably compared to Archie I felt that he might have been a little rusty. He was definitely not in the same class as Archie. I especially remember that I had a camera, a 35mm with a flash, and I remember very well that he was under the impression that he would be on TV. I went back two years later, but I don't think I would have considered him good enough or interesting enough to have him recorded for the Living Country Blues series. So that was the only time I ever met him that evening for a brief time— maybe an hour or so, you know.[3]

Küstner's assessment is contrary to the high esteem that many of their musi-cal compatriots had for Leroy and Willie Gaines. His fateful decision not to record Leroy Gaines may have been a great loss for blues history, but alas, it was not meant to be. Using a Bob Dylan idiom, the Gaines Brothers stayed "com-plete unknowns" who would have faded into total obscurity, were it not for the glowing ways in which Archie Edwards spoke of them.

AN INTERVIEW WITH JOHN CEPHAS

—Dr. Barry Lee Pearson[1]

Bowling Green, the county seat of Caroline County, Virginia, lies some ninety miles southwest of Washington, DC, on U.S. Highway 301. "Bowling Green" John Cephas lives in a house he built himself in the rural community of Woodford, five miles outside Bowling Green. Over the years his life has been divided between Woodford and Washington, where he was born [on September 4, 1930] and where he worked as a carpenter until retiring in 1987. Today, when not on the road playing the blues, he tinkers with his cars, boats, and tractors, and pursues the life of a gentleman farmer.

Cephas's music derives primarily from two formidable African American institutions, the church and the country house party. His father owned a guitar, but his earliest inspiration and instruction came from his aunt, Lillian Dixon, who, along with her friend Haley Dorsey, introduced him to the blues. Cephas' grandfather, John Dudley, first exposed him to rural nightlife and country "breakdowns," teaching him songs that were then favorites on the house party circuit and are still in his repertoire today. His other primary teacher was his cousin, David Talliaferro, one of the best guitar players in Caroline County.

Cephas had given up performing in the late 1960s, but a chance encounter with Alabama pianist Wilbur "Big Chief" Ellis rekindled his interest. Cephas and Ellis met harmonica player Phil Wiggins at the Smithsonian Folklife Festival in 1976 and, together with bassist James Bellamy, formed the Barrelhouse Rockers. Ellis moved back to Alabama less than a year later, however, and died there in 1977. Since then Cephas & Wiggins have carried on as a duo, quickly earning a reputation as the top acoustic blues act in the Southeast. John Cephas received a National Heritage Award in 1989 in recognition of his musical talent, his teaching efforts, and his determination to keep the Piedmont blues tradition in the public eye. He continues to participate in workshops and other public presentations and serves as a board member for the NCTA.

Like Cephas, Phil Wiggins is a Washington, DC, native [he was born on May 8, 1954]. A self-taught harmonica player, he learned from community traditions and from listening to records of harmonica legends Sonny Terry, Little Walter, and Sonny Boy Williamson II. His highly vocal harmonica style also draws on his grandmother's old-fashioned lined-out hymns and on the style of Washington guitar evangelist Flora Molton, with whom he worked off and on until 1976. His style merges the soulfulness of church vocals with the good-time sound of house party blues. Today, he and Cephas enjoy worldwide recognition as the leading exponents of the Piedmont or East Coast blues tradition that embraces the style of Blind Boy Fuller, Gary Davis, Sonny Terry, and Brownie McGhee.

As far back as I can trace my family's existence was that my family most likely came up the Rappahannock River as slaves, and they were disembarked at Port Royal. Most of the black people in this area, this is where they came from. And they were sold into slavery in Caroline County, Spotsylvania County, and farther south of here. And then they settled mostly in the Norfolk area where my great-great-great-great-grandfather was a slave, and then later, after the Emancipation Proclamation, he was given the forty acres and a mule. The mule is dead, but the land that was given to the family is still intact over there. I grew up in a segregated society, to everybody in the community; they were so close that we almost were considered family although we might not have been birth kin. But it was just like one big family and what influenced me came out of this community I was raised in.

I was born in Washington, DC, in what is known as Foggy Bottom. That was supposed to be a bad part of town at that time, but that was a real good experience. During that period of time, I think that families were much closer together and you lived in neighborhoods where everybody knew everybody. In contrast, today it's very different because I don't care where you live, everybody's strangers. But we were all one big happy family. A lot of my relatives lived nearby in the same neighborhood and they visited each other's houses. We shared music together. It was so much that we shared together.

When I was young, seven or eight years old, my mother taught me and my brother Ernest how to sing. We were a duet. She brought us up and would rehearse us during the week, during the daytime. My father was out working for one of the construction companies, and my mother used to have us practicing. And boy, when I used to hit them bad notes or didn't sing in tune, my mother used to whap us. My mother . . . she really taught me about how to sing, how to use your voice. So we sang in the church under the direction of my mother for years, until I got up to about ten or twelve years old.

When I was eight or nine years old, my aunt Lillian introduced me to the blues. She had a boyfriend named Haley Dorsey and he was very good at playing the guitar. He used to come to the house and spent time with my aunt and every time he would come around he would bring his guitar. I was attracted to that sound, that blues, you know, when I was young. Aunt Lillian, she was a guitar player herself. So I used to listen to her and Haley play the blues. Blues was around the house all the time. Sometimes she would play the guitar and I would stand there, so young I wasn't even realizing what I was hearing, but I was so fascinated with it. And my aunt knew that I was interested. So even at that early age she would give me the guitar and in her spare time she would try to show me how to play. I was always asking her, "Will you show me how to do this?" And she would show me different chords on the guitar. And I did learn a few chords and it kind of just always stuck with me. I was always trying to pick out something on the guitar.

My real inspiration in life was my grandfather, John Dudley. He was quite the guy. He was always respected in the community as one who was really cheerful, as one who could really sing, one who would like to party. Almost everybody knew him and knew him as a person that on the weekends there was going to be a party where there's going to be plenty food, plenty to drink, and plenty good times. Yeah. That was my grandfather. He taught me the song about "Going Down the Road Feeling Bad," taught me about "Railroad Bill." Then he used to play a lot of those songs like "Hand Me Down My Walking Cane." Oh man, there were so many songs. And then he used to sing like the barbershop songs, "Oh I Wander Today From the Hills," "Maggie," to "Watch the City Below, "songs like that. "The Old Mill Stream" and songs of that nature that they would barbershop on. We used to do all that together. Get all the family, my mother and my aunt, my brother, my father, and we used to sing all those songs.

[My grandfather] was a guitar player, a gambler, a ladies' man. And sometimes I've been associated with being the sole heir of John Dudley. When I was young, he used to come around to the house in Foggy Bottom and say, "Hey, boy, come on. I'm going down the road. I want to take you with me." We used to go down in Virginia. My grandfather used to get us and take us down to the country together and show me all about where my roots were. Show me my cousins, our homeplace and where he was born. And I was really impressed by that. He loved those country breakdowns and he used to have them at his house. As a matter of fact, I had a cousin named Jim Henry Coleman from down in Virginia used to make liquor. So my grandfather used to sell liquor and he used to drink it too. I think the very first drink of liquor that I took in my life my grandfather kind of oversaw that. I was with him at my cousin Jim Henry's house and he had some of that still liquor. I was just a young fellow, but I remember he and my brother and all of us were together. My grandfather told me, he would say, "Boy, you got to start. You got to cut your teeth, boy, and be a man." He would say, "You won't be a man until you can drink this. You got to stand up and drink it like a man." So he gave me some of that stuff and that stuff liked to kill me. Yeah, he was the kind of guy that introduced me to all those things: corn liquor, music, country parties, and all those good times.

I can remember they would have house parties and they would send us upstairs to bed. All the kids would be upstairs and they would be partying downstairs. A lot of times you couldn't go to sleep for all of the music and frolicking that was going on. But we weren't participants. That didn't come until later years when they kind of loosened the reins on you. You know, the older people used to have the reins on you. They wouldn't expose you to too much of what they were doing during that time. But I would hear the sound in my ear, you know. The words that they were singing and how they would be affected by it. And it kind of affected me in the same way. Even though I was going to church I always had that aspiration to go there to be with that other crowd. Of course the people in the church, especially my mother, kind of frowned upon that even though they were doing the same thing. They would go to church on Sunday, but on those Friday and Saturday nights they would gather at each other's houses for those country breakdowns and hoedowns where they dance and drink corn liquor and just have a good time.

I grew up in a religious home. My father was a Baptist minister and all of my young years, even before I was attracted to the blues, I was always encouraged to play religious music. If I'm interested in music, this was the way to go. As I grew up, and when they found out that I was kind of interested in blues, man, they say: "This is the wrong way to go. Don't go to the houses of ill repute." But whenever they would party like on the weekends, Fridays or Saturdays when other people would come over, the first thing they would say was, "John, go get your guitar and come out and play a few numbers for some of the people here in the house." And they would partake of the blues too. But they would always encourage me: "No, no don't do this, don't do this, please don't do this." But I didn't look at it like that. A lot of times they say, "Oh God, this is Satan's music. This is devil's music. Those people are getting drunk and they're down in there having a good time with women and they're doing all these things of ill repute. For God's sake, don't do this." But when the band struck up, they was right there.

My father bought a guitar. So at that time I had already been exposed to the blues. I was actually playing a little bit of open-key stuff and slide that he didn't know anything about. So he bought himself a guitar and he used to hide it in the closet and he wouldn't allow me to touch it. But every time that he would leave, I'd go to the closet and get his guitar and I'd play it. Almost every time he would inevitably catch me, or know that I had been fooling with it, and give me a licking over it. One way he used to catch me, a couple of times I'd break a string on there. And I got where I could tie them back up and tighten it back up. And he'd go and look, see the string tied up and say, "Oh, you've had the guitar." So I got many a thrashing over the guitar. So one day I had been after his guitar again and he just told me, "Well, I can't stop you and I'm getting tired of whipping you. It don't look like I'm ever going to be able to play it, so I'm going to give it to you. Here's the guitar if you want to play it." That gave me a chance to play it as much as I wanted, after he almost killed me trying to keep me from playing it. And I really went for broke then, because I didn't have to be ashamed of it or try to hide it.

I learned "John Henry" in open tuning, what we called Sebastopol. In fact, that's the first way I learned to play guitar was in Sebastopol, because once you tune it up you didn't have to finger too much. You just have to like play on the dots of the guitar and you make plenty good music, or use a slide. I mean, I used to just take one string, and strung it up on a board or somehow. I'll tell you what they used to use a lot: when they used to make them brooms, a broom had wire around the top of it, take that wire off the broom when they throw that broom away and string it up on something, put a bridge on the bottom and slide up and down to change key. I used to play in open tuning then because I didn't know too much about how to tune it up. But I could tune open tunings, or I'd get somebody to tune it up for me to play in standard tuning. I didn't start really participating at those house parties until I was a teenager. At least I didn't start drinking corn liquor until I was about fourteen years old. Then I kind of got more exposed to the intricacies of it, the real lowdown blues. Every chance I would get I would try to go down where they were playing the blues and dancing. It just came naturally to me. Blues drew me like a magnet. It was part of me, part of my heritage, part of my soul.

The families had no other place to go. In the black community, wherever they lived, all the black people, they were there together. And what they would do is that on the weekends, my cousin lived right down the road from me. Another cousin live right down the road from me; my brother and sister live right down the road from me. We would congregate at one of the family members' houses. And that's where we would have our fun. That's where we have our house parties, you know. And it was so integral and it was so family-oriented that almost every weekend, everybody would be wherever the party was. And the blues was just a medium that kind of drew them together. That wasn't the only thing that drew them together. Just being in a segregated society, for survival, drew the black people together.

So on weekends we'd gather together at somebody's house. A lot of them were primitive instruments they would play. Homemade. Somebody might have a guitar that he had made. He might have some percussion instrument that he made. He might have some bones or spoons. And then they did have store-bought instruments, but they weren't of good quality. But anything that a guy could make music from, if he was just beating on top of a can or pan or either a washtub string band. They used just about anything you could think of to make instruments. In later [years], they were able to buy instruments. Saxophones, guitars, banjos, fiddles, and what have you. We had one guy that was really good on the banjo, Harold Hill. He inspired a lot of guys to play the banjo. He could pick it or claw-hammer it either one. I played with banjo players. I even tried to play banjo myself. I could play it a little bit. I started to buy one a little while ago. But the banjo is so expensive now I don't know if I want one or not.

I had a cousin named David Talliaferro who was a great influence on me. He was six or seven years older than me and he was one hell of a guitar player. I'll tell you the truth, David was the best guitar player around, the best in Caroline County, Virginia, maybe all of Virginia. Didn't nobody fool around with David Talliaferro. But he was just a country boy and never got exposure. He died about twenty-five years ago. But he really taught me a lot, I'd say 80 percent of what I know on the guitar. He just played those raw blues. He taught me to play the thumb-and-finger style, like the other Piedmont guitar players do. We called that style the "Williamsburg Lope." You know, trying to get the guitar to say what you want it to say while keeping the rhythm behind it. I used to sit for hours on end just playing and singing to myself, trying to get that three-finger style of picking. When I first discovered I had it, man, that was an experience. I think I went out and got plastered. Once I got that, I started feeling comfortable with the guitar. I could sit down and play what I wanted and it sounded like I wanted it to sound. David and I kind of teamed up and we would go around together on the weekends and play at parties or just about any affair on that house-to-house circuit. And the more I played, the better I got.

David was the best I worked with back then . . . if he would play. He wouldn't play unless you gave him something to drink. Then in order to keep playing, he'd have to have something more to drink, and then soon he'd get drunk and then he couldn't play anymore. Well, I guess that's characteristic of a lot of other blues players. Of course, back then I had quite a tolerance for alcohol. I could drink David under the table and still be going strong. Of course, I'm paying for it now. But back then we would just play music and drink corn liquor. Man, I've drunk so much of it, I'm going to tell you the truth, it used to run out of my ears.

Then I had another cousin, John Woolfolk, and sometimes he would go around and play with us. And he had a sister who could play too, and she used to give house parties. In this part of Virginia certain people were noted for having gatherings at their houses. One place in particular was my cousin's, Christine Woolfolk. She used to have something almost every weekend. It was just like going to a juke joint. Christine used to fool around with the guitar. She would just do it in fun and frolic. She might say: "Give me that guitar. Let me play; learn to do this." She might do one number and that's it or something like that. She wouldn't want to get competitive. Absolutely not. It wasn't proper for a woman to do that.

Even here in DC, they would have rent parties and have entertainers, some-body playing the guitar. That would draw a lot of people. But we never made any money, just all we could eat and drink. When I got older and started working, I still preferred to be down in the country even though it's a long drive back and forth to Washington. I must have driven that 301 highway a million times, because even years ago I would head for the country on the weekends. I don't think I can remember a weekend when I got off work on Friday evening that I didn't have somewhere to go. See, everything started on Friday and kept on just the whole weekend. Man I couldn't wait to get out of town.

Out in the country everybody knew everybody, so you knew what you could do and what you couldn't do. So it wasn't much of a problem. Of course, there used to be a fight every now and then. Like if somebody gets jealous because he thinks somebody else is shooting at his woman. I tell you, them guys used to be aggressive, particularly about the girls. Yeah, that's what most of them get to fighting about, them girls. Especially after you get a little high, you know, and the music gets jumping and you're dancing on the floor. You better not dance with nobody else's woman too long. And not too many times. And maybe one of those women was cheating on somebody. Well, they used to fight and cut, shoot each other over that.

And sometimes the parties used to get turned out. If you weren't involved in it, you just pick up your stuff and go over to somebody else's place. And then I've been to parties where I've been involved in actually fighting. We started fighting maybe one or two o'clock. If somebody that's a friend of mine gets in a fight, we fight all night long or fight until everybody gets too tired and go home. Yeah, get black and blue and bloody if one of those free-for-alls starts. Boy, I'll tell you, back in the country things could get rough. Everybody gets steamed up drinking that corn liquor and someone starts fighting. I've been in free-for-alls where everybody would be fighting and nobody knows who's fighting who. Breaking all the windows out, tearing the door down. I've been to quite a few of those. But all that's faded out. Mainly, I guess, because black people have become more affluent now and they're involved in so many other things. They're free to travel and to go where they want to. They have a little bit of money now and there's no need for a house party because their lifestyle has absolutely just changed.

Drinking and staying up all night long kind of got to me after a while. We would play those old juke joints and be on the road all the weekend, going from place to place, and I got tired of that. And then there was the headaches from some of those bad weekends when you drink too much. So I just gave up playing the guitar altogether. I didn't want to play any more music. I didn't want to play guitar for about five or six years. As a matter of fact, I played at a party one night and left my guitar and I didn't go back to get it. That was in the late '60s.

Then one night I went out to a birthday party. A girlfriend invited me to this party. I hadn't played for a long time. So I went there, but I didn't take a guitar. There was a guy she introduced me to. His name was Big Chief Ellis. She introduced us and told me that he was a well-known blues piano player. And she told him, "Chief, John plays the guitar." So he and I just started talking and what have you. Well, the same evening the hostess of the party said, "Say, John, why don't you get your guitar so Chief can hear you play?" I said, "Oh, shucks, I don't feel like fooling with no guitar." But then Chief said, "Man, why don't you go on and get your guitar. I'd like to hear you play." So then I said, "Okay," and I went home and got my guitar and brought it back. All the people were sitting around in there and they wanted to hear blues. So I struck up a few tunes. Chief said, "Man, you play a mean guitar. Boy, you can really play that thing." I said, "Well, I'd like to hear you play sometime." So then the girl that had the party said, "You know, I've got a piano downstairs in the basement. Why don't you guys go down there and hook up a little bit."

Chief and I agreed and went downstairs. And, boy, when he started playing the piano, I said, "Man, this guy is ready!" He was playing the blues. Stuff that I love, like Walter Davis. And believe me, when I heard them, it was rebirth. So we played and all the people that was upstairs came downstairs. I guess it was about ten o'clock when we hooked up and we played until the next morning at daybreak. Straight through. We was drinking and having a heck of a time.

So Chief told me, "Man, I've been looking for a guitar player like you." He started telling me about some of the things he was doing, playing festivals and all, and asked if I would come and play with him. At first I told him I wasn't interested. But he would call me every day to ask me to come over to his house and play. I can never forget, I used to try to duck Chief sometimes. I wouldn't answer the phone because I thought it was Chief telling me to come and play, and I didn't want to get involved with playing. Finally, I started going over to his house in the evenings, and me and him would play. I was really catching on to what he was doing, and we got it together and made a good connection. Then I went out and played a few festivals with Chief and then people started to hear me and Chief playing. And then we started getting gigs and more gigs. And I was almost just eased back into it, you know. I'd never played really for money until I had met Big Chief Ellis. And really I was unaware that people were interested in that blues type of music I was playing, that black man's country folks music. So Chief and I, we played together for about five or six years, traveling around to different places. Big Chief played that old barrelhouse piano, which was unique because very few people can make the piano roll the way he could. And I'll tell you, it really went good with the type of blues guitar that I played.

In 1976 we were playing at the American Folklife Festival in DC, down on the Mall. That's where we met Phil Wiggins, who was playing with Flora Molton, a gospel singer out of Washington, DC. I was playing with Big Chief. We had Johnny Shines, Sonny Rhodes, and other blues musicians there. So in between one of our breaks, we were planning on having a jam session after we were off stage. And we heard him playing that harp, Chief and I. So we kind of conspired. I was telling Chief, "Man, the way that guy plays that harp, we ought to try to talk that guy into coming and joining us." So Chief say, "Yeah, we ought to do it." So Phil agreed. Then we started off with a group called the Barrelhouse Rockers. It was four of us: Chief, James Bellamy on bass, Phil on harmonica, and me on the guitar. I guess we played together until, I think it was 1977. Chief had a heart attack down in Birmingham, down in his home. He went home, I guess for his final rest, he went back home and died.

I would still get calls from people to come and do a gig just by myself. So I did a couple of gigs, but I kind of felt uneasy. I just wasn't really into it. So I asked Phil, "Why don't you come and we do a couple gigs together." So Phil agreed and we really had a good, tight sound together. So then we started getting a little notoriety as a duo and we just progressed until the present day. Over the last twenty years we've played just about any place you could imagine. We've been all over the country. We've been all over the European Community too. Scandinavia, Germany, France . . . we've been all over Africa and South America for the Arts America program. We've been to the Soviet Union and China, Mongolia and Australia. So I guess you could say we've been all over the world playing. I'd still go anywhere to play the blues and to teach people about Piedmont blues. But I think it takes a certain kind of person to handle the aggravation of being on the road so much. It's definitely a strain. I mean, we've been on the road so long that I keep a bag packed all the time. When I come home, I just take out all the dirty clothes and put in some other clothes and set my bag by the door.

I like all kinds of music, and if I like it I try to learn it. I used to listen to Merle Travis a lot, and I learned quite a few of his songs and some of his techniques, some of his style—and Skip James, Blind Boy Fuller, Gary Davis. I first heard Skip James on recordings and the minute I heard him I was just drawn into his repertoire. I mean, he was so different and the music was so eerie, so bluesy, the minute I heard it I was drawn into it. But I'll play everything from gospel to country and western. Phil and I try to give the audience different styles in our shows: ragtime, lowdown blues, more uptempo stuff. But basically, we stay close to the Piedmont sound because that's our roots.

ARCHIE EDWARDS: BARBERSHOP BLUES

—Dr. Barry Lee Pearson[1]

Archie Edwards describes his music as "good old country blues." Although he owns an electric guitar and can play some "Chuck Berry and Jimmy Reed," he prefers the acoustic sound of the 1920s and 1930s. Following a typical pattern, Archie played as a youngster, then put his music away for a while. However, he later began to play again and, motivated by the presence of John Hurt, he brought his music to the public. Now he is a mainstay on the Washington blues scene. Edwards and a handful of other performers, including John Cephas and Phil Wiggins, Flora Molton and John Jackson, are keeping East Coast country blues alive.

Archie was born in 1918 in Rocky Mount, Virginia, and grew up in a musical family back in the country around Union Hall, Virginia. His father was a major inspiration but the recordings of Blind Boy Fuller, Blind Lemon Jefferson, John Hurt, Furry Lewis, and Buddy Moss provided his early repertoire. Archie is, in a sense, a blues historian and can interpret the songs and the styles of his early heroes. But he is also an extremely creative songwriter with a great talent for blending traditional material with his own ideas to produce a special brand of East Coast blues. His repertoire includes ballads such as "Stagolee," "Frankie and Johnny" and "John Henry" which he learned from his father. He has many original compositions to his credit, several of which are available on his first album, *Living Country Blues USA, Vol. 6: The Road is Rough and Rocky*, produced by Siegfried Christmann and Axel Küstner in 1980 for the German L+R label (L+R 42.036). His only previous recording was a 45, "The Circle Live Boat," backed by his tribute to John Hurt, "The Road Is Rough and Rocky." His association with and admiration for John Hurt has deeply influenced his life and Archie is dedicated to keeping John's music and memory alive.

Archie has performed all over the DC area in concerts and at house parties. He has worked clubs like the Ontario Place, Childe Harold's, and McGuire's Tavern on Capitol Hill. He has performed at the Smithsonian Festival of American Folklife several times and has also been to the Philadelphia Folk Festival, the Hudson River Festival, the Maryland Folklife Festival, and the Folklore

Society for Greater Washington's Annual Festival at Glen Echo. He recently toured Europe with the American Folk Blues Festival. I first met him in 1976 at the Maryland Festival when he was performing with the late Mother Scott. As impressive as his blues playing was then, it has improved and now includes Blind Lemon Jefferson and Jimmie Rodgers pieces played on the ukulele! He has also resurrected a slide guitar style he learned from his father.

Archie moved to Seat Pleasant in the 1950s. He has been a barber, a truck driver, cab driver, and a special police officer. Recently he retired from government work, he is now content to drive his cab and play music. He is available for bookings and can be reached through Barry Pearson, Folklore Archives, English Department, University of Maryland, College Park, Maryland.

Archie's words are taken from several interviews and taped conversations which took place in his barbershop, my home, and at the University of Maryland. The interview was edited by Archie and myself.

Archie Edwards:

I was born in Franklin County, Virginia, a little place out in the country. I started playing the guitar when I was about seven years old, back in the country. My father played the guitar very well, and the harmonica—everything. He was really a harmonica player, Oh boy! And the five-string banjo—he'd whip a five-string banjo to death but he never did do anything with it.

So I got interested in it from his playing. There was no radios, televisions at that time and the only music we heard was someone playing a banjo or guitar every now and then.

How I got started, people would come to the house, sit down and jam. Pick the guitar, play the banjo, harmonica, all that stuff. He had some friends that played and on Saturday night back in those days people didn't have nothin' to do but walk five or ten miles and come by his house, you know, eat dinner, drink whiskey, and play the guitar. My father had a buddy named Boyd Maddox who would do that quite often. Now he played real good guitar. So he would come to our house on Saturday night and stay till Monday morning sometimes. So one Saturday night in March, I reckon around the early '30s, I was a little child. So my father and this fellow were playing the guitar and my mother fixed dinner. So they put the guitar on the bed, you know in the country there, the bed was in the living room. So he put the guitar on the bed and we were all sitting around the fire there.

So there was one note that that man made on the guitar, one note ringing like crazy in my mind, in my head, you know. So in those days, you know, children were not supposed to touch anything that belonged to anyone else. If you did, you just got tore up. But this note that this guy had made on the guitar, it sounded so pretty and one mind told me, "If you can just get over there to that bed and make that note just one time real low, you'll have it made. If I could make that one note I knew I would be able to play the guitar. I finally got the courage to sneak over there to the bed and I picked up the guitar and I made the note. That was the old "Red River Blues" but I think I dropped down a little too heavy with that and my daddy heard it, my father, he said, "Who in the world is that in there in the living room playing that guitar?" that man said, "Uncle Roy, that's your boy playing that guitar." Sure enough, it was Uncle Roy's boy and Uncle Roy's boy has been playing ever since.

So that's when I started, when I was about six or seven years old. I started on what you call the old "Red River Blues," but I didn't get a whipping either and that's one thing my father didn't whip me for. Said, "Now, wait a minute, as young as he is he done made a note. I like that."

My father was a sharecropper so I grew up on the farm. I didn't pick any cotton 'cause I grew up in Virginia but I did pluck a lot of tobacco. We grow tobacco, call it priming tobacco. Pick off about eight or ten leaves. Rest of it, take a tobacco knife and whack it out, call it cuttin' tobacco.

Then I started working at the sawmill when I was about sixteen. I did a little sawmilling and a lot of farmworking, you know. And someone had guitars, you know. We had this little camp out there in the bushes, not too far from the sawmill, and we would go out into the woods and cut logs and haul them down to the mill and saw lumber all day.

At night we'd go back to the camp and we would sit around. Some of the boys would play poker and some would pitch horseshoes and do this and that. But I would sit around and pick the guitar and listen to other guys play. So I got to the point where I was pretty popular at the sawmill camp with the guitar. That was in '36, '37. In '37 I left the sawmill and I worked for a doctor.

What style music did your father play?
My father used to play "John Henry" and "Frankie and Johnny." Of course they had a different way of playing, play in Sebastapol, play with a slide, "John Henry" and "Frankie and Johnny." That was my father's favorite piece. I use a slide but I don't call it no bottleneck. What I use is more up to date—I use a piece of blow down pipe off a hot water tank.

My father made corn liquor. Franklin County was the corn liquor capital of the world. We would carry wood for them when I was a young boy. They would give us some, a little bit, a half a gallon, a great big gallon and pretty soon we'd have two or three gallons of liquor saved up. Somebody come by there to buy some liquor, if my dad didn't have any, well, we'd sell it to them. Get four or five dollars. We kept the spare change, buy new shoes or a shirt. Started off knowing how to handle it 'cause we didn't drink it, but I wish we had, cause that corn liquor was good, you know. My daddy, he made the best.

They had a little Gene Autry guitar cost five dollars. So me and my brothers had to get the money to selling moonshine, selling a little whiskey. Me and my brothers figured to get it together, that's only a dollar and a quarter apiece, so we sent up there and got it brand new, guitar case, instruction book, and everything, and, brother, we took off from there. Started off with a Gene Autry guitar back in the '30s.

I had learned to tune before that, but the Gene Autry five-dollar guitar was the first one that I ever really learned to play and carry it out and win the public with it.

I used to listen to Deford Bailey, you know. He was the guy who played "Up the Country Blues" and "Muscle Shoals Blues" and he was from Tennessee. You know, he was one of the early famous stars of the early Nashville Grand Ole Opry.

And my sister bought an old record player and we started playin' that old record player and listening to old blues like John Hurt and Blind Lemon. But my oldest brother would go to parties at night and he would pick up old recordings from anybody that he could get 'em from, and bring 'em home, you know. And we'd put 'em on the old record player and we would listen to them. So my younger brother Robert—we would listen to the records and I would pick the guitar and if I'd make a mistake he would stop me and tell me where I made the mistake, and he would play and I'd listen and I'd correct him. So we both learned professionally at home before we was fourteen, fifteen years old.

I got into it a little deeper than my father because he was never gifted enough to listen to the records, see, and get the chords from the record player and get the chords like the professionals play. Now I can listen to a record twice. I'll play it just like the record like the artist played—like Blind Lemon, Frank Hutchinson, all those old-timey dudes, you know. And every time we get a hold of a record I'll play it around three times and whip it out on the guitar.

About everything I play now is stuff that I heard as a kid, that is any old tunes that I play—of course, I wrote a few tunes of my own. But the old tunes—the old "Kansas City Blues," "Evil Eye Mama," "Bearcat Mama Blues," and all that stuff, Blind Lemon, Blind Boy Fuller stuff, I heard this when I was a kid because it was stuff my daddy played.

Growing up in the country, now this is how I got a chance to be exposed to the public when I was about twelve or thirteen, my brother had an automobile. Back in those days your parents didn't let you out until you were about eighteen. My brother had an old Model A Ford, he was about nineteen. So he'd go to a party and if there was nobody to play the guitar he'd come back home and ask my mother to let me go play the guitar. So I kind of enjoyed that because it gave me a chance to get out in the public. So I'd jump out of bed, get dressed, grab my little guitar, jump in the car with my brother, and go sit and pick the guitar for the rest of the night.

So most of the time I used to play for house parties but in those days people didn't have much to pay you. About the only thing I got out of playing when I was a kid was a soda and a couple of pieces of hot fried chicken. At these house parties I wasn't old enough to drink whiskey so the proprietor or whoever was in charge of the house party would always give me cold sodas and hot friend chicken, biscuits—very good. 'Cause the people always keep a tub of ice, ice cold Pepsi-Colas, always frying hot fried chicken, baking those homemade biscuits. So, man, I got a chance to get a grape soda, hunk of chicken on a biscuit. I was satisfied. Yeah, a really good time. I really enjoyed it.

Once you in a little community where everybody get to know everybody, they can get together and have some fun. Now the thing about it, certain times if the guys ten, fifteen, twenty miles away would hear about it they'd come in and try to take the girls over and then that would be the problem. Now down in Union Hall—if they had a community party you wouldn't have any problem but sometimes guys from Roanoke or thereabouts—"Let's see if we can find a country party." They stop and ask questions. "So anybody giving a party tonight?" "Yeah, this and this person giving a party."

And then they crash the party. They ain't got no women with them, they come in to the party, get a few drinks, next thing you know they corner somebody's girl over there you know. Dudes get tough on it, have a few little fist fights.

But in those days—news couldn't travel too fast. You could drive through a little town, you didn't see no one to ask questions 'cause people went to bed so early you could drive right through the town not see a damn soul, so you don't know nothin'.

"Hey man, who's givin' the party tonight?" Sometimes it's "Such and such person," sometimes it's "Who are you?" I'm so and so. "Where you live?" Uh-Uh. Nobody's giving a party tonight because they don't want you there.

But getting back to my guitar now. I played the guitar for myself all the way down through life. But during the time I was in the service, I kinda passed the guitar up. And as well as I played before I went in the service, I got back out of the service—picked up the guitar and couldn't get a single note. So when I went to bed that night—I said to myself, well, I know I used to play the guitar but what happened? And the next morning I picked it up and played it. Just overnight picked the guitar and went back to playin' again.

So I had quite a few experiences while I was in the service because one of the greatest experiences that I had in the service during the time I was in Camp Blanding, Florida. The guy—Howlin' Wolf was down there in the same camp that I was in. So I got a chance to play his guitar and he heard me play and he advised me to continue to play because he liked what I was doing so that made me feel pretty good.

John Hurt was my idol and I learned to play "Stagger Lee" and "Candy Man Blues" you know, and then I started picking up a little bit on Blind Lemon Jefferson and another great musician named Furry Lewis. I learned a little something from him. So I just kept putting pieces together. Got to the point where I could play pretty good. So there's one song that I played on Saturday night I called the "Saturday Night Hop" because I hopped out of bed just about every Saturday night to go somewhere and play that song.

Now Mississippi John Hurt, there's a story about him that you will never believe to save your life. I learned to play his pieces when I was a kid. I learned them in about 1931, 1932. And from then until 1964 I still played his songs and I always had a feeling I would meet him someday. In the back of my mind I knew one day I would meet Mississippi John Hurt. So I kept picking the guitar, and then I went, I was stationed in Mississippi. We was in a little town called Centreville, Mississippi, and I asked a lot of people around Centreville, Mississippi, if they knew Mississippi John Hurt. Well, some of the old-timers around there knew him but they didn't know where he was. He had kinda faded out. So I stayed in Mississippi about two, three years and didn't find John Hurt.

I didn't find John Hurt, but I always had it in my mind I would meet him. That was in '63 and Sunday paper came and I didn't throw it away. I put it on the chair on my side of the bed. So on the Thursday I believe it was, I picked it up and was reading it and I found the picture of this man sitting, in the newspaper, playing the guitar, and I read it and it said Mississippi John Hurt is now appearing in Washington, DC, at the Ontario Place nightly. I said, well, I didn't find him in Mississippi but I found him in Washington.

I told my wife, "You see this? Now this is the man I been looking for all my life." I said, "Now he's here in Washington. I'm going down there and meet him and play the guitar with him."

She said, "Oh well, don't you think that's quite a bit step for somebody like you," say, "that man's a pro." I said, "I don't care. I'm going there to meet him and we going to have a time," and sure enough I did. I called down to the club to check it out. I picked up the telephone and called down there to the Ontario Place and I asked them if it was true that John Hurt was playing there and they said, "Of course he's down here. Playing every night." And I said, "That's what the paper said and I didn't believe the paper." He said, "Do you know John Hurt?" I say, "Yes, I sure do." He says, "Are you from Mississippi?" So I said, "No, I'm not." "But how do you know John?" I said, "Well, it's kind of a funny thing. We have a mutual understanding I guess between the two of us." I said, "I just happened to learn some of his music when I was a little boy and once I learned his music I figured I knew him. We have something in common so that's how I know him."

So I went down and met John and called to him. Man, me and that cat got hung up on some damn guitar. You talk about a hell of a time.

It was a beautiful thing between me and John Hurt 'cause for the last three years of his lifetime he'd come to my house when he wasn't on the road. He'd come to my house and we'd sit and play all night and I'd go to his house and we just had ourselves a doggone good time.

I talk to his wife now, pick up the phone and call in Mississippi. Ella Mae, his little granddaughter, came to Washington and stayed out in Seat Pleasant with me and my wife when she went to college.

I met a lot of people at festivals, Mance Lipscomb, he was a tough man. I met him when I was at the festival down at the Mall in 1970, we had a long conversation. And Skip James, he'd been here and played and sang with me and of course the Gaines Brothers, Willie and Leroy Gaines.

We'd have Saturday night gatherings at the barbershop. The Gaines Brothers and I, different people sit around play the guitar, swap songs, drink a few beers, a little whiskey. The Gaines Brothers with their guitar playing have been the biggest aspect of the barbershop recently but I had Mother Scott out here too. John Hurt used to come, at least I used to go down to his house to pick him up, bring him over to the barbershop during the time he was home, wasn't on the road or at a gig or something. He would sit around play the guitar. I would cut a few heads of hair and join him, you know. So we would have a heck of a good time cutting hair and playing the guitar during those times.

I worked with Mississippi John Hurt about three years but then he went back to Mississippi and passed away. About three years after he passed away I decided to get back out in the music world again and I thought I better do something to take to the people to let them know I did know John Hurt so I wrote the song titled "The Road is Rough and Rocky."

Another thing, you won't believe this, I was coming through Georgetown one night a few years ago and it was a rainy night and I was just cruising along there with nothing to do. So this bellboy came out to the corner and flagged me, you know. So I stopped for him and he said, "Follow me in here to the hotel," hotel in Georgetown. He said, "Follow me right through here and wait, I'll bring you a passenger out." So he went on in and came back out and I saw this blind man and this lady with him. So he gets in the cab and says, "Take me to the Cellar Door."

So I back on out and got on M Street there, going on down to the Cellar Door, so I asked him I says "Who's playing at the Cellar Door tonight?" he says "I am," he says, "I'm Sonny Terry." I says, "Sonny Terry? Man, I been knowing you for the longest time." He says "How do you know me?" I says, "Well back in the '30s, I was coming from school one evening and I passed by a place called Clayton Barnard's filing station and the guy sold liquor there. So I saw these two white fellows in a '30 Chevrolet coach, and they had these two colored fellows with them. So the blind boy with the gray guitar, solid metal guitar, was Blind Boy Fuller and that was—Sonny Terry was the young man that was wavin' at us, you know, walking past the highway there."

So it was about thirty years later after Mississippi John Hurt was discovered. I was at John Hurt's house one day and he was talking. And we brought up Blind Boy Fuller's name and so I asked him, "What kind of guitar does Blind Boy Fuller play?" He says, "Blind Boy Fuller plays a solid metal gray dobro."

I say, "Well, I saw the guy when I was a kid." So it was. It's true and when I told Sonny Terry about this, he says, "Man, you got a better memory than I have. But I know you too. You're the man that plays that old steel pan Gretsch guitar and sounds like Blind Boy Fuller." I say "Yeah." He says "You are rough." He says, "Come down to the club, tell them you're my guest and see the show." So I went down and saw the whole show, sent me over beer and everything.

I never heard of too many who played the blues here in Maryland except Buster Brown. Now he was living out here in Capitol Heights. The boy that come out with his harmonica thing about "Fannie Mae." He was from out there. Now Roy Clark, he lived up the highway in Maryland. He's a local boy but he's in bluegrass, plays guitar, banjo, everything, and Roy Buchanan, a rock 'n' roll man, they all got farms up there in Prince George's County out Palmer Highway.

Over in Virginia there's John Jackson and John Cephas. You find blues in most any southern state because hardship has prevailed in all southern states. Blind Boy Fuller, he was from North Carolina, Gary Davis, Jesse Fuller, Elizabeth Cotten. Those Carolinas have come up with some beautiful guitar pickers. I think you could find blues around any country town where boys get together on a Saturday tonight, drink some whiskey, and stomp their feet. Yeah, the guitar is pretty famous on the East Coast.

Now, I'm gonna keep my taxicab in shape. If they think I'm gonna work myself to death after I retire they must be crazy. I'm tired of working for the government. I gave them thirty-two years. No more. Now unless I do make a hit with the record then they can get some (tax money). Now I'm my own boss.

I love to play the guitar. That's not really work. Working with something that you love, you don't worry about it. I'll play for hours and hours. That's something that I want to do. Enjoyment takes the stress and strain out of whatever you're doing. If you like to do it, no problem, but anything that you do, if you don't like to do it, it will drive you crazy.

Like I quit that job as a police officer. I made up my mind to get that burden off of me because it was worrying me to death, 'cause, see, I was doing my job but the other people wasn't doing their job. When the clients come in to the building, instead of the workers coming downstairs to see them, to help the clients, so the clients can go about his business feeling good, why they'll wait to the last minute. They wait till the client starts raising hell, then they want me to get the client out of the building. Why, you got to be crazy. I'm not gonna use no physical stress and strain on this client. You got to see him. Throwing him out of the building is not gonna solve the problem. You don't throw a man out of the building when he's mad and hungry 'cause he's coming back. Right? He gonna shoot up somebody when he come back. People got to be crazy—I ain't nobody's fool to fight and tussle with nobody when he has the right to be here too, that's stupid.

Archie, do your blues, your songs, come out of these experiences in your life?
Some of it is actually everyday living, some of it is the hard times, hardship that people go through, and then again sometimes you just sit down and start imagining things. You might not have ever seen it. That's like when I wrote that song about "Call my baby long distance 'cause I want to talk to her so bad, when the operator asked me for my money took every cent I had." Man, I didn't ever do nothing like that, but I was just imagining if I was in that predicament.

Like an artist paints a picture, an artist sits down and starts to thinking about certain things and I might start writing a song about it but I don't experience it.

Roosevelt Sykes told me almost the same words about "It's like an artist."
It is an artist but an artist will put his on a piece of paper; you put yours through your body out through your fingers on the guitar. You can imagine the blues, anybody with a mind can sit down and imagine yourself to be in the worst predicament in the world and not have it be true. You can imagine yourself being a bum standing on the corner—no shoes on but have a pocket full of money but you can imagine that—and start writing. But most of the blues did originate from the living, everyday trend, but not anymore. It all depends on what you want to concentrate on, what predicament you imagine yourself in—or see somebody having a hard time. An artist might draw a picture, everything that they put on the paper is not real, but they can imagine it and some person come and look at it say, "My God, that person is—look at that expression on his face, look at how he's dressed. He had a hard time in life."

Sometimes I take stuff that I've heard and rearrange it but most of the stuff that you hear me do today, if I say it's mine, it's something I did myself, something I just picked out of the blue sky.

Because you take a bluesman, they think alike—somewhere down the line they think alike. It is something that they have seen or done or had done to them, or something like that. So bluesmen think their life kind of coincides.

People have gone as far as they can go with music. They have to come back to home base again. Gone so far out it has no place else to go. So it comes back home to start all over again so this is what brings me in, you know, I'm here waiting for them. So this is about one of the best things I ever done in my life, hung on to the blues.

The greatest feeling that I have ever had in my life is to be able to sit and tell people that I did it myself. And it's lookin' so good now, so if I don't make a dime I still think I've got a lot out of it, 'cause it's good to be able to say that all down through life the thing that I believed in and what I did is beginning to come back to the front again, you know. It bring you up. I feel mighty good about being able to play the guitar. Many people used to say, "Why don't you play jazz guitar, why don't you do this, why don't you go to school to study, you know, get into this deep stuff?"

I say, "Oh, no, this is deep enough. This is actually deeper than you think." See, most people don't know actually how deep blues is and once you know how to do it yourself, you'll know how deep it is, 'cause it's the next thing to a spiritual.

I'm trying to keep the blues—what you call black heritage—I'm trying to keep it rolling. Yeah, and it doesn't matter who I teach it to, 'cause Mississippi John Hurt asked me, he said, "Brother Arch," he said, "Whatever you do, teach my music to other people." He said, "Don't make no difference what color they are, teach it to them." He said, "Because I don't want to die and you don't want to die. Teach them your music and teach them my music."

ELEANOR ELLIS

Eleanor Ellis is one of the pillars of the acoustic blues scene in Washington, DC. She arrived in 1976 from her home state of Louisiana. By the early 1980s she befriended and was mentored by the great local players such as Flora Molton, John Jackson, John Cephas, and Archie Edwards. It is a testament to the kindness and inclusiveness of the DC musical elders to embrace a young white Southern woman with a thick Louisiana dialect as one of their own.

Eleanor Ellis started playing in her early teens and had been a performing musician since the early 1970s, playing upright bass and guitar in the roots music scene—folk and bluegrass. She was a member of two bluegrass bands, the Green Valley Cutups and Bill C. Malone's famed Hill Country Ramblers. As a student at New Orleans's Newcomb College at Tulane University, she frequented the Big Easy's famed French Quarter to pick up all she could from that vibrant music scene. She recalled, "I found the DC area to be full of gig opportunities. By the time I met Flora and began to play with her, I had been playing my music in public—solo and with small groups—for over ten years, and had become known in the DC area, as well as keeping a connection with New Orleans (Jazz and Heritage Festival etc.).[1]

She is today a celebrated master of the country and Piedmont blues, one of the most significant women in the acoustic genre internationally, with a fluid command of acoustic blues fingerpicking styles. Anybody who meets her will know that, while petite, she is a strong-willed artist who has paid her dues on multiple levels. She plays with a natural elegance, always reflecting a sense of beauty in the music, expressive with feeling. Eleanor Ellis, with her trademark flaming red hair, sings with a rich, strong voice coupled with exquisite, refined guitar picking, and a wide-ranging song repertoire of the regional blues traditions. During her long career, she was also an active music journalist, writing about her mentor, blues and gospel singer and guitarist Flora Molton, in *Living Blues* magazine, documenting the biographical legacy of the famed DC street singer. She was Flora's driver, musical partner, and close personal friend. She backed Flora on two albums that stand as important classics: *I Want to Be Ready to Hear God When He Calls*, and *Flora Molton*, recorded for Radio France.

She reminisced:[2]

I met Flora Molton when I was asked to chauffeur her to the 1983 Oxon Hill Blues
Festival that was put on by Myron Samuels. We hit it off and she actually asked me
to play with her and to back her on guitar. Playing, touring, and recording with
Flora Molton, and having her as a personal friend, was an important part of my
musical life. People like Neil Harpe, Archie, John Cephas, and John Jackson were
also influential on me. It was a great time of getting better on the guitar and knowing these really wonderful people. Just knowing those people was great and musically they all had a big part in my development. But playing with Flora helped to
form me as a musician as much as than anything. I played guitar with her from the
early 1980s until her death. We had a great time together. It was a wonderful experience which I will never forget.

Today, Eleanor Ellis is in her absolute prime, an indelible and wonderful prac-
titioner of the truehearted Piedmont blues. When she takes the stage, she plays
the blues with virtuosic ease, comfortable fluidity and joyous feeling. The elders
of the DC blues scene have been frequently cited that they wished for people to
carry on the music after they were gone. Eleanor Ellis fulfilled that wish beautifully. Today, she is the elder, an inspiration for younger acoustic blues players,
and especially women, such as the talented Erin Harpe, one of the important up
and coming blues musicians, to whom Eleanor was a teacher and mentor.

She performs with varied musicians from the DC area and beyond, including
the Phil Wiggins Tidewater Trio with Rick Franklin. She also performs with Bill
Ellis, Andy Cohen, Neil and Erin Harpe, Jay Summerour, and many others. She
is in a duo with harmonica player Pearl Bailes called Alligator Pears, a Southern
term for avocados, and in a trio, Backporch Blues with Eric Selby on percussion
and Jay Summerour on harmonica.

Eleanor Ellis is active as a teacher with private students and in national
blues workshops. Besides all the other activities, as international performer and
teacher, she was a founding member of the DC Blues Society and the Archie
Edwards Blues Heritage Foundation.

Notably, she is producer and editor of a superb video documentary *Blues
Houseparty* which now takes an important part in the history of the Piedmont
blues, as many of the featured artists have since passed. This video, narrated by
Phil Wiggins, documents a party at John Jackson's house with a major jam session that includes just about everybody on the local scene in the 1980s.

Phil Wiggins stated, "It is always a great pleasure and an adventure to play
with Eleanor Ellis. She is a great guitar player. Her hard work shows when we
play together. When we are learning a song together she makes great choices
off-the-cuff and then works on them and comes up with something even bet-

ter. Her guitar playing ranges from rhythmically strong, fat tone to beautiful chimes. And she has a voice like an angel."

Eleanor Ellis reminisced:

Archie was very supportive and always said nice things and always asked me to play. He called me "the white Memphis Minnie" or something like that. He had a nice compliment anyway. The guys in the barbershop were just really nice people. I never felt anything but that from them. They were very accepting and very encouraging. I was very flattered when somebody like NJ Warren would ask me to play things; they really liked what I did.

It's always just wonderful to play with Phil. Phil is so intuitive; he's so sensitive. He's so knowledgeable and just such a good musician that it's really fun to play with him. When you add Rick Franklin, who is so much fun and I love him forever, it's really fun. That trio is great. And you know Phil is such a good songwriter too. It's really interesting to see what he comes up with in the way of material because he's always listening, he's always finding things he wants to do, or he's writing these amazing songs. He's a great songwriter. And it's really been great to play with both of those guys.[3]

Her album *Comin' a Time* on Patuxent Music is an outstanding representation of the current vibrancy of the DC blues.

ARCHIE'S FAMOUS BARBERSHOP

The epicenter of the acoustic blues scene was the original barbershop, located at 2007 Bunker Hill Road in Northeast Washington, DC. On Saturday afternoons at 1 PM, the proprietor Archie Edwards, from Franklin County, Virginia, closed shop and musicians of all skill levels showed up for jam sessions. The liquor bottles came out, everybody smoked and drank and, between the social banter and fellowship, they played the blues. By all accounts there was so much smoking that nicotine and cigar smoke stained the walls. An old refrigerator in the back held the supplies. Archie drank Budweiser and liked mixing moonshine and orange juice. It was his kingdom. He was in charge and the king of the hill.

For any community to thrive and sustain, a central meeting place is needed to bring like-minded people together, coupled with people willing to lead, support, and nurture. The barbershop was that central pivot for the acoustic blues community, perhaps the single largest determinant for the long-term cultural success of the roots blues in Washington. The acoustic blues scene, centered in Archie's barbershop, flourished and was sustained over decades through a healthy combination of friendship and rivalry, a sense of musical kinship and shared mission, mutual respect, and competition. People were drawn to the barbershop to play, learn, and exchange. Over the years, players of all stripes came through, both locals and transients. Mississippi John Hurt, a musician whom Archie idolized and emulated, became his friend when Hurt was brought to DC. Hurt and Archie became friends and often jammed together at the barbershop. In his song, "The Road is Rough and Rocky," Archie sang, "John Hurt was my best friend. Now the poor boy is dead and gone. Poor boy is dead and gone." Eleanor Ellis reminisced:

> Archie told me that he looked for John Hurt when he went in the service but he never could find him. I think he was driving a cab at the time—it was always half mystical—and he said, "I told my wife, 'Save the Sunday paper, there's something in it I need to see.'" So, he went out, he was driving around in the cab. He came back and he saw an ad that John Hurt was playing at Ontario Place Club, which was in DC at the time—yeah. So, he went down there, and that was how he met him. Now,

that's a story I heard. Apparently, Skip James was on the same bill, and he was so drunk that he was bent over, and so Archie was telling John Hurt, "I can play guitar. You want me to play, I'll play." So finally Skip James was in such bad shape Archie came up and finished up the gig with John Hurt. Archie wasn't that fond of Skip James. He said Skip James had kind of nasty disposition.[1]

Archie was a skilled fingerpicking and slide guitarist in the Piedmont style, the same fingerpicking technique used by John Hurt.

Everybody came to Archie's—professionals and amateurs, photographers, writers, musicologists, musical novices, and blues fans, black and white. The doors were open to everyone. It was a scene, a community of blues fans. For some of the noteworthy characters, Archie's was the main place for their musical participation. They may have been relatively unknown, but they were good, and in some cases extraordinary. Most of the regulars at the barbershop never achieved fame, working day jobs just as Archie did. Some were retired, some just getting started.

Michal Baytop reminisced:

Archie had this personality I just couldn't resist. I never met anybody like him before in my life. Through him I met all of his friends, like Eleanor and John Cephas and Phil and John Jackson. The grasp that he had on the music—he was like a walking encyclopedia, and he could sit there and tell you about all these people with little anecdotes. Archie would get into explaining things and he was a fountain of knowledge.

He made me understand a lot of things. One of the things that always tickled me was that John Jackson, John Cephas, and Archie—who we called "the Big Three"— all three of them would play the same song so differently. Then Archie would say something like, "Ah, man, John Jackson, you promised me you wouldn't play my song. Doggone it, now you're playing my song." But they didn't sound anything alike at all. . . . Archie used to tell these stories about these great musicians that used to come by the barbershop. They were gone and forgotten. Nobody would remember those guys because they weren't that famous but they were great. Little Jimmy Smith, Leroy Smith, NJ Warren, Louisiana Red, Larry Johnson. Archie would always bring up the Gaines Brothers, because they were a good example of the caliber of musicians that came through the barbershop, good friends of Archie and fine players. Everybody at the barbershop listened to Archie's stories and even if we had not met the Gaines Brothers, soon we would know them well enough to tell stories about them.

If you wanted to hang around Archie, unless you were Mr. Bones, you had to play guitar.[2]

Eleanor Ellis recalled, "Archie was very supportive and always said nice things and always asked me to play. He called me 'the white Memphis Minnie' or something like that."

There are and were some interesting characters and fine musicians coming through:

Michael Baytop

Bluesman "Big Mike" is a towering figure at 6'8", a powerful presence, always sharp-dressed and debonair. He was born in Washington, DC, in 1948, and is one of the important members of the local acoustic blues scene, an impressive personality in the old and new Archie's barbershop. He was a student of Archie Edwards and everyone at the famous barbershop that he could pick something up from.

Himself an accomplished performer, he is today a blues elder, storyteller, and a symbolic leader of the current barbershop scene. He was also a teacher and mentor to Miles Spicer of the M.S.G. Acoustic Blues Trio. Baytop is a popular performer, workshop teacher, and friend to all who cross his path, a gentleman and a fine musician who sings, plays guitar in the Piedmont style, harmonica, and bones, which he learned directly from Richard "Mr. Bones" Thomas.

He made a terrific album of Frank Stokes covers with Rick Franklin, titled *Searching for Frank*, a beautiful tribute to the Memphis picker and minstrel, which stands as one of the best tributes to Stokes. Both Rick Franklin and Michael Baytop came up through the Archie's barbershop experience, and this album aptly showcased their own skills as fingerpickers and singers. Phil Wiggins referred to the album as one of his all-time favorites. It's roots music at its finest, clean, delightful, lovely and perfectly played in the Piedmont style. Phil indicated that he had hoped to cooperate on future projects.

Then something tragic happened. Michael Baytop had a stroke that stopped the important ambassador of the local blues in his tracks. For a long time, he could not perform, a setback that would have ruined the musical passion in many. Yet, Mike persevered despite the struggle it took just to walk and talk. Now, in 2017, he is back to singing with his friends and even playing bones.

He is full of stories about the time with Archie and the gang at the barbershop. His oral history is what keeps the memories of wonderful characters alive:

When I first came into Archie's barbershop, I was about thirty-five years old. A friend of mine brought me to Archie's shop to meet him. Archie was a little teeny guy, but he took up so much space. He was like 290 pounds in that little teeny body. Archie was about sixty or seventy years old, and there were these two young guys in their twenties—and Archie was setting them straight—"Yeah, because I said so"—he was jumping down their throats. One of the young guys was trying to tell his friend, "Hey, man—no, this old dude can't talk to me like that." Archie said, "I can talk to you any way I want to talk to you. In my shop, I can talk any way I want." I thought that is one of the meanest little guys I ever met. He could care less what size this guy was. He had my undying admiration after that. He didn't care or give a whit how big this guy was. Archie just fascinated me . . . You could sit there, just between Mr. Bones and Archie and listen to them all evening long. They'd tell you story after story. Then you found out they were "true" stories. I mean you had some big liars in the barbershop spinning tall tales. But, the thing was that Archie and Bones, they didn't lie. Those guys were for real . . .[3]

Mr. Bones

The well-respected bones percussionist, Richard "Mr. Bones" Thomas was a barbershop regular. Bones are two carved flat pieces of either wood or bone that are used as clappers. Phil Wiggins still refers to him as "a real sweetheart of a guy. He had a beautiful smile. He was real easygoing." Mr. Bones recorded a superb album *Blues 'N Bones* in 1989 with Archie Edwards and the DC harmonica player Mark Wenner, who achieved international fame with the blues-rock bar band the Nighthawks. Mr. Bones may have ranked among the best players of this traditional percussion instrument. The Archie Edwards Blues Foundation reports:

Mr. Bones was a fixture in the Washington music scene for at least seven decades. Born in Pomonkey, Maryland, on July 30, 1922, he was raised in Washington, DC, from the age of six months. He developed an interest in the bones at the age of six, after seeing a vaudeville performance by Sammy Davis Jr. He crafted his first set of bones from the wood of a cigar box. He then began fashioning them from wood and finally settled upon using 6- to 7-inch beef rib bones—a process that takes approximately nine months. Mr. Bones met Archie Edwards in 1989 at the recording of *Blues and Bones*. After making the recording, they performed at the Chicago Blues Festival; and, in 1997, they performed at the St. Louis Blues Festival. He also recorded with Michael Roach on the CDs *Ain't Got No Home* and *The Blinds of Life*. His amazing talent on the bones and his winning personality made Mr. Bones a crowd favorite when he performed with members of the barbershop. He was a hit at the Smithsonian Folklife Festival, the Bull Durham Blues Festival, Blues in the Burg (where he was a featured performer), the DC Blues Society Festival, and other local festivals. He also performed community service benefit shows at hospitals, schools, and civic events.[4]

Joe Watson

Joe was one of Archie's friends, a regular, and a true character who spent much time hanging around the barbershop. Everybody who remembers him says that he basically only knew one song, which he played consistently, and very well at that. The Archie Edwards Blues Foundation reports:

> Joe Watson was born in Goochland, Virginia, and moved to Washington, D.C., in 1941. He worked at the Harrington Hotel for 40 years before retiring. Joe and Archie were very good friends, as evidenced by their constant banter and insults aimed at each other. He played the guitar and sang. He is most famous for his song "Can Do Bad By Myself," a Barbershop favorite.[5]

Napoleon Brundage

He was a DC local by way of New York City, originally from Georgia, a capable harmonica player, and a regular at the barbershop. He played Hohner Special 20 harps, a serious player who picked up the harp late in life. He used to be a record store owner in Washington, DC, and a music lover with a good ear. Most of his style was developed in the barbershop.

NJ Warren

Navy veteran NJ Warren was an affable, polite guy from Pine Bluff, Arkansas, and he played in a slow, languid, typically Delta style and sang in an ethereal, deep, gravelly voice. Unlike the other players at the barbershop, he did not play the intricate fingerpicking style popular in the Piedmont. If he was here today, playing on a back porch in the Mississippi Delta someplace, the blues world would whip itself into a frenzy for having "discovered" a truly authentic roots and blues player. But at the time, he was just another local retired DC guy that was part of the Archie's barbershop scene, a fixture of the local blues scene and by all accounts quite the ladies' man.

Theorin O'Neil

The Archie Edwards Blues Foundation reports:

> Theorin O'Neil, who liked being called Mr. O'Neil, was from Pittsylvania County, Virginia, which bordered on Franklin County, Archie's home. However, they did not meet and become friends until they both moved to the Washington, D.C., area.

Although Mr. O'Neil's guitar playing style was different from Archie's, their common roots were still evident. Mr. O'Neil was a tall, reserved, and sober man. He was also shy and very dignified. He was a regular at the barbershop for many years until his failing health prevented him from attending the Saturday sessions. A truck driver for a moving firm until his retirement, Mr. O'Neil enjoyed gardening. He and his wife raised six children.[6]

M.S.G. Acoustic Blues Trio

The M.S.G. Acoustic Blues Trio consists of Miles Spicer, Jackie Merritt and Resa Lynne Gibbs. Miles Spicer, the trio's fingerpicking guitarist, was a student of DC blues musician Michael Baytop, who was a founder and president of the Archie Edwards Blues Foundation and who had studied under Archie Edwards. Resa Lynne Gibbs sings and plays percussion and Jackie Merritt sings and plays harmonica and bass.

The M.S.G. trio is unique in that it is one of the few, maybe the only, contemporary blues trio fronting two women. The trio is semi-pro, and they have stayed mostly regional, but their musicianship and musical vibe is simply wonderful, as evidenced by invitations to major festivals such as the Chicago Blues Festival. They have also played the prestigious Kennedy Center Millennium Stage. This ensemble plays a heartwarming repertoire of both traditional and original acoustic blues, gentle, lighthearted, reaching all the way back to the spirituals, to gospel, all with a true folk blues, back-porch feeling. Miles Spicer expressed their approach to music with, "grace, bliss, hope, joy," uplifting qualities that regular folks normally don't associate with the blues, but which blues fans know to be true. "We love what we do. We are honored to carry on traditions. We hope that the love we have for the music and for each other is obvious and infectious."

The multi-instrumentalist Jackie Merritt plays harmonica, guitar, bass, and taps bones. She learned this percussion technique, in which bones or spoons are clapped rhythmically, directly from Mr. Bones Thomas, who was a key member of Archie's barbershop scene. She recalled:

He was just such a sweet, generous man and he was always smiling from one ear to the other, this big grin. And I would come to the barbershop to try to sit in to play next to Phil, and every time I would show up I would start listening to the bones, and I wanted to play the bones. I always sat next to him. He pretty much showed me my whole way of playing. My style is his style, the way I hold the bones, everything is based on what he showed me. And then I found out years later that at the time most people only played with one hand and he played with two back in the day.[7]

She started harmonica late in life with her musical passion, and she teaches painting and drawing at a local community college. Phil Wiggins was an inspiration and her harmonica teacher. The trio's remarkable lead singer, the golden-voiced Resa Lynne Gibbs, is also a percussionist. She perfectly rounds out the ensemble with her rich, powerful, and soulful singing that draws deeply on spiritual and gospel roots. Resa is a physical therapist by day and a musician by night. She is a vocal instructor who teaches occasionally at the prestigious Country Blues Workshops at Centrum, in Port Townsend, Washington.[8]

Miles Spicer philosophized:

> Music is a continuum. It just builds on itself. So, we're taking all of our individual references and influences. We have the template of influences, which is the music that the masters created, and that is our standard. So, with that in mind, it's not a matter of creating or re-creating the songs that have been done from the '30s and the '20s as much as creating modern music with those songs as the template.[9]

Erin and Neil Harpe

Erin Harpe is from Annapolis, Maryland, and now makes her home in Boston. She was exposed to the blues from childhood on, and she mingled in and around Archie's barbershop. Erin is today one of the rising stars of the blues, a guitarist and singer who performs both solo and backed by her full band, the Delta Swingers, a rollicking, rocking roots band. As Erin said, "It's more the Charles River delta blues than the Mississippi delta blues."[10] Ironically, while the band plays a diverse set, Erin Harpe's musical heritage is essentially Piedmont fingerpicking blues, a musical form that has surrounded her for her entire life. She performs often as a solo acoustic performer, presently mostly on the East Coast and around Boston.

Erin Harpe is the daughter of the famed musician, artist, and old-time guitar expert Neil Harpe of Annapolis. Neil is well known in the blues community for his vintage guitar instrument business and he was himself an integral part of the Maryland and DC blues scene, as a friend of the Archie Edwards's barbershop cadre and founding member of the DC Blues Society. Neil is an exceptional visual artist and among his work is a realistic portrait of Archie Edwards, sitting in his barber chair, playing guitar. Young Erin grew up in the music world her father exposed her to, the blues all around her. Erin picked up the guitar in her teen years, and once she did it came fast and natural. Seemingly everything she had internalized musically manifested itself and she soon emulated Memphis Minnie, as so many other women blues singers before her have done. Her mentor, however, was Eleanor Ellis, both as role model and as occasional teacher, while Neil Harpe was undoubtedly her greatest musical influence. Her current repertoire includes a wide range of deep blues including Memphis Minnie, Randy Newman/Bonnie Raitt, Mississippi John Hurt, Hammie Nixon, Bessie Smith, Lonnie Johnson, Slim Harpo, Fred McDowell, Henry Thomas, Taj Mahal, Tommy Johnson, and many more—a set list that will light the fire of any country blues fan.

Phil Wiggins once played a duet with Erin. "She was fabulous. An incredible player who had really found her own stride. It was one of the best performances. I loved playing with her. She was so amazingly good. I was really surprised at the real deep roots sounds that she brought out of me. She turned into a world-class blues singer."

Erin's father Neil Harpe was a former student at the Corcoran School of Art. He found his way to the acoustic blues through the college scene:

I got into this kind of music at an earlier period, when I was in high school in the late 1960s, living in Annapolis, and there were a number of people who were coming through Annapolis frequently who were into this music, primarily Max Ochs and Mike Stewart, aka Backwards Sam Firk, and Tom Hoskins and John Fahey from time to time. And these people were fairly frequently around town. I had been really more of a "folknik"—before that played folk music and maybe a little bit of bluegrass and old-time country music. But as soon as I discovered this music and fingerpicking, I pretty much lost interest in any other kind of music. So fast forward a little bit. I went to college, ended up at American University in Washington, D.C., where I encountered Mike Stewart, who at that time was living in D.C. And he and Nick Perls were in town. Max Ochs, who is still alive and kicking—he plays all the time. He's active in the music scene. Eventually I'd get out and play music and ran into Eleanor Ellis at an open mic along with Rick Franklin. Eleanor was playing music with Flora Molton, and she introduced me to a lot of people in the D.C. area, because I had been living in Annapolis until then. Met Phil and John Cephas and Archie. I ran into Archie at the D.C. Folk Festival. I used to many times share the stage with John Jackson and a lot of these people. We played in numerous concerts and blues venues and folk festivals. John Jackson was always glad to see me. Warner Williams often when I'd run into him, the first thing he wants to know is how my daughter is doing, because my daughter plays this kind of music now, and it's gone to yet another generation, and Warner always says, "How's that little girl of yours?"[11]

Ben Andrews

This player, who died a tragic death in 2011, was a founding member of the DC Blues Society and a well-known and highly regarded member of the local acoustic blues community. He was one of the most brilliantly talented, and also the most troubled, of the acoustic blues community.

Ben started to study guitar at age eight and gravitated to blues after hearing Sonny Terry and Brownie McGhee and Big Joe Williams at the Smithsonian Folklife Festival on the Mall. The Mapleshade recording artist was a virtuosic player of world-class skill. He had regular gigs at the Grog and Tankard and Madam's Organ clubs. He was internationally renowned and widely accepted within the barbershop community as one of the best players in the region. Michael Baytop recalled:

> Ben Andrews sometimes got gigs for Archie and me. That was one of the reasons I got to play with Archie and Mr. Bones, because Ben was easygoing. Ben was about my age, and he was a superb player and he loved playing with Mr. Bones and Archie. He would bring Bones and Archie along on tour to different parts of the country. The only thing they didn't like was the way he'd be drinking when he drove. They would say, "Mike, you want to come with us?" At first Ben didn't like that and he would say, "I don't want him coming." They were like, "No, Mike don't go—we don't go." After a while we got to be all right. After Archie passed Ben still wanted Mr. Bones to come along and play with him. Ben let me open the show and then Ben would take over with Mr. Bones. So, it was fun for me too.[12]

Ben performed solo and also with the Blue Rider Trio, with Jeff Sarli on bass and Mark Wenner on harmonica. Mark Wenner was part of the DC blues community, the harmonica player for the famous internationally renowned blues rock band the Nighthawks and a founding member of the DC Blues Society. Although not typically a part of the barbershop scene, he was well known and highly regarded by all. Phil Wiggins, in particular, respects Mark's playing and regards him as one of the top harmonica players nationally. Mapleshade Records founder Pierre Sprey recalled:

> But Mark's signature harp sound, playing electric with the Nighthawks, has not prevented him from developing as a virtuoso acoustic harmonica player, often seen on stage with all kinds of acoustic blues greats. I first saw him at a mid-eighties blues festival in D.C. in a head-to-head cutting contest with one of the greatest acoustic harmonica players in the country, Phil Wiggins (of Cephas & Wiggins fame). To this day, that half-hour exchange remains the most exciting blues harp playing I've heard in my life. Around this time, Mark was having a lot of fun sitting in regularly with Ben Andrews at Ben's weekly solo gig at Madam's Organ in the heart of Washington's jumping Adams Morgan music scene. Fans loved their collaboration; out of that grew the Blue Rider Trio.[13]

Warner Williams and Jay Summerour

The Maryland-based acoustic blues duo of the National Heritage Fellow Warner Williams on guitar and Jay Summerour on harmonica has been active for more than thirty years. Sometimes they are billed as Little Bit a Blues with Eric Selby on drums. In and around the DC region they are a regular fixture, an integral part of the musical landscape. Like Cephas & Wiggins, they carry on the guitar-harmonica tradition of Sonny Terry and Brownie McGhee, a duo that Jay Summerour has often described as his idols.

Williams was born in Takoma Park in 1930 to a musical family. He's been playing for most of his life, first within the family and then in house-parties, picnics and festivities, as was typical for the entertainers within the African American community. For a while he was a street busking kid, earning change on the streets of Maryland and Washington, DC, and he's worked street corners all his life. He's played and sung in church, in taverns, and juke joints. Truly a guitar virtuoso who can play many styles including blues, country, hillbilly, gospel, and anything in between, he is at home no matter what style, including the pop music of the time. Dr. Barry Lee Pearson defined him as a songster and cited that Williams won a prize on a local radio program playing Ernest Tubb's "Walking the Floor Over You."[14] This song was also beloved by John Jackson, and is an example of the integration of the Piedmont Blues to include all kinds of influences, including blues, ragtime, country, Appalachian mountain music, and popular music from radio shows, especially the Grand Ole Opry. He has often cited influences including Blind Boy Fuller, Lightnin' Hopkins, and Muddy Waters, to country artists Hank Williams, Ernest Tubb, and Gene Autry, as well as jazz, big band, and popular tunes.

To say that he lives to play, and loves to play, would be a vast understatement. Even now, in his late eighties, Williams, who sings in a weathered, ethereal tenor going on baritone, likes to be called "Guitar Man" and is usually seen in wraparound sunglasses and a cowboy hat, is seemingly insatiable. When on tour, sometimes in his famous white van with cow horns and stick-on letters "Guitar Man," after a gig, long after all his musical partners have gone to sleep, he can still be found in the hotel lobby playing and singing to entertain the night clerks, sometimes to their enjoyment and sometimes to their annoyance. Late-arriving hotel guests get their cameras out and photograph the insatiable old bluesman. In the mornings, he is already back before everyone, sitting in the hotel lobby ready to sing and play his wide repertoire of country blues, entertaining people as they show up for breakfast. Even now, after more than seventy years of playing, he is a captivating singer and picker who will thrill any audience.

Jay Summerour, born 1950 in Rockville, Maryland, is the soulful counter-part to Williams, a great harmonica player and percussionist who learned harmonica from his grandpa, Smack Martin, who played the juke joints. He's spent the last thirty years partnering with Warner Williams, sometimes singing and whistling with Williams, mostly backing up swiftly on harmonica. He plays the traditional style, filling it in just right, never overplaying and tastefully accentuating the songs. He may be subtle, but he has the chops and skills and he carries on a long tradition of country blues harmonica players with elegance. Whatever they play has a rustic, ethereal tone, a reflection of two lifetimes of playing while working full-time jobs to support their families. Williams drove a garbage truck for the Maryland-National Capital Park and Planning Commission to support his wife and eight children. Summerour was a school bus driver.

There is often a sad irony in the blues, and certainly when it comes to the careers of this superb duo, call them songsters, bluesmen, or whatever. The *Washington Post* called Warner Williams "one of the last great songsters" and reported that after he was bestowed the nation's highest award for traditional musicians, the National Heritage Fellowship—Master of Traditional Arts—an award won by B.B. King, John Lee Hooker, and Bill Monroe, among others, he was still busking in the Washington, DC, Metro station at Shady Grove.[15] They are still not getting their deserved global recognition, considering their musical skills, range of repertoire and sheer excellence, despite several excellent, critically acclaimed albums on the Patuxent, Smithsonian Folkways, and Orchard record labels.

Harmonica player Jay Summerour is the good-natured, affable spokesperson for the duo, which is sometimes accentuated by drummer Eric Selby. Williams is taciturn; he speaks through his guitar. When he does offer a few words, it's few indeed. Summerour told the story:

> I guess that was about thirty years ago and I was traveling around with a bunch
> of different bands and I came home and Warner was at my cousin's house, and
> they wanted him to meet me. He came over to my apartment and he had his gui-
> tar with him, of course—he always did. We sat down on the couch and played
> music, and we've been playing together ever since. He used to do open mics all the
> time—so he started taking me with him. We would go to Gallagher's and Susanne's
> American Kitchen and lots of places in Gaithersburg and play open mics. We did
> that for about maybe five or six months—and Nick Spitzer from the Smithsonian
> heard about us and he found us and asked us if we wanted to do a recording for
> the Smithsonian. So that's how we first got started with the Smithsonian Folkway
> Records. We did our first tape maybe in '94. And we did our first CD in 1999.
>
> We used to go to Archie Edwards's barbershop. Back then it was just Eleanor
> Ellis, Phil Wiggins, Archie, Mike Baytop, NJ Warren, and Mr. Bones all playing

around the barbershop. Archie and Mike Baytop and NJ and Mr. Bones—they used to ride out to my house in Rockville, and then they came to my house in Poolesville.

I got started in harmonica because my grandfather Smack Martin used to play. My grandfather played with this guitar player from across the street named B. Cliff—who used to play a lot of gospel and blues. Matter of fact, Mr. Warner used to play there too in the backyard. You'd get a whole lot of musicians used to sit around in this neighborhood—Mr. Warner, my grandfather, my uncle—just a lot of guys got together every weekend to play. I always said that I'd like to sit around and play music like them—that's what I wanted to do for a living. I never knew that I would, but I always said I'd like to. I mean, people used to come from all over and listen to that. My mom played with a women's softball team called the Wonderettes, and they used to have blues bands perform all the time, so I'd see all those blues bands come to the ballpark. They'd have ballgames, cookouts, and dances at night. And they'd play blues—James Brown, Little Richard, all these guys—Etta James, Koko Taylor—they used to call it the chitlin circuit. I was about nine years old when I first started playing baseball and hearing all these guys. So that's where I got it from.

Warner used to be on a TV show—him and his dad. His dad used to play a fiddle and guitar—everything. They used to go to downtown D.C. from Takoma Park—Warner lived at New Hampshire Avenue where you first come to the district line in Maryland and Takoma Park. They used to catch the bus down to Foggy Bottom and play down there all the time on the corner down in D.C. When Warner got married he moved out to Olney from there. He's been playing a long time. He used to play with a big-time band and a soul band, the Moroccans, and blues band back in the day, and they were pretty good too. But they played all the dances and juke joints. He's been around for a long time. A lot of people know Warner.

We never toured internationally because Warner wouldn't fly. We've been asked a couple times by the Smithsonian and other promoters and stuff, but he wouldn't fly. He took a train actually out west to Port Townsend in Washington. When it takes five hours for other musicians to be home it takes us five days.

We have played many gigs. We played the opening of the World War II memorial, the Library of Congress concert series, the Smithsonian Folklife Festivals. We've stayed really busy for a long time—and people have treated us good. Nick Spitzer took us down there to do the New Orleans Jazz Fest, and I think we were the only acoustic duo to play there.

We played a whole lot with the people from the barbershop. U.S. congressmen would hire us, we played for a president from Africa when he came here. Dr. Barry Lee Pearson helped us a whole lot and wrote a bunch of articles on us. He had us do music seminars at Maryland University, and got us involved in the Middleburg Festival and a lot of festivals. He helped us a whole lot. He really did a lot of publicity stuff on us. Yeah. He's always been there for us. Between him and Nick Spitzer and Mark Puryear, they have really promoted us a whole lot in our careers.

In addition to playing with Warner, I have also been playing with other musicians for a long time. I always get hired by a bunch of different bands or sit in with them. It all started back when I used to sit in on this band, Small Talk, that played around Silver Spring, a Southern rock band. Then I hooked up with the Starland Vocal Band. I was a stage manager for them and they let me play with them and sing. They helped me a whole lot getting started. I was with like Billy Price and Willie Dixon and a whole lot of people at this place called Desperados in D.C. so I got pretty well known. I started doing stuff with Eleanor Ellis. I play in the ensemble Back Porch Blues with Eric Selby. I played with Memphis Gold on his CDs. Mike Baytop and I did a soundtrack for a play called *Color Me Dark* that started at the Kennedy Center and went all around the world. So, I've been playing with a bunch of different people.

We both had had day jobs. I drove a school bus and he worked right beside me at the bus lot and he worked at the Park and Planning Commission, which was right beside each other. We would leave work and go to open mics or something and play. People started coming around and when we played the places were packed. A lot of people followed us around. That's how Nick Spitzer heard about us. The biggest gig we ever did was open up for Jackson Browne on the 4th of July for 400,000 people. And at the Wolf Trap gig with Joe Louis Walker and Junior Brown and at the Folk Festival in Maine in Bangor.[16]

After Archie died

Eleanor Ellis reminisced, "After Archie died the group of friends and regulars thought that if we all put in a little bit of money, maybe we could keep the shop open and we could pay the rent. We decided to form a nonprofit organization."[17] Miles Spicer recalled:

We had just an amazing run of luck when Jeff Glassie was introduced to the barbershop. When he came to our first meeting we were talking about forming a foundation. He raised his hand and said, "Well, I'm a corporate lawyer and we can incorporate you. I work with nonprofits all the time—and I'll take you on pro bono." So, we got our 501(c)(3) incorporation done through his law firm for free. That's how the Archie Edwards Blues Heritage Foundation was created in 1998, to perpetuate Archie's legacy and to keep the jams going. In the years that followed the foundation has held workshops and concerts by professional acoustic blues musicians. Visitors come from all over the country and the world.[18]

At the time of this writing, the "new" barbershop—the Archie Edwards Blues Heritage Foundation—is located in a former used bookstore in Riverdale Park, but before this book could go to press it was announced that they lost their lease and will seek a new home. The current building is simple but functional, anything but fancy. The members preserved Archie's old barbershop chair in what looks more like a clubhouse than a museum, because in this place it's not only about the past but is dedicated to carrying the music into the future. The walls are adorned with some of the original photos, plus new images of more recent times. A small stage, a piano, an honor-system refrigerator, and a long guitar rack indicate that this place is alive, and indeed, on Saturdays the local musicians come from near and far to join in to jam sessions, just as they did in the old days. Musicians of various skill levels congregate. The new barbershop swells to capacity when renowned musicians tour and play the small venue. Recent performances have included a range of acoustic blues luminaries: Guy Davis, Scott Ainslie, Lauren Sheehan, Piedmont Blūz, Austin Walking Cane, Jerron Paxton, Rory Block, Mary Flower, Del Rey, and many more. Just about everybody signed their name on the bathroom wall, which has now become an enshrined part of the history.

The late Dennis Herndon was a board member of the foundation. He explained:

> We have done performer workshops, hands-on workshops on to how to fix harmonicas, how to fix your guitar, how to do sound for acoustic performing and recording. We are totally separate from the D.C. Blues Society, which is mostly electric. We are an all-acoustic scene. Other than amplification it is all acoustic music. Right now, we have a mailing list of over 400 members. We perform at local concerts and festivals, where we also have informational tables.[19]

This type of non-profit, community-based, self-directed entertainment is becoming more popular all over the country. Old churches and warehouses are being converted for locally orchestrated events, run by the locals for the community. This community-centered entertainment is not unique, but on a national level the Archie Edwards Blues Heritage Foundation is outstanding in that it is seemingly the only organization dedicated to acoustic blues, with the core mission of offering educational programs, concerts, jam sessions— and most importantly, carrying on the important function of offering a central meeting place for musicians and music lovers.

ACKNOWLEDGMENTS

Phil Wiggins and Frank Matheis send many thanks to the following:
Special thanks to Margaret Judge Pooley, for her great help with transcriptions and proofing. Advisors: Dr. Barry Lee Pearson, Lorna Owen, Eric Pooley, Dr. David Evans, Dr. Adam Gussow, Dr. Bruce Conforth, Brett Bonner, Jas Obrecht, and Elijah Wald. David Evans for his excellent editing. Interview contributors: Axel Küstner, Barry Lee Pearson, Dennis Herndon, Eleanor Ellis, James Early, Jeff Place, Jay Summerour, Jim Greene, Joan Fenton, Margo Blevin, Julia Olin, Lauren Sheehan, Lee Talbot, Marc Pessar, Max Ochs, Michael Baytop, Miles Spicer, Jackie Merritt, Resa Lynn Gibbs, Neil Harpe, Erin Harpe, Paddy Bowman, Pete Reiniger, Trish Byerly, Valerie Turner, Benedict Turner, Rick Franklin. Photo contributors: Axel Küstner, Paul Kennedy, Bibiana Huang Matheis, Fernando Sandoval, Augusta Blues Week Archives, Smithsonian Folklife Festival Archives, Archives of the late Myron Samuels, John Cephas Archives with Lynn Sellers Volpe, Archives of the Travellin' Blues Workshop—Paddy Bowman, Dexter Hodges, Michael G. Stewart, and Julie Fox.

Phil thanks:
Frank Matheis, Rhabyah Khaliq, Flora Molton, John Cephas, John Jackson, Archie Edwards, Chief Ellis, Dr. Barry Lee Pearson, Otis Williams, Martha, Eliza, and Wendy Wiggins, Matt Watson, Judy LaPrade, Mark Puryear, Peter McCracken, David Eisner, Margo Blevin, Joan Fenton, Beth King, Brittany Hicks (and all the folks at Augusta), Valerie and Ben Turner, Charlie Pilzer, Mike Pitulo, Bernice Johnson Reagon, Diana Parker, James Early, Ralph Rinzler, Dan Shehe (and all of the folks at the Smithsonian Institution), Jeff Place, Pete Reiniger (and all the folks at Folkways), Clifford Murphy, Barry Bergey, Cheryl Schiele (and all the folks at the NEA), Julia Olin, Madeleine Remez (and all the folks at the NCTA), Thea Austin, Jennifer Cutting (and everyone at the Library of Congress), Jon Lohman (and everyone at the Virginia Folklife Program at the Virginia Foundation for the Humanities), Chad Edward Buterbaugh and everybody at the Maryland State Arts Council, and my fellow musicians: The Chesapeake Sheiks, House Party, Tidewater Trio, Dom Turner, George Kilby Jr., Corey Harris, Ben Hunter, Joe Seamons.

Frank thanks:
Special thanks to my book partners Phil Wiggins and Margaret Judge Pooley. All those who helped me get here: Berta Lehmann, Bibiana Huang Matheis, Maya Matheis, Sigrid Stupelman, Stuart Marwell. My creative team: Leo Marino III, Paulina Manzo, Felipe Galindo. My magazine editors: Brett Bonner, Kate Goldsmith, Lance Ringel, Cary Wolfson, John Sinclair. My radio friends: Randy Milroy, Michael Kleff, Thomas Meinhard, Monika Künzel. My former music partner: Lowry Hamner. My record label colleague: Tom Mindte. Many thanks to the excellent publishing team at the University Press of Mississippi.

NOTES

Preface by Frank Matheis

1. We recommend following up by reading the works by Dr. Barry Lee Pearson, professor in the English Department at the University of Maryland. In *Virginia Piedmont Blues: The Lives and Art of Two Virginia Bluesmen*, Pearson chronicles the life and times of bluesmen John Cephas and Archie Edwards, in what stands as the most extensive biographies of these musicians.

Introduction

1. Barry Lee Pearson, *Virginia Piedmont Blues: The Lives and Art of Two Virginia Bluesmen* (Philadelphia: University of Pennsylvania Press, 1990), 266.

2. John Jackson, personal conversation with Frank Matheis, at Clearwater Festival, New York, 1994.

3. Pearson, *Virginia Piedmont Blues*, 80.

4. Gene Rosenthal, "An Open Letter to Frank Matheis," Frank's personal Facebook page, July 2016.

5. Alan Lomax was a folklorist who spent his career documenting folk music traditions from around the world. He undertook field trip with a portable tape recorder and collected thousands of recordings on acetate and aluminum discs from 1933 to 1942 under the auspices of the Library of Congress and later for his independent archive, starting in 1946. His collection of recordings has now been digitized and preserved by the Association for Cultural Equity.

6. Dr. Lornell's *Virginia's Blues, Country, and Gospel Records, 1902–1943: An Annotated Discography* is an important work documenting the regional blues. Interested readers should also check out the albums *Virginia Traditions: Western Piedmont Blues* (Smithsonian Folkways Archival BR 100003, 1981), with extensive liner notes by Kip Lornell, Brett Sutton, Dell Upton, and Mike Mayo; and *Virginia Traditions: Non-Blues Secular Black Music* (Smithsonian Folkways Archival BR 100001, 1978), produced by Kip Lornell.

7. Barry Pearson, "Rappahannock Blues: John Jackson," *Smithsonian Folkways Magazine* (Summer 2010). http://www.folkways.si.edu/magazine-summer-2010-rappahannock-blues -john-jackson/african-american-music/article/smithsonian.

8. As the John Hurt biographer Dr. Philip R. Ratcliffe pointed out to Frank Matheis in an email of January 5, 2017, John Hurt never felt at home in the run-down neighborhood where he was moved to. The meaning here is his connection to the African American community and especially to Archie Edwards.

9. Dick Waterman, "John Hurt; Patriarch Hippie." *Sing Out!* (February/March 1967): 7.

10. As the John Hurt biographer Dr. Philip R. Ratcliffe pointed out to Frank Matheis in an email of January 5, 2017, the New York recording was actually completed in December 1928.

11. Sheldon Harris, "Mississippi John Hurt," *Blues Who's Who* (Cambridge, MA: DaCapo Paperback, 1979), 257–58.

12. Waterman, "John Hurt; Patriarch Hippie," 7.

13. Axel Küstner, interview excerpts from taped conversation, in liner notes to *Archie Edwards: The Road is Rough and Rocky* (Original Field Recordings, Vol. 6, Living Country Blues USA), 2–3.

14. Pearson, *Virginia Piedmont Blues*, 59–60.

15. Pearson, *Virginia Piedmont Blues*, 59–60.

16. Eddie Dean, "Skip James' Hard Time Killing Floor Blues," *Washington City Paper*, November 25, 1994. http://www.washingtoncitypaper.com/articles/9345/skip-james-hard-time-killing-floor-blues.

17. Leland Talbot, taped interview with Frank Matheis, January 18, 2016.

18. Harris, *Blues Who's Who*, 273.

19. Pearson, *Virginia Piedmont Blues*, 61.

20. Pearson, *Virginia Piedmont Blues*, 236–38.

21. Josh Shaffer, "Elizabeth Cotten," Our State—Celebrating North Carolina, July 29, 2014. www.ourstate.com.

22. Peggy Seeger, "About My Family." www.peggyseeger.com. Accessed January 9, 2016.

23. Elizabeth Cotten Biography. www.elizabethcotten.com. Accessed January 9, 2016.

24. Elizabeth Cotten Biography. www.elizabethcotten.com. Accessed January 9, 2016.

25. L. L. Demerle, "Remembering Elizabeth Cotten." www.eclectica.org. Accessed January 10, 2016.

Chapter One. The Early Years

1. There is no evidence to corroborate that Bessie Smith played guitar professionally. She may have played on an amateur level and she could have taught basics to Esther Mae Scott. Or, the anecdote could have been slightly changed over the passage of many decades, or misunderstood along the way. Perhaps Esther Mae actually said that she learned guitar during her time *with* Bessie Smith, rather than *from* Bessie Smith.

Chapter Two. The Cephas and Wiggins Years

1. Ralph Rinzler (1934–1994) was one of the primary movers and shakers in American folk and traditional music. He helped established the Smithsonian's Folklife program and managed it for decades. He was active in the folk song revival in the 1950s; he learned to play banjo and mandolin, later joining old-time music group the Greenbriar Boys. Ralph learned tunes from Woody Guthrie in Washington Square Park, traveled with Mike Seeger through Appalachia, and "discovered" Doc Watson. He organized performances with Pete Seeger, Bob Dylan, Mary Travers, and Bernice Johnson Reagon.

2. Joseph T. "Joe" Wilson, born and raised in the Blue Ridge Mountains of East Tennessee, was a folklorist and journalist who served as the executive director of the National Council for the Traditional Arts (NCTA). He was perhaps the greatest supporter of John Cephas, and

Cephas & Wiggins, and their de facto manager. Joe Wilson was a tireless supporter of folk and traditional music of every kind, including bluegrass, early Appalachian mountain music, and blues. He embraced many traditional artists and served as their champion, and he stands as one of the powerful supporters of the music of the Blue Ridge region. At the NCTA he was involved in the preservation and archiving of all sorts of folk music and arts of the region. In 2001 the National Endowment for the Arts awarded a National Heritage Fellowship to Wilson, an award also bestowed on John Cephas, largely by the support of Joe Wilson.

3. Bess Lomax Hawes (1921–2009) was the youngest child of folklorist John A. Lomax. Bess joined her father and brother Alan as a researcher at the Library of Congress, where they directed the Archive of American Folk Song. She was an important figure in the establishment of public folklore programs throughout the United States. In Washington, DC, at the Smithsonian, she was deputy director for presentation for the 1975 and the summer-long 1976 Bicentennial Festival of American Folklife.

4. L+R Records 1980. Executive Producer Horst Lippmann. Produced and recorded by Siegfried A. Christmann and Axel Küstner. Recorded in Washington, DC, and Woodford, Virginia, in 1980.

5. There was already another famous harmonica player by that name, Mojo Buford.

6. Cajun fiddler Dewey Balfa, from Mamou, Louisiana, was a 1982 National Endowment for the Arts National Heritage Fellow, an award often referred to as the "Living Legend" award. Phil also won this award in 2017.

7. Produced by Horst Lippmann. Reissue produced by Jerry Gordon. Licensed from L+R Records. Tracks 1–10 were recorded April 9, 1983, at Gypsy Studio in Falls Church, Virginia, by Mike Rivers: St. James Infirmary, I Saw the Light, Sick Bed Blues, Piedmont Rag, Dog Days of August, Roberta, Highway 301, Hoodoo Woman, Louisiana Chase.

8. Algia Mae Hinton died on February 8, 2018.

9. *Bowling Green John Cephas and Harmonica Phil Wiggins* (Flying Fish Records, 1984). Produced by Joe Wilson: Reno Factory, Cherryball, Dog Days of August, Staggerlee, Hard Time Killing Floor Blues, John Henry, I Saw the Light, Roberta. Recording and remix by Pete Reiniger, production Larry MacBride and Joe Wilson. (Also issued as cassette *Let It Roll: Bowling Green*, 1985 on Marimac produced by Larry MacBride.)

10. Cinecom Entertainment Group. Starring Chris Cooper and James Earl Jones. DVD.

11. Phil was bestowed the same National Heritage Fellowship in 2017, but more about that later.

12. Produced by Joe Wilson. Recorded and mixed by Pete Reiniger, in Fairfax, Virginia: Black Cat on the Line, Richmond Blues, Weeping Willow, Guitar Man, Police Dog Blues, Corrine, Careless Love, Brownsville.

13. Produced by Joe Wilson, joined by Daryl Davis on piano and Don Rouse on clarinet. Jeff Hopper on bass. Recorded in Springfield, Virginia, by Bruce Loughry; digital editing Dave Glasser at Airshow Studio in Takoma Park, Maryland. Darkness at the Delta was recorded live at the Barrymore Theater in Madison, Wisconsin: Flip, Flop, Fly, No Lovin' Baby Now, One Kind Favor, Evil Twin Blues, Today I Started Loving You Again, Too Old to Dream, Darkness on the Delta, Blue Day Blues, Standing at Judgment, The Backbiter, Devil Got My Woman, Banks of the River.

14. Big Boss Man, Mama Let Me Lay It On You, Prison Bound Blues, Jesus Is Mine, Little Red Rooster, Blake's Rag, A Shanty in Old Shanty Town, Broke Down Engine, Good Morning Little School Girl, St. Louis Blues, The Things I Used to Do, Sick Bed Blues, Burn Your Bridges, Going to the River, Prison Blues, Keep Your Hands Off Her.

15. 1995. Produced by Joe Wilson. Recorded and mixed by Pete Reiniger at the Hot Spot, in Hyattsville, Maryland, which was essentially Pete's house. Several cuts recorded by Bruce Loughry at Bias Studio in Springfield, Virginia. Editing and mastering by David Glasser at Air Show in Springfield, Virginia: Action Man, Man Without a Future, Screaming and Crying, No Ice in My Bourbon, The Blues Will Do Your Heart Good, Caroline in the Morning, Backwater Blues, Going to the River, Cool Down, Special Rider, Hard Liquor, Nine Pound Hammer, Right of Way Blues, Twelve Gates to the City.

16. Black Rat Swing, I'm a Pilgrim, Reno Factory, Guitar And Harmonica Rag, Goin' Down the Road Feelin' Bad, Eyesight to the Blind, Louise, Chicken Can't Roost Too High for Me, Pony Blues, Burn Your Bridges, I Ain't Got No Lovin' Baby Now, West Carey Street Blues, Richmond Blues, Rising River Blues.

17. Produced by Joe Wilson. Recorded with Pete Reiniger at Private Ear Studio in Hyattsville. Some tracks recorded by John Vengrouskie in Silver Spring: Mamie, Meeting the Mule, Spider Woman, Trouble in Mind, Jelly Roll, Walking Mama, A Lot of Them Blues, Illinois Blues, I Was Determined, Sounds of the Blues, Worried Life Blues, Me and My Chauffeur, Slow Blues, Leaving Blues, Pigmeat.

18. Produced by Joe Wilson. Recorded by Ronnie Freeland. Burnt Hill Studio, Clarksville, Maryland. Live recordings for the first national tour of Masters of the Steel String Guitar by Pete Reiniger: Stack and the Devil, Railroad Bill, Last Fair Deal Gone Down, Sickbed Blues, The Pimp in the Pink Suit, Burn Your Bridges, Darling Cora, Forgiveness, Bowling Green Strut, Darkness on the Delta, Reno Factory, Somebody Told the Truth, Something Smells.

19. Produced by Joe Wilson. Ann Rabson on piano, Daryl Davis on piano, and Andrew Volpe on bass. Recorded by Bill McElroy at Slipped Disc in Ashland, Virginia. Mastered by Bill McElroy and by Don Stout and Bruce Iglauer at Colossal Mastering in Chicago, Illinois: Ain't Seen My Baby, I Did Do Right, Catfish Blues, Susie Q, All I've Got Is Them Blues, Dirt Road, Broke and Hungry, Three Ball Blues, Brother, Can You Spare A Dime?, I Won't Be Down, Seattle Rainy Day Blues, The Blues Three Ways.

20. Produced by Dr. Barry Lee Pearson. Recorded by Bill McElroy at Slipped Disc in Ashland, Virginia. Mastered by Pete Reiniger, Smithsonian Folkways Recordings: Richmond Blues, Going to the River, Keep Your Hands Off My Baby, Black Rat Swing, Mamie, Crow Jane, Dog Days of August, John Henry, Pigmeat Crave, Prison Bound Blues, Key to the Highway, Going Down the Road Feeling Bad, Careless Love, Great Change, Reno Factory, Step It Up and Go.

Chapter Three. Carrying on the Legacy on My Own

1. *Phil Wiggins & The Chesapeake Sheiks Live at Montpelier.* Silverbirch Records. 2014. Recorded live at the Montpelier Arts Center, Laurel, Maryland. Ian Walters piano, Matt Kelley guitar, Marcus Moore violin, Eric Shramreck bass. All sing backing vocals.

2. *Phil Wiggins & Dom Turner.* 2014. Recorded and mixed at Oceanic Studios, Sydney, Australia by Jim Moginie: Roberta, Jimmy Bell, Going Down South, No Ice in My Bourbon, Louis Collins, Special Rider Blues, Stop and Listen, Some of These Days, No Fools No Fun, New York City, Sitting On Top of the World, Last Fair Deal Gone Down, Let the Mermaids Flirt with Me, When You Got a Good Friend.

3. Civil and human rights activist and folklorist Worth Long was a blues historian, cultural worker, Smithsonian folklorist, and festival organizer. He brought a long-standing interest in black music to his work with the Smithsonian (which began in 1970). He was nominated for a Grammy (with Ralph Rinzler and Barry Lee Pearson) for *Roots of Rhythm and Blues: The*

Robert Johnson Era (1993), a recording with Columbia Records that grew out of a Smithsonian project of the same name.

Flora Molton

1. Eleanor Ellis, "Flora Molton—From a Little Girl I've Been Singing, Singing, Singing," *Living Blues* (May/June 1989): 24.
2. Bernice Reagon, "The Lady Street Singer," *Southern Exposure* (Summer 1974): 39.
3. Ellis, "Flora Molton—From A Little Girl I've Been Singing, Singing, Singing," 26.
4. Reagon, "The Lady Street Singer," 40.
5. Eleanor Ellis, interview with Frank Matheis and Phil Wiggins, Archie's Barbershop, Riverdale Park, Maryland, November 10, 2014.

John Jackson

1. Verified in phone conversation by Frank Matheis with UK blues musician Gypsy Bill Williams, who stated, "I only knew him as Mississippi John Jackson."
2. John Jackson in personal conversation with Frank Matheis in 1994.
3. Barry Lee Pearson and Cheryl A. Brauner, "John Jackson's East Virginia Blues," *Living Blues* 63 (January/February 1985).
4. Trisha Byerly, personal interview with Frank Matheis, November 9, 2014.
5. Barry Pearson, "Rappahannock Blues: John Jackson," *Smithsonian Folkways Magazine* (Summer 2010). http://www.folkways.si.edu/magazine-summer-2010-rappahannock-blues -john-jackson/african-american-music/article/smithsonian.
6. Pearson, "Rappahannock Blues: John Jackson."
7. Byerly interview with Frank Matheis.

Esther Mae "Mother" Scott

1. William Mackay, "Esther Mae Scott Dies, DC Singer, Composer," *Washington Post*, Oct. 17, 1979.
2. "Mother Scott, Musical Leader" (obituary), *Washington Star*, October 17, 1979.
3. David Goren, "Mother Scott," *Sing Out!* 27, no. 6 (1979): 14.
4. "Mother Scott, Musical Leader."

Wilbert "Big Chief" Ellis

1. Editorial, "Wilbert Big Chief Ellis. Interviewers Ira Selkowitz in 1976 and Susan Day in 1977," *Living Blues* 63 (January/February 1985): 28–29.
2. Bob Rusch, "Big Chief Ellis: Oral History," *Cadence* (March 1978): 6.
3. Rusch, "Big Chief Ellis: Oral History," 6.
4. "Wilbert Big Chief Ellis. Interviewers Ira Selkowitz in 1976 and Susan Day in 1977," 30.
5. Harris, "Mississippi John Hurt," *Blues Who's Who*, 174–75.
6. "Wilbert Big Chief Ellis. Interviewers Ira Selkowitz in 1976 and Susan Day in 1977," 30.

Bill Harris

1. A reference to the fact that Washington, DC, has a predominantly African American population with white people having settled the surrounding suburbs. Recollection by Frank Matheis as a guest in the club.
2. James Rupert, "Jazz Guitarist Bill Harris Dies at Age 63," *Washington Post*, December 7, 1988.
3. Y. Leah Latimer, "A Jazzed-up Day for Bill Harris," *Washington Post*. November 9, 1978.
4. Rupert, "Jazz Guitarist Bill Harris Dies at Age 63."

The Festival of American Folklife (Smithsonian Folklife Festivals)

1. http://www.festival.si.edu/about-us/mission-and-history/smithsonian.
2. James Early, personal interview, November 13, 2014.

The Gaines Brothers

1. Pearson, *Virginia Piedmont Blues*, 68.
2. Pearson, *Virginia Piedmont Blues*, 60.
3. Quotations from Axel Küstner from an interview with Frank Matheis, May 9, 2015.

An Interview with John Cephas by Dr. Barry Lee Pearson

1. Barry Lee Pearson, "John Cephas," *Living Blues* 145 (May/June 1999): 15–19.

Archie Edwards: Barbershop Blues by Dr. Barry Lee Pearson

1. Barry Pearson, "Archie Edwards: Barbershop Blues," *Living Blues* 63 (January/February 1985): 22–26.

Eleanor Ellis

1. Eleanor Ellis, email to Frank Matheis, February 15, 2019.
2. Telephone interview with Eleanor Ellis, 2012.
3. Telephone interview with Eleanor Ellis, June 18, 2017.

Archie's Famous Barbershop

1. Interview with Eleanor Ellis, Archie Edwards Blues Heritage Foundation, Riverdale Park, Maryland, November 11, 2014.
2. Interview with Michael Baytop, Archie Edwards Blues Heritage Foundation, Riverdale Park, Maryland, November 11, 2014.

3. Michael Baytop, Eleanor Ellis, and Miles Spicer, personal interview with Frank Matheis, November 11, 2014.

4. "Generation to Generation," Archie Edwards Blues Heritage Foundation. http://www .acousticblues.com/Generation/gen2gen.html.

5. "Generation to Generation," Archie Edwards Blues Heritage Foundation. http://www .acousticblues.com/Generation/gen2gen.html.

6. "Generation to Generation," Archie Edwards Blues Heritage Foundation. http://www .acousticblues.com/Generation/gen2gen.html.

7. Personal interview with Jackie Merritt, November 8, 2014.

8. Personal interview with Resa Gibbs, November 8, 2014.

9. Personal interview with Miles Spicer, November 8, 2014.

10. Telephone interview with Erin Harpe, December 27, 2014.

11. Telephone interview with Neil Harpe, November 23, 2014.

12. Interview with Michael Baytop, Archie Edwards Blues Heritage Foundation, Riverdale, Maryland, November 11, 2014.

13. Mapleshade Artists: Mark Wenner. http://www.mapleshaderecords.com/artists/mark_ wenner.php.

14. Barry Lee Pearson, Liner notes to *Classic African American Songsters* (Smithsonian Folkways SFW CD 40211).

15. Justin Jouvenal, "For Guitar Man Warner Williams, Passion Outshines Spotlight," Washington Post, September 5, 2011.

16. Jay Summerour, telephone interview, June 1, 2017.

17. Interview with Eleanor Ellis, Archie Edwards Blues Heritage Foundation, Riverdale Park, Maryland, November 11, 2014.

18. Interview with Miles Spicer, Archie Edwards Blues Heritage Foundation, Riverdale Park, Maryland, November 11, 2014.

19. Phone interview with Miles Spicer, 2014.

INTERVIEWS CONDUCTED
BY FRANK MATHEIS

Transcribed by Margaret Judge Pooley
Baytop, Michael. Personal interview. November 11 and 15, 2014.
Blevin, Margo. Personal interview. July 2017.
Bowman, Paddy. Telephone interview. April 22, 2015.
Byerly, Trish. Personal interview. November 9, 2014.
Early, James Counts, and Phil Wiggins. Personal interview. November 13, 2014.
Ellis, Eleanor, and Phil Wiggins. Personal interview. November 10, 2014.
Ellis, Eleanor. Personal interview. June 18, 2017.
Fenton, Joan. Personal interview. July 18, 2016.
Franklin, Rick. Telephone conversation. May 30, 2017.
Gibbs, Resa. Personal interview. November 8, 2014.
Herndon, Dennis. Personal interview. November 11, 2014.
Harpe, Erin. Telephone interview. December 27, 2014.
Harpe, Neil. Telephone interview. November 23, 2014.
Hurt, Mary Frances. Telephone interview. January 4, 2016.
Jackson, John. Personal conversation. 1994.
King, Beth. Personal interview. July 18, 2016.
Kennedy, Paul. Personal interview. December 25, 2014.
Küstner, Axel. Personal interview. May 9, 2015.
Merritt, Jackie. Personal interview. November 8, 2014.
Olin, Julia. Personal interview. December 16, 2014.
Pearson, Barry Lee. Personal interview. March 1, 2016.
Pearson, Barry Lee. Personal interview. November 12, 2016.
Pessar, Marc. Telephone interview. May 29, 2017.
Ratcliffe, Phillip. E-mail correspondence. August 8, 2018.
Reiniger, Peter. Telephone interview. December 10, 2016.
Place, Jeff and Phil Wiggins. Personal interview. November 13, 2014.
Sheehan, Lauren. Personal interview. July 15, 2015.
Spicer, Miles. Personal interview. November 8, 2014.
Spicer, Miles. Personal interview. November 11, 2014.
Summerour, Jay. Telephone interview. June 1, 2017.
Talbot, Leland. Telephone interview. January 18, 2016.
Turner, Valerie, and Benedict Turner. May 29, 2017.
Weinstock, Ron. Telephone interview. December 25, 2014.
Wiggins, Martha. Telephone interview. March 2, 2017.
Wiggins, Phil. Countless interviews in person and via telephone from 2013–18.
Williams, Gypsy Bill. Telephone interview. 2012.

Phil Wiggins jamming with Ben Hunter, 2016. Photo by Frank Matheis.

The duo of Warner Williams, a National Heritage Fellow, and Jay Summerour, 2018. Photo by Bibiana Huang Matheis.

DISCOGRAPHY

Musical research and liner notes from:

Bowling Green John & Harmonica Phil Wiggins. *Original Field Recordings Vol. 1, Living Country Blues USA*. L+R Records LR 713123, 1981.

Cephas & Wiggins. *Dog Days of August*. Flying Fish Records FF70394, 1984.

Cephas & Wiggins. *Guitar Man*. Flying Fish FF70470, 1989. (W. C. Handy Award winner)

Cephas & Wiggins. *Flip, Flop & Fly*. Flying Fish FF70580, 1992.

Cephas & Wiggins. *Cool Down*. Alligator Records ALCD4838, 1995.

Cephas & Wiggins. *Homemade*. Alligator Records ALCD4863, 1999.

Cephas & Wiggins. *Somebody Told the Truth*. Alligator Records ALCD4888, 2002.

Cephas & Wiggins. *Master of the Piedmont Blues*. Cracker Barrel Series CB110, 2002.

Cephas & Wiggins. *Shoulder to Shoulder*. Alligator Records ALCD4910, 2006.

Cephas & Wiggins. *Richmond Blues*. Smithsonian Folkways Records SFW CD 40179, 2008.

Cephas & Wiggins. *From Richmond to Atlanta*. Bullseye Blues 11661-9633-2, 2000.

Cephas & Wiggins. *Bluesmen*. Chesky Records JD89, 1993.

Cephas & Wiggins. *Sweet Bitter Blues*. Evidence Music ECD 26050-2, 1994.

Phil Wiggins & Dom Turner. Independently produced PWDT001, 2014.

Phil Wiggins & The Chesapeake Sheiks. *Live at Montpelier*. Silverbirch Records, 2014.

Various Artists. *Roots of Rhythm and Blues: A Tribute to the Robert Johnson Era*. Columbia CK 48584, 1992.

Various Artists. *True Blues*. Telarc 33815-02.

Flora Molton and the Truth Band. *Original Field Recordings Vol. 3, Living Country Blues USA*. L+R Records CDLR 712928, 1981.

Flora Molton. *I Want to Be Ready to Hear God When He Calls*. Patuxent CD257, 2014.

Various Artists. *Virginia Traditions: Western Piedmont Blues*. Smithsonian Folkways Archival BR 100003.

Various Artists. *Living Country Blues: An Anthology*. Evidence ECD26105, 1991.

Big Chief Ellis. Trix 3316, 1995.

Various Artists. *American Folk Blues Festival '81*. L+R Records CDLS 42022, 1981.

Various Artists. *American Folk Blues Festival '82*. L+R Records LR CD 2052, 1982.

Archie Edwards. *Original Field Recordings Vol. 6, Living Country Blues USA*. L+R Records CDLR 712621, 1981.

Archie Edwards. *The Toronto Sessions*. Northern Blues NBM0006, 2001.

Archie Edwards. *Blues 'N Bones*. Mapleshade Productions 56952, 1994.

Various Artists. *Barbershop Blues Vol. 2: Don't You Weep and Moan*. Archie Edwards Blues Heritage Foundation, 2012.

John Jackson. *Don't Let Your Deal Go Down*. Arhoolie CD 378, 1965.

John Jackson. *Country Blues & Ditties*. Arhoolie CD 471, 1968.

John Jackson. *Front Porch Blues*. Alligator Records ALCD 4867, 1999.

John Jackson. *Rappahannock Blues*. Smithsonian Folkways SW CD40181, 2010.

Frank Hovington. *Gone with the Wind*. Flyright Fly CD66, 2000.

Roy Dunn. *Know'd Them All*. Trix 3312, 1993.

Moses Rascoe. *Blues Live at Godfrey Daniels*. Flying Fish FF70454, 1990.

Various Artists. *Classic American Ballads*. Smithsonian Folkways SFW 40191, 2006.

Various Artists. *Classic Appalachian Blues*. Smithsonian Folkways SFW 40198, 2010.

Various Artists. *Classic Harmonica Blues*. Smithsonian Folkways SFW 40204, 2012.

Various Artists. *Classic African American Songsters*. Smithsonian Folkways SFW 40211, 2014.

Various Artists. *Classic African American Ballads*. Smithsonian Folkways SFW 40215, 2015.

Various Artists. *Classic Piedmont Blues*. Smithsonian Folkways SFW 40221, 2017.

Eleanor Ellis. *Backyard Blues*. Independently produced, 2014.

Eleanor Ellis. *Comin' a Time*. Patuxent Records CD 138, 2007.

Warner Williams & Jay Summerour. *Little Bit a Blues*. Patuxent Music CD 038, 1999.

Warner Williams & Jay Summerour. *Blues Highway*. Smithsonian Folkways SFW 40120, 2004.

Warner Williams & Jay Summerour. *Down 'N' Dirty*. Patuxent Music CD 163, 2007.

Mike Baytop & Jay Summerour. Patuxent Music CD 314, 2018.

Franklin & Baytop. *Searching for Frank*. Patuxent Music CD 156, 2007.

Rick Franklin & Tom Mindte. *Dancing with My Baby*. Patuxent Music CD 246, 2013.

Franklin & Harpe. *Doin' the Dozens*. Patuxent Music, 2007.

Franklin, Harpe and Usilton. *Hokum Blues*. Patuxent Music CD 022, 1999.

Neil Harpe. *Hokum Blues*. Hokum Blues HB 1002, 2007.

Piedmont Blūz. *Country Blues Selections*. Independently released, 2015.

The Blues Rider Trio. *Early Morning Blues*. Mapleshade Productions 12132, 2007.

M.S.G. Acoustic Blues Trio. *The Flood*. Independently released, 2016.

Doc Watson. *Country Blues Collection*. Sugar Hill Records SUG CD 3966, 2003.

Lightnin' Wells. *O Lightnin' Where Art Thou?* Blind Lemon Records 29348, 2017.

Lauren Sheehan. *Some Old Lonesome Day*. Independently released, 2016.

Lauren Sheehan. *The Light Still Burns*. Wilson River Records, 2013.

Lauren Sheehan. *Two Wings*. Wilson River Records, 2005.

Lauren Sheehan. *Rose City Ramble*. Wilson River Records, 2011.

Lauren Sheehan & Zoe Carpenter. *Tillamook Burn*. Independently released, no date.

Skip James. *The Complete Early Recordings*. Yazoo Records, 2009.

Skip James. *Blues from the Delta*. Vanguard 79517-2, 1998.

Mississippi John Hurt. *Avalon Blues: The Complete 1928 OKeh Recordings*. Columbia Records CK 64986, 1996.

Mississippi John Hurt. *Legend*. Rounder Records CD 1100, 1997.

Mississippi John Hurt. *Avalon Blues 1963*. Rounder Records CD 1081, 1991.

Carrying On the Legacy, a CD featuring the music by contemporary Piedmont Blues musicians, is available on the Patuxent Record label (Patuxent CD-321).

BIBLIOGRAPHY

"Africa and the Blues: An Interview with Gerhard Kubik." Afro-Pop.com radio interview transcript. April 2007.

"African Diaspora Program Book." Smithsonian Folkways. http://media.smithsonianfolkways .org/docs/festival/1975_Program_Book_African_Diaspora.pdf.

Bastin, Bruce. *Red River Blues: The Blues Tradition in the Southeast* (Music in American Life series). Urbana: University of Illinois Press, 1995.

Bowman, Paddy. From original typed internal memo notes "Bios—Travellin' Blues Workshop." Undated, circa 1980.

Bowman, Paddy. Memo draft for press release about Elizabeth Cotten. Circa 1980.

Carlson, Mary E. "University of Virginia Profiles: Chuck Perdue Preserves, Documents Folk Culture from the Inside." *UVA Today.* October 8, 2007. https://news.virginia.edu/content/ uva-profiles-chuck-perdue-preserves-documents-folk-culture-inside.

Churchman, Deborah. "Guitarist John Jackson: Using Music to Communicate." *Christian Science Monitor,* June 30, 1983. http://www.csmonitor.com/1983/0630/063008.html.

Cohn, Lawrence. "Mississippi John Hurt: The Dramatic Rediscovery of a Near-Legendary Blues Singer/Guitarist." *Down Beat* (July 1964): 22–23.

D'Arcy, David. "Interview with Bernice Johnson Reagon." *Heavenly Sight.* August 5, 2010. www .heavenlysight.org.

Dean, Eddie. "Skip James' Hard Time Killing Floor Blues." *Washington City Paper.* http:// www.washingtoncitypaper.com/articles/9345/skip-james-hard-time-killing-floor-blues . November 25, 1994.

Demerle, L. L. "Remembering Elizabeth Cotten." *Eclectica.* Accessed January 10, 2016. http:// www.eclectica.org.

DelGrosso, Rich. "Cephas & Wiggins: Voices from the Piedmont." *Blues Revue* 103 (December/ January 2007): 8–14.

"Elizabeth Cotten Biography." ElizabethCotten.com. Accessed January 9, 2016. www.eliza bethcotten.com.

Ellis, Eleanor. "Flora Molton—From a Little Girl I've Been Singing, Singing, Singing." *Living Blues* (May/June 1989).

"Festival Mission and History." Smithsonian Institution. http://www.festival.si.edu/about-us/ mission-and-history/smithsonian.

Fox, John Hartley. Liner notes. *Mississippi John Hurt: Legend.* Rounder CD 1100.

"Generation to generation." Archie Edwards Blues Heritage Foundation. http://www.acoustic blues.com/Generation/gen2gen.html.

Garrigue, Andy. Phil "Harmonica" Wiggins—The Other Half of the Best Acoustic Duo. *Blues Review Quarterly* 6 (Fall 1992): 17–21.

Goren, David. "Mother Scott." *Sing Out!* 27, no. 6 (1979): 14.

Grossman, Stefan. "Interview with John Fahey." Accessed January 10, 2016. www.guitarvideos.com.

Harrington, Richard. "Sweet, Holy Blues." *Washington Post*, June 24, 1983.

Harris, Sheldon. *Blues Who's Who*. New York: DaCapo, 1979.

Harris, Sheldon. *Blues Who's Who*. New York: DaCapo, 1994.

Hokkanen, Niles, and Russell Reppert. "Bowling Green Blues." *Acoustic Guitar* (May/June 1991).

"Joseph Wilson: Folklorist, advocate and presenter. Silver Spring, MD and Trade, TN." National Heritage Fellowship 2001 Press Release. 2001.

Joyce, Mike. "For Bill Harris, a Tribute with Distinction." *Washington Post*, July 26, 1988.

Joyce, Mike. "The Blues' East Side Story." *Washington Post*, August 29, 1990.

Küstner, Axel. Liner notes. *Archie Edwards: The Road Is Rough and Rocky*. Original Field Recordings Vol. 6. Living Country Blues USA.

Latimer, Y. Leah. "A Jazzed-up Day for Bill Harris." *Washington Post*, November 9, 1978.

Lorenz, Stephen. "Cosmopolitan Folk: The Cultural Politics of the North American Folk Music Revival in Washington, D.C." Diss., George Washington University. 2014. ProQuest Dissertations Publishing, 3615789.

Lornell, Kip. *Virginia's Blues, Country, and Gospel Records, 1902–1943: An Annotated Discography*. Lexington: University Press of Kentucky, 2015.

"Legacy Honorees: Bernice Johnson Reagon." Smithsonian Folklife. http://www.folklife.si.edu/legacy-honorees/bernice-johnson-reagon/smithsonian.

Mackay, William. "Esther Mae Scott Dies, D.C. Singer, Composer." *Washington Post*, October 17, 1979.

"Mark Wenner." Mapleshade Records. http://www.mapleshaderecords.com/artists/mark_wenner.php.

Matheis, Frank. "The Country Blues is Dead, They Say." The Country Blues. 2014. http://www.thecountryblues.com/?s=the+country+blues+is+dead%2C+they+say&x=0&y=0.

Matheis, Frank. "Eleanor Ellis." The Country Blues. http://www.thecountryblues.com/artist-reviews/eleanor-ellis/.

Matheis, Frank. "Erin Harpe." The Country Blues. http://www.thecountryblues.com/artist-reviews/erin-harpe/.

Matheis, Frank. "MSG Trio." The Country Blues. http://www.thecountryblues.com/artist-reviews/m-s-g-acoustic-blues-trio/.

Matheis, Frank. "Phil Wiggins—On His Own But Not Alone." *Living Blues* #234, vol. 45, no. 6 (2014): 8.

Matheis, Frank. "Rick Franklin." The Country Blues. http://www.thecountryblues.com/artist-reviews/rick-franklin/.

"'Mother Scott,' Musical Leader." Obituary. *Washington Star*, October 17, 1979.

Pearson, Barry. "Archie Edwards: Barbershop Blues." *Living Blues* 63 (January/February 1985): 22–26.

Pearson, Barry. "Bowling Green John Cephas and Harmonica Phil Wiggins: D.C. Country Blues." *Living Blues* 63 (January/February 1985): 14–21.

Pearson, Barry Lee. "John Cephas." *Living Blues* 145 (May/June 1999): 15–19.

Pearson, Barry. "Mother Scott." *Living Blues* 63 (January/February 1985): 36.

Pearson, Barry. "Wilbert 'Big Chief' Ellis." *Living Blues* 63 (January/February 1985): 28–35.

Pearson, Barry Lee. *Jook Right On—Blues Stories and Blues Storytellers*. Knoxville: University of Tennessee Press, 2005.

Pearson, Barry Lee. "Rappahannock Blues: John Jackson." *Smithsonian Folkways Magazine*. Summer 2010. http://www.folkways.si.edu/magazine-summer-2010-rappahannock-blues-john-jackson/african-american-music/article/smithsonian.

Pearson, Barry Lee. *Sounds So Good to Me: The Bluesman's Story.* Philadelphia: University of Pennsylvania Press, 1984.

Pearson, Barry Lee. *Virginia Piedmont Blues: The Lives and Art of Two Virginia Bluesmen.* Philadelphia: University of Pennsylvania Press, 1990.

Pearson, Barry Lee, and Cheryl A. Brauner. "John Jackson's East Virginia Blues." *Living Blues* 63 (January/February 1985).

Ratcliffe, Phillip. *Mississippi John Hurt: His Life, His Times, His Blues.* Jackson: University Press of Mississippi, 2011.

Reagon, Bernice. "The Lady Street Singer." *Southern Exposure* (Summer 1974).

Robertson, Ellen. "Legendary Piedmont Blues Guitarist John Cephas Dies at 78." *Richmond Times-Dispatch*, May 5, 2009. http://www.richmond.com/entertainment/article_365c1c65 -4047-5fd7-8c2d-d39ceb00f55e.html.

Rosenthal, Gene. "An Open Letter to Frank Matheis." Facebook.com. July 2016. https://www .facebook.com/thecountrybluesDOTcom.

Rupert, James. "Jazz Guitarist Bill Harris Dies at Age 63." *Washington Post*, December 7, 1988.

Rusch, Bob. "Big Chief Ellis: Oral History." *Cadence* (March 1978): 6.

Seeger, Peggy. "About My Family." PeggySeeger.com. Accessed January 9, 2016. www.peggy seeger.com.

Selkowitz, Ira, and Susan Day. "Wilbert Big Chief Ellis." *Living Blues* 63 (January 1985): 28–30.

Shaffer, Josh. "Elizabeth Cotten." Our State—Celebrating North Carolina. Accessed July 29, 2014. www.ourstate.com.

Skelly, Richard. "Saturday Night Music: An Interview with John Cephas and Phil Wiggins." *Sing Out!* 33, no. 2 (Winter 1988): 12–17.

Waterman, Dick. "John Hurt: Patriarch Hippie." *Sing Out!* (February/March 1967): 7.

Waterman, Dick. Blues Forum Google Group statement. groups.google.com/forum/#!topic/bit .listserv.blues-l/hHcE-iTkulQ. February 1, 2002.

Zito, Tom. "'Guest Lecturer': Blues-Packin' Mamma." *Washington Post*, October 24, 1970.

INDEX

The authors Phil Wiggins and Frank Matheis at Augusta Blues Week, 2016. Courtesy of Frank Matheis.

ABOUT THE AUTHORS

World-renowned blues harmonica virtuoso **Phil Wiggins**, a 2017 NEA National Heritage Fellow, is the primary informational source, expert advisor, and guiding force of this book project. For forty-plus years the musician and teacher has been an integral member of the Washington, DC–area acoustic blues scene and in the center of the East Coast acoustic blues. He has personally known, performed with, and befriended almost all players of the period between 1975–2015, in the region and beyond. He lived the history, was part of it, and he continues the legacy of this musical tradition to this day, as performer and educator and a proponent of the Piedmont blues, the rural folk tradition of the mid-Atlantic region. Among his many activities, he was the former president of the Washington, DC Blues Society. He was a partner in the legendary blues duo Cephas & Wiggins, with "Bowling Green" John Cephas, for thirty-three years since they first connected at the Smithsonian Folklife Festival in 1976. Cephas & Wiggins were Alligator Records artists and multiple W. C. Handy Award winners, including Entertainers of the Year and Best Traditional Blues Album in 1987. They were fixtures on the festival and workshop circuit as minstrels, teachers, folklorists, storytellers, and proponents of the rich African American folk tradition. Widely considered one of the world's top harmonica players, Phil Wiggins has befriended and performed with a wide range of traditional acoustic blues personalities nationwide and internationally. Cephas & Wiggins performed worldwide as cultural ambassadors for the U.S. State Department to Europe, Africa, Central and South America, and the Caribbean. The Kennedy Center sent Cephas & Wiggins to China and Australia. In 1988 they even performed at the Russian Folk Festival in Moscow. In Washington, they received the high honor of performing at the White House for President Bill Clinton and his family. Cephas & Wiggins produced three albums on the Flying Fish label and three on Alligator, plus a few on smaller labels, such as Chesky. They enjoyed a fruitful career that lasted until John's death in 2009. After the death of John Cephas, Phil Wiggins partnered with West Virginia bluesman Nat Reese, another pillar of the local acoustic blues scene, until Nat Reese's death in 2012. Phil Wiggins is now in his twenty-fifth year as teacher at the Augusta Heritage Center of Davis & Elkins College in Elkins, West Virginia. He was participatory in getting Blues

Week at Augusta started at a time when there was no comparable program in the United States. He also teaches at the Port Townsend Acoustic Blues Workshop in Washington State, where he was the artistic director for five years. Plus, he continues to play an active role in the National Council for Traditional Arts. He actively performs with key acoustic blues players on major world stages.

Music journalist **Frank Matheis** is the scribe for the project, writing the story as told by Phil Wiggins and adding supporting essays. For five decades, Frank has been a serious listener and student of roots and blues music, as well as a DJ, radio producer, and music journalist. As regular contributing writer to *Living Blues* magazine, and formerly to *Blues Access* magazine, he is also the publisher of a website dedicated to the acoustic blues: thecountryblues.com. Frank has had direct connection to the acoustic blues scene in and around Washington, DC, since his studies at the University of Maryland in the late 1970s. He has published over five hundred music articles and spent a decade on the radio in New York and Connecticut hosting blues and roots shows on WKZE-FM and WVKR-FM. As radio producer, his roots and blues documentaries have aired on Deutschlandradio, and numerous stations in the USA and Australia. He is recipient of the New York Festivals 2003 Best International Documentary award for *American Folk Music from Hawaii to Quebec*, produced in German for the German NPR Deutschlandradio, as well as other radio awards.

CPSIA information can be obtained
at www.ICGtesting.com
Printed in the USA
LVHW090121040222
710079LV00003B/195